THE POST-SOCIALIST CITY

CONTINUITY AND CHANGE IN URBAN SPACE AND IMAGERY

JOVIS
diskurs

THE POST-SOCIALIST CITY

CONTINUITY AND CHANGE IN URBAN SPACE AND IMAGERY

ALFRUN KLIEMS / MARINA DMITRIEVA (EDS.)
WITH THE ASSISTANCE OF
LOUISE BROMBY AND CHRISTIAN DIETZ

INTRODUCTION: THE POST-SOCIALIST CITY   6
CONTINUITY AND CHANGE IN URBAN SPACE AND IMAGERY
Marina Dmitrieva, Alfrun Kliems

1. THEORETICAL CONCEPTS

REPRESENTATIONS AND IMAGES OF "RECENT HISTORY"   16
THE TRANSITION OF POST-SOCIALIST LANDSCAPE ICONS
Mariusz Czepczyński

TOWARDS BANALIZATION?   34
TRANS-FORMING THE LEGACIES OF THE POST-SOCIALIST CITY
Lydia Coudroy de Lille, Miléna Guest

A CUMBERSOME HERITAGE   52
POLITICAL MONUMENTS AND BUILDINGS OF THE GDR IN REUNITED GERMANY
Arnold Bartetzky

2. ARTISTIC REALIZATIONS

URBAN "TRUTHS"   68
ARTISTIC INTERVENTION IN POST-SOCIALIST SPACE
Cynthia Imogen Hammond

SCREENING THE POST-SOVIET METROPOLIS   86
REPRESENTATIONS OF URBANITY IN CONTEMPORARY RUSSIAN CINEMA
Eva Binder

THE GOLDEN CITY AND THE GOLDEN SHOT   104
IMAGES FROM PRAGUE AFTER THE VELVET REVOLUTION
Alfrun Kliems

3. DISCURSIVE RECODINGS

POST-TOTALITARIAN AND POST-COLONIAL EXPERIENCES   120
THE PALACE OF CULTURE AND SCIENCE AND DEFILAD SQUARE IN WARSAW
Małgorzata Omilanowska

CULTURAL POLICY AS THE POLITICS OF HISTORY   140
INDEPENDENCE SQUARE IN KIEV
   Wilfried Jilge

THE PRESENCE OF THE RECENT PAST   156
DIFFICULT TRANSFORMATIONS OF A "PARADIGMATIC SOCIALIST CITY":
DUNAÚJVÁROS
   Béla Kerékgyártó

PROJECTED HAPPINESS   170
OLD MYTHS AND NEW AMBITIONS IN A BUCHAREST NEIGHBORHOOD
   Carmen Popescu

BUCHAREST AS A BATTLEGROUND, 1989–2009   196
   Augustin Ioan

4. ECONOMIC CONDITIONS

TURBO URBANISM IN PRISHTINA   210
   Kai Vöckler

ASTANA, ALMATY, AND AKTAU   230
ARCHITECTURAL EXPERIMENTS IN THE STEPPES OF KAZAKHSTAN
   Philipp Meuser

POST-SOCIALIST OR POSTMODERNIST?   248
THE SEARCH FOR A NEW URBANISM IN ARMENIA
   Tigran Harutyunian

LIST OF AUTHORS   264

IMAGE CREDITS   268

INTRODUCTION: THE POST-SOCIALIST CITY

Continuity and Change in Urban Space and Imagery

Marina Dmitrieva
Alfrun Kliems

Disintegration is a form of renewal,
at least for a moment.
There's more to be said for clinging to the fragments,
which are real, than to the whole,
which for now is just a promise.
Karl Schlögel, *Marjampole*, 2005[1]

In *Marjampole, or Europe's Return from the Spirit of the Cities*, Karl Schlögel describes the cities of Eastern Europe from a traveler's perspective, and maps the changes they have undergone since the breakdown of the socialist systems. Schlögel's essays trace a new physiognomy of the continent, a Europe from the perspective of its cities—also or especially from the perspective of the East.

Schlögel's observations take as their departure point urban fragments—train stations and docks, shopping malls and neon signs, bazaars, building façades, palaces of culture, tenements. This approach gives each of the post-socialist cities in the region its own specific face that extends beyond any overarching, schematic concept applicable to all of them.

Our grasp of the whole—in this case "the" post-socialist city—will also be schematic at best. It is in this sense that we use the term "post-socialist city" less as a precise concept and more as a heuristic category allowing us to examine specific phenomena in particular cities and relate them to each other. We see this as our contribution to the discussion that for about ten years has revolved around catchphrases like urban reconstruction, socialist spaces, urban remembering and forgetting, the future of the past, cities after the fall, transit spaces, life after communism, iconic landscapes, and place identity. More specifically, this volume is concerned with the post-socialist character of urban centers in Eastern Europe from the nineteen-nineties until today, including post-Soviet Asia, with particular attention paid to urban development.

Since urban transformations are not only realized in buildings, streets, squares, and architectural ensembles, but also in art—in imaginations of the urban—we have asked art historians, literary scholars, and film theorists to contribute to this book as well as architects and historians of architecture, geographers, and urbanists.

The common starting point of these contributions is the observation that urban development under socialism was highly politicized and did not function without the rigorous exercise of power in city planning and a corresponding, ideologically charged understanding of art. Socialist ideas and concepts influenced the planning of cities, industrial areas, and suburban settlements. After the fall of the walls, this socialist legacy has now come to be reflected in the transformation of the cityscapes as well as in the artistic responses to them. It lives on even after the collapse of the state socialisms, whether the inhabitants of the post-socialist cities want it to or not.

On the other hand, what was created by rigid socialist urban planning—at times without consideration for evolved social, economic, or demographic contexts—came into conflict with the parameters of a market economy after the political changes. That which was built under socialist auspices and that which was constructed and continues to be constructed under post-socialist conditions do not coexist peacefully, but rub up against each other uneasily. It is this very potential for tension that gives the post-socialist urban landscape as well as the artistic reflections on it their characteristic vitality.

The example of the post-socialist city shows once again that building as well as the artistic response to what is built are imaginative acts. Building is no less an act of the imagination as is the reflection on what is built. The planning of urban spaces, floating urban discourses, and images of the city in the fine arts, in literature, and in film all share this characteristic, but so do the material and economic aspects of planning and building and the artistic responses to it. All of these practices have to do with the human imagination, with the ability to respond artistically and creatively to the world, to cities, and, in this case, to the transformation of cities after the end of socialism.

A survey of the contributions to this volume reveals common ground and similarities between the cultural reinterpretations, recodings, and ruptures characterizing the post-socialist city from Eastern Europe to Asia. The conflict over the political subjugation of space shines through all the facets in a myriad of ways, with utopian spatial fantasies on the one side and imaginative efforts towards emancipation in art on the other. The perspectives collected here can be broken down into four larger complexes: theoretical concepts, artistic realizations, discursive recodings, and, finally, economic conditions.

1. Theoretical Concepts

The introductory contributions to this volume focus on the theoretical grounding of the phenomenon of the post-socialist city. They take a broader approach to its architectural and artistic legacy and provide a comparative overview of similar practices in different cities.

Mariusz Czepczyński analyzes representations and images from recent history, with a specific interest in the—sometimes more, sometimes less—labyrinthine trajectories of post-socialist icons. His study is informed by the idea of the cultural landscape as a system of representation and is based on his own observations, interviews, and media such as the Internet and advertisements. Socialism, Czepczyński argues, left behind an ideological landscape, and along with it thousands of icons waiting to be reinterpreted. He describes the reappreciation and new representation of old icons as exemplary of the liminal, and concludes that liminal times generate liminal landscapes.

Like Czepczyński, Lydia Coudroy de Lille and Miléna Guest also explore the transformation of the legacy of post-socialist cities. They refer to this transformation as a banalization, on both a material and a functional level. Their concept of banalization, however, is not axiological and in no way implies a judgment of "good" or "bad." The authors are rather interested in understanding the double process of value loss and value increase in the course of systemic change. Their examples are desacralization, minor shifts in meaning, and patrimonialization.

Arnold Bartetzky closes the introductory section with an analysis of monuments that represent a specific problem in the artistic treatment of the socialist inheritance. He is particularly interested in the current debate surrounding some statues of socialist leaders. Bartetzky refers to the monuments in question as cumbersome and unwieldy heritage. Focusing on the territory of the former GDR, he compares the contemporary—and widely diverging—reactions to statues of Karl Marx in Berlin, Leipzig, and Chemnitz. Bartetzky concludes that the change in ideological context is not the only reason monuments are removed or reinterpreted, but that there are also arbitrary factors at work, such as cultural initiatives, prominent local figures, or media campaigns—making it impossible to make generalized predictions as to the future fate of most of these monuments.

2. Artistic Realizations

The second block of texts takes as its object art projects in urban space, city films, and literature, in order to understand what inspires artists about urban space and the different ways in which they engage with it and become involved in it themselves.

In her contribution, Cynthia Imogen Hammond takes a look at artistic interventions in the post-socialist city. She understands urban interventions as mostly anonymous, illegal, and therefore oppositional acts in public space that blur the lines between art, vandalism, and politics. More specifically Hammond emphasizes Krystian Czaplicki aka Truthtag and his "truthtags." These are styrofoam objects the artist attaches to buildings, walls, and stairs, bringing these elements into a spatial and architectural dialogue with the three-dimensional graffiti. Hammond classifies these objects as *renegade ornaments*. They can be found particularly in cities that have been marked by developments such as the Westernization of formerly socialist space, the manufacturing of memory for tourist consumption, and the celebration of the pre-Soviet aspects of the urban environment.

Eva Binder discovers the phenomenon of Westernization in the city films of contemporary Russian cinema. In her essay, she traces the iterations of the post-Soviet metropolis in current films by directors such as Valerii Todorovskii, Aleksei Uchitel', Aleksei Balabanov, and Piotr Buslov. City films, such as the action and mafia thrillers by Balabanov and Buslov, use Moscow—and to a lesser degree, St. Petersburg—as integral elements of the narrative. At the same time, the cities on the screen invite viewers to compare them to real cityscapes. In order to assess the transformation of images that has taken place in recent decades, Binder first addresses Perestroika cinema, where she finds parallels to the Soviet cinema of the nineteen-twenties, before she turns to post-Soviet cinema. She concludes that the representation of Russian cities on film has undergone a value shift both in terms of content as well as aesthetics, which is linked to the loss of status of social elites.

Alfrun Kliems considers the case of the Czech underground, which puts forward an image of Prague strikingly at odds with the traditional theme of the "city of three peoples" made up of Germans, Jews, and Czechs (Tripolis Praga). She finds this new image in the Prague novels of the cult novelist Jáchym Topol and their film adaptations, in which post-socialist Prague is presented as a divided city. Topol is interested in the sociocultural fissures in urban space after the collapse of communism, refusing the trend of reviving the multicultural legacy of the Central European cities by casting a romanticized look back at the Tripolis Praga and its store of memories. Topol's work realigns values: from the elitist Prague modernism shaped by written language he moves by way of gutter slang to the speakers of a post-Babylonian "Kanak language."

3. Discursive Recodings

In this section, exemplary surveys show how the contemporary treatment of socialist buildings, apartment blocks, and whole city districts has led to controversy. Topics range from a former socialist drawing board city in Hungary, to a residential district in Bucharest and its revaluations throughout its history, to politically contaminated buildings and squares like the Palace of Culture and Science in Warsaw and the Independence Square in Kiev. The essays go back in time and include historical architectural planning in their analyses. Concluding the section is a spirited article on architectural battles in today's Bucharest.

First, however, Małgorzata Omilanowska introduces us to the Warsaw Palace of Culture and Science and Defilad Square. For twenty years now, the Palace has posed a challenge for Polish architecture and urban planning. Omilanowska asks to what extent this can be considered a post-totalitarian or even post-colonial problem. The discussions surrounding the Palace are increasingly focusing on the fact that it and the development around it are not only perceived as a product of Stalinism, but also as the result of Soviet oppression: designed by Russian architects, built out of Soviet material, constructed by Soviet workers, and declared a gift for the Polish people. Omilanowska describes this doubling of totalitarianism and colonialism as an ideological fusion for which there is, at present, no solution.

Wilfried Jilge shows how Kiev's Independence Square became a stage on which the Ukrainian state's politics of history is acted out. The decision in 2001 to fundamentally redesign the square and construct an ensemble of monuments there is inextricably linked to the functioning of state cultural production. The eclectic and kitschy features of the square perpetuate a tradition that Jilge calls "Soviet in form, national in content." The attempt was made, he argues, to establish "national historic" symbols and themes in as monumental a way as possible, an approach that reflects the Ukrainian government's contradictory understanding of history.

The idea of throwing up socialist industrial cities in the middle of the countryside seems no less imported. Béla Kerékgyártó introduces just such a city in his essay on Dunaújváros, with a focus on the urban development of the nineteen-fifties. Dunaújváros, once known as Stalin City, is considered a paradigmatic socialist drawing board city, comparable with Nowa Huta in Poland or Eisenhüttenstadt in the GDR. It was planned in a dogmatic fashion, which ran counter to real conditions and spontaneous development on the ground. Furthermore, the creation of a livable urban environment always had to take second place to the need to increase the volume of new housing. Kerékgyártó concludes with a discussion of the attempts in recent years to use educational institutions and art projects to introduce urban life into a city that does not, in reality, function like a city.

Carmen Popescu also considers earlier planning stages—in this case dating back to the turn of the twentieth century—in her study of the development of the Floreasca district in the northeast of Bucharest. By foregrounding the tension between existing construction and the district's changing image, Popescu shows how paradoxical the labeling of residential areas can be. The Floreasca district has been the object of a variety of myths of fortune and glamour throughout its history; myths that blur the lines between built reality, the social composition of the population, and imaginary projection. Popescu explores this by delving into the "prehistory" of the district, analyzing its historical layers, and then concluding with an ethnographically inflected look at the present.

Augustin Ioan chooses the essay genre to critically engage with contemporary Bucharest and its designers. According to Ioan, for the last twenty years the Romanian capital has been a post-socialist battleground with gated communities at its outskirts. A solution to the problem was presented in the guise of the so-called *Pact for Bucharest*, a manifesto by the city's residents, among which numbered a few planners and architects. Ioan acknowledges the good will and positive intention behind the manifesto, but nevertheless finds it to be amateurish, narrow-minded, provincial, and naïve. What is lacking, he suggests, are real visions for the future. Ioan asks questions that cut across the current debate: why do we view private property as our enemy? Why should we prefer the small and simple to the large and complex? And why are we always waging war against the new?

4. Economic Conditions

The final section leaves behind East Central Europe and turns first to Southeast Europe and then to Asia. The five cities presented here (Prishtina in Kosovo, Astana, Almaty, and Aktau in Kazakhstan, and Yerevan in Armenia) are all capitals, trading hubs, and/or cultural centers that attained a new status on the political map after the collapse of state socialism in the last decade—a status that now requires an architectural response.

Kai Vöckler uses Prishtina as an example of turbo urbanism, a vivid term he employs to describe the uncontrolled building taking place in post-conflict cities, such as Belgrade, Skopje, and Novi Sad. Vöckler argues that what we have here is a new kind of urbanization, whose roots can be found in the absence or weakness of those institutions that should be regulating building processes. Added to this are the rapid growth of the urban population as a result of migration and the presence of foreign organizations with their staff. Vöckler calls this latter phenomenon *Unmikistan*, from the acronym for the *United Nations Interim Administration Mission in Kosovo* (UNMIK). One effect of turbo urbanism's spontaneous building, aimed only at making a quick profit, is the absence of public facilities. Architects are not used, and the resulting architecture looks the part: a mish-mash of styles with historic-looking elements of décor.

Philipp Meuser's article turns to cities in Asia that are growing at least as quickly as those in Southeast Europe, whereas here it is a matter of *too* much political involvement in city planning. Meuser compares the architectural experiments in Astana, Almaty, and Aktau, paying particular attention to the attendant economic changes. Astana, Kazakhstan's new capital, has become a "two-speed city" and is on its way to becoming a megalomaniac city. Almaty, meanwhile, has remained the economic and cultural center of the country, despite having been politically disempowered. There are also new projects such as Rem Koolhaas' science city, an attempt to revive the Soviet concept of the *naukograd*.

Tigran Harutyunian goes back to the nineteenth century to describe a similar development surrounding the recasting of Yerevan as megalopolis, and argues that the Armenian capital is still looking for its new urban identity. Will it be a post-socialist or a postmodern city? On the one hand, post-Soviet architecture was influenced by the postmodern context in which it was designed; on the other, Western postmodernism was more than just an architectural revolution. This, however, is less true for post-Soviet postmodernism, which is most of all a result of the political collapse and shift in values, and has less to do with irony and dialogue.

This last block of texts, with its emphasis on the economic conditions of urban planning, not only shifts our perspective from Europe to Asia, but we find here a different perspective on the part of the objects as well: in Asia, Abu Dhabi is the ideal, not Moscow, London, or Paris.

Twenty years after the political ruptures of 1989/91, there seems to be a certain amount of common ground in the transformation processes of urban, post-socialist space—despite all the cultural, political, and social differences between the cities in question and despite their divergent conditions and traditions. This common ground is created if nothing else by the necessary response to the rupture in the image of the city and the clash between the socialist legacy and post-socialist appropriation, transformation, and upheaval. Planners, architects, artists, and residents took part in conflicting attempts to upgrade or destroy what was old, to create new architectural relationships or revive buried ones, and, in a striking number of cases, to cover over fissures and decay with gaudy color and kitsch—and so, ironically, to preserve it for the present.

We can also identify several different approaches taken in the region to constructing the future: a "Western European" upgrading and forced revitalization of historic city centers; an "American" stratification of residential neighborhoods according to income; and, finally, a rank "Asian" growth of cities.[2] Often, each of these approaches can be found in one and the same city—in brick and concrete, as a promise or a threat.

Acknowledgements

The idea for this book was born after an eponymous panel put on by the editors at the "IXth International Conference of the European Association for Urban History" (Lyon, August 27–30, 2008). At a meal following the panel, the participants decided, more or less spontaneously, to expand or revise their talks for publication and bring them together in a volume. We are very grateful to our colleagues for their willingness to do so and for the stimulating discussions at the conference. Their work formed the foundation of this project. In the ensuing months, other scholars with a variety of specializations contributed articles on the topic, and we would like to express our heartfelt thanks to them as well.

The publication of this book would not have been possible without the support of the *Center for the History and Culture of East Central Europe* (Geisteswissenschaftliches Zentrum Geschichte und Kultur Ostmitteleuropas) at the University of Leipzig, where the two editors are part of the research project "Imagining the Urban in East Central Europe: City Planning—Visual Culture—Poetry" (Imaginationen des Urbanen in Ostmitteleuropa. Stadtplanung—Visuelle Kultur—Dichtung). The printing of this publication was made possible by the German *Federal Ministry of Education and Research*.

We would also like to thank Louise Bromby, Laura Bruce, Millay Hyatt, and Peter Kovalsky for their translations and assistance in editing the texts. Without the help of Christian Dietz, who not only gave the articles a uniform format but also managed and arranged the images, this book would have been much less attractive. We are particularly grateful to him. Finally, we would like to thank the ıovis Verlag Berlin team for their professional support of this project.

Endnotes

1 First published in German in 2005: Karl Schlögel, *Marjampole oder Europas Wiederkehr aus dem Geist der Städte* (Munich: Hanser, 2005), 65. Transl. by John Kerr in Karl Schlögel, "The European Archipelago," in *The Europe beyond Europe. Outer Borders, Inner Limits*, ed. Manfred Sapper, Volker Weichsel and Andrea Huterer (Berlin: Berliner Wissenschafts-Verlag, 2007), 9–36 (special issue *Osteuropa*).

2 See: Kiril Stanilov, ed., *The Post-Socialist City. Urban Form and Space Transformations in Central and Eastern Europe after Socialism* (Dordrecht: Springer, 2007), 11–15.

THEORETICAL CONCEPTS

REPRESEN-TATIONS AND IMAGES OF "RECENT HISTORY"

The Transition of Post-Socialist Landscape Icons

Mariusz Czepczyński

Iconic Landscape as the Representation of Societies

In new cultural geography, as introduced by Denis E. Cosgrove and John B. Jackson,[1] cultural landscape is interpreted as a unique composition that represents the relationships of powers and history in a system of signs, written in many layers, reflecting aesthetic, political, ethical, economic, infrastructural, legal, and many other elements.[2] Cultural landscape can be seen as the main composer, as well as the living transmitter of culture, a picture consisting of symbols rather than of facts.[3]

Landscapes are the bodily expressions of the way of thinking, the experience and the hierarchical values of each group of society, as well as of each individual. The context is central to the understanding of the landscape, as it frames and embodies economic, social, and cultural processes.[4]

Landscape, in a similar way to language, can operate as a representational system. Signs, names, buildings, places, and spaces can be read and interpreted as geosymbols.[5]

Landscape is one of the most visible and "communicative" media, through which thoughts, ideas, and feelings as well as powers and social constructions are represented within a culture. Representations through landscapes are therefore central to the process by which the meaning of space is produced.[6] Members of the same culture share the same values and meanings and must reveal the same or a similar system of communication, based on mutually understood codes and signs. The representational function of landscape can be explained by the interpretation of icons, which play a similar role as words in a language system. The iconographical interpretation of a landscape, as highlighted by Cosgrove,[7] pays specific attention to the development of the study of the landscape as a way of seeing or representing the world. The aesthetic view of landscape has been explained as a way of conceptualizing and signifying the world. The landscape idea represents a way of seeing in which people have "represented to themselves and to others the world about them and their relationship with it, and through which they have commented on social relations."[8] This force, more abstract than material, is based on identity and symbolic links. Through their iconography, groups share the same representations, the same visions of the world and values, uniting them within the common space of belief. Iconography creates stable identities and helps to maintain these identities by resisting generalized circulation and partitioning space.[9] Cultural urban landscape is a system of representation, by which all sorts of objects, buildings, features, people, and events are correlated in a set of concepts or a mental representation we carry in our heads.[10]

The collapse of communism left highly ideological landscapes and thousands of icons to be reinterpreted. This essay aims to present iconic landscape repositioning practices in the post-socialist nations of Central Europe, defined as the former members of the so-called Eastern Bloc, which are now part of the European Union. The process of the rearrangement of icons is facilitated by the politics and practices of reminiscence and oblivion, and will be demonstrated by a set of examples from various cities around Central Europe. The study is based on interviews, regional media studies, internet discussion groups, a variety of published and dispersed materials, as well as the author's own comparisons, observations, and interpretations.

Crossing the Eras: Liminal Times—Liminal Landscapes

In times of profound and structural transformation, the landscape represents social and cultural trends and tendencies, sometimes hidden under a layer of declarations and practices. The transformation or liminal state is characterized by ambiguity, openness, and indeterminacy. Liminality is a period of transition, during which our normal limits relating to thought, self-understanding and behavior are relaxed, opening up the way to something new. People, signs, places, or things may not complete a transition, or a transition between two states may not be fully possible. Those who remain in a state between two other states may become liminal on a permanent or long-term basis. Victor Turner[11] gained notoriety by exploring Arnold van Gennep's[12] structure of the rites of passage and expanding theories on the liminal phase. Such liminal times can be branded by liminal landscapes: the landscape is no longer typical for the previous regime and planning, but at the same time quite different from the aspired ones. The liminal transformation of the Central European cultural landscape consists of multiple separations, transitions, and reincorporations, expressed in political statements, everyday practices, and living spaces. The burdensome meaning of communism was usually left deeply coded into both the external and internal structure of urban landscapes. The problem of dealing with the meanings and forms of the post-socialist leftovers has been one of the most significant issues of post-socialist landscape management. The 1989 "autumn of nations" brought not only an overturn of the communist dictatorships, but also the opportunity of finding new paths towards the future—freed from traces of fear, cowardice, or renunciation.[13]

Urban cultural landscape can be perceived as the visual scheme illustrating the relationship of power and control from which it has emerged.[14] The core meaning of a landscape is coded through symbols written into the setting. The meaning becomes especially visualized while it is being transformed, or during the liminal time. Power, control, and resistance as well as needs, lifestyles, and values are the foundations of the cultural landscapes debate. City scenery reflects powers, needs, and aspirations as well as glorious and tragic history, all of which are written into the symbols and signs. The urban landscape projects and communicates the view of the dominant element of society to the remainder of the population, through the symbols scripted into the setting.[15] The iconographical comprehension of a cultural landscape is based on the reinterpretation of landscape features as icons or visualized ideas. Symbolic images are turned into solid rock/brick/concrete/steel features, while cultural icons become landscape icons through the process of conceptualizing and signifying the world. The power written into the visible forms of urban structures features particularly strongly in totalitarian regimes, especially communist ones. In consequence, the place-memory discourse becomes more noteworthy in transitional societies, when a changing political and social system implies changing reminiscences and recollections of the past.[16]

History, Memory and Landscaping Policies

Memory and memorizing policy can be seen as the way in which the past is represented, and often becomes an important political resource. Memory can also be an important factor in social negotiations, as Michel Foucault says: "… if one controls people's memories, one controls their dynamism. It is vital to have the position of this memory, to control it, administer it, tell it what it must contain."[17] Power, control, history, and memory become core foci of a struggle over past and historical policies. Commemoration as well as oblivion is part of historical policy, which finds its material form in cultural landscape features.[18]

Central European countries have been undergoing a vast reinterpretation and repositioning of the "recent past." More than twenty years after the collapse of the Iron Curtain and the Berlin Wall, nations such as Hungary, the Czech Republic, Romania, and Poland are still confronting their communist legacy. The reinterpretation of the socialist past is an integral part of social and cultural transformation, in many cases as important as political or economic change. For most of the time they were in power, communist regimes and their leaders were active in ideological "place making," based on the creation of significant structures and coding ideas into architectural shapes. Communism celebrated the city and its landscape as the ultimate expression of political life and national spirit. The cultural landscape was the result of these constant negotiations and actions. Many major landscape features became political statements and proclamations. As a cultural declaration, a landscape icon carries the values and ideas embedded into it via related texts, memories, connotations, and implications.

Societies can be analyzed as communities connected by memories and obliviousness.[19] Every community needs some emotional binders incorporated into its institutions, symbols, and narrations. As much as any other political statement, socially produced and constructed cultural landscapes can be seen as "centers of human meaning as well as a mode of social control and repression."[20] Mechanisms of restraint are usually rooted in the past, while the interpretation of the past is frequently a political assignment. At the same time, artificial materializations of the past produce meanings and construct reality. For Orwell, the past—manifested in the memory practices of commemoration and rejection—influences contemporary identities and, to a further extent, future opportunities and developments.[21] Baker argues that the past influences or even determines the present.[22] He also points out the fact that the representations of the past tend to minimize diversity and complexity, bestowing past experience with an overriding sense of unity.[23]

Political control over memories can be institutionalized and facilitated by special historical institutions, established to explain, interpret, and disseminate a real/preferred/factual/

chosen or favored version of history. Institutions such as the *Instytut Pamięci Narodowej* (Institute of National Remembrance—Commission for the Prosecution of Crimes against the Polish Nation), the *Institutul de Investigare a Crimelor Comunismului* (Institute for the Investigation of Communist Crimes in Romania), and the Estonian-based *Foundation for the Investigation of Communist Crimes* were established with the aim of clarifying and adjusting the ambiguous communist period. The process of reminiscence and recognition has been facilitated by a set of political decisions, procedures, and bureaucratic practices.[24] Officially approved memories, particularly in totalitarian states, sometimes become a law and "legitimate truth," multiplied and propagated by the media and other institutions.

Memory is "archived" not only in national archives and in people's minds, which can be a very changeable and unstable form of storage, but also in written form, as well as in material artifacts such as landscape features. Cultural landscape can be analyzed as an icon of memory, but we must bear in mind the weaknesses, threats and subjectivities implied by its human character, very clearly visible in the selective process of recalling. The process of the selection of memories is conditioned or determined by several factors, most of which are related to the past. The result of recall and remembering is visualized and fixed in the material and intellectual features of the cultural landscape, facilitated by political and economic powers. Both the burdens and glories of history have their landscape representations, which can be read if a decoder and reader are found. The materialized and institutionalized features of memories sometimes become authorized elements of memorial policy, especially in authoritarian regimes, aimed at the abusive control of memory.[25]

History and heritage—that which we opt to select from the past—are used everywhere to shape emblematic place identities and support particular political ideologies.[26] What is kept and what is not kept is an indicator of ambitions, desires, and aspirations. The cultural and political history of a nation, society, or city has been constantly negotiated and materialized in its physical surroundings as an identity, based on what is remembered or rather recalled. "Even the landscapes that we suppose to be most free of our culture may turn out, on closer inspection, to be its product."[27] Landscape is read and appreciated through the cultural and historical memory that people give to it. "Vast and seemingly impersonal historical and/or economic 'forces' have always been the aggregate products of the choices that were made by individuals."[28] The process of the reinterpretation of memories is most clearly visible in transitional societies, where political, economic, and cultural factors enhance the redefinition of the past.

As pointed out by Turner, the liminal transformation of iconic landscapes can be summed up in three main categories or approaches, related directly to the phases of liminality: separation, transition, and reincorporation.[29]

Icons Assigned to Oblivion

According to Turner, separation is the first phase of liminality, which began just after the first free elections in 1989 and 1990. Sorting out the "good" and the "bad" has started this epistemological transformation, while "landscape cleansing" followed directly after the process of separation. Political iconoclasm has been typical revolutionary behavior, aimed at the reconstruction and reinterpretation of the past by eliminating unwanted icons that strongly represent the old system.[30] Unwelcome elements and qualities have been flushed out from the landscape, to make cities more habitable and acceptable for liberalized societies. Many of the unwanted codes and symbols, names and labels were eliminated by the physical destruction of features that were difficult to reinterpret, followed by the elimination of social practices and memories. The removal, renaming, rededication, or simply the reuse of the symbolic heritage of a discredited regime was, in itself, simple enough, providing "a new onomatology of places."[31] It seems that a considerable proportion of post-socialist societies would rather "put history aside" and not allow its painful memories to be evoked. Beginning in the early nineteen-nineties, the political aspect of cultural landscapes in post-socialist cities began to disappear. Since many sculptures and names directly conveyed ideologies and icons, many people believed that these landscape features mimed the communist system of concepts. The elimination of mimetic structures and objects was the most spectacular, theatrical, and often most remarkable part of post-communist landscape transformation.

The fate of the monuments of iconographical socialist heroes illustrates the political and social transformation in liminal societies. Several of the old icons in bronze were melted down to provide material for new statues, or were sold to private collectors; Cracow's Lenin went to Italy, the one in Berlin ended up in Holland. Some others appear to have "disappeared and been forgotten"; Sofia's Lenin statue, for example, which was removed in the late nineteen-nineties due to a road reconstruction, was never returned to its former place, and the Bucharest Lenin Monument was taken down from its high pedestal in front of the *House of Free Press* and laid down beside the kitchen wall of the suburban palace of Mogoşai (▶ 1). In every country in the region, many statues were literally repositioned, de-pedestaled, and removed to peripheral locations, the Hungarian examples of this being the best documented and analyzed.[32]

Established in 1993, the most famous and biggest "Cemetery of Public Monuments of the recent Past" has been recently renamed as *Memento Park Budapest*. The Statue Park in district of Szobor contains dozens of monuments, reliefs, and plates that have been relocated from the streets and squares of the Hungarian capital—including Lenin, Marx and Engels, memorials to the Soviet Soldier, the communist Martyrs, the Republic of Councils, and many more.[33] In 2001, a Lithuanian anti-communist entrepreneur opened a private theme park known as Stalin World or *Grūto Park*, 120 kilometers southwest of Vilnius. Two Lenins, Stalin, Brezhnev, and Dzerzhinsky, together with Mother Russia and many more sculptures and exhibitions, are displayed on twenty hectares of woodland. Another one, *Kozłówka*, established in the eastern part of Poland during the de-Stalinization period in 1956, is a much more modest collection of Marxist memorabilia, based on the "storage of unwanted icons." From the middle of the nineteen-nineties, a small sculpture park in Uniejowice, in southwestern Poland, grew rapidly as the neighboring municipalities were more then happy to donate their unwanted Monuments of the Soviet Army or local Polish communist heroes.[34] Probably the most "liminal," in a very broad sense of the word, is Moscow's *Sculpture Park* near Gorky Park, where contemporary art is on display alongside a random collection of former leaders, including Dzerzhinsky, Stalin, Brezhnev, Kalinin, numerous soldiers, and Soviet emblems, with hardly any interpretations (▶ 2). These specific theme parks are mostly visited by tourists, and have for the most part become just another interesting attraction rather than a history lesson.

World War Two memorials, predominantly dedicated to the Red Army, were easy targets for reinterpretation as soon as the Soviet Army withdrew.[35] Tanks, obelisks, and grand sculptures of victorious soldiers have evoked many bad memories, since the presence of the soldiers was followed by the tyranny of the communist regime. The monuments were often

1

1   Oblivion in silence: Bucharest's Lenin Monument, now abandoned in the suburbs, Mogoşai, Romania, 2005.

located in central parts of cities, at major crossroads, or on hills, constantly reminding locals of who they should be grateful to. After 1989, many of the Soviet war memorials were removed from the most exposed and central locations (▶ 3). Those in cemeteries were maintained and protected according to international conventions and treaties governing war graves. The most dramatic and best-known recent elimination of a post-communist icon was seen on the streets of the Estonian capital Tallinn at the end of April/beginning of May 2007. The removal of the "Bronze Soldier" from the city center brought a new dimension and significance to the discourse on icon separation. The memorial of a Soviet soldier, 1.83 meters high, was erected in 1947, close to the remains of a few Soviet soldiers buried nearby. Estonians say that the memorial symbolized Soviet occupation, while its supporters say it celebrated heroes who fought against the Nazis. The monument was removed from its original site in the early morning of Friday, April 27, and taken to a military cemetery a few days later. On the Friday evening, a crowd of more than 1,000 demonstrators gathered where the monument had stood.[36] The varying social constructions, attitudes, and representations of the "Bronze Soldier" mirror the different attitudes towards history evoked by the different fears and expectations of various social groups. There is no question that the Red

2

3

2   Storage of an unnecessary icon: Stalin Monument at the Sculptures Museum near Gorky Park, Moscow, Russia, 2008.
3   Hidden icons: former memorial of the Soviet Army, moved from a central square to a peripheral cemetery, Gdynia, Poland, 2005.

Army suffered high casualties while liberating Central European countries from the Nazis, but the goodwill engendered by this liberation was expended many times over during the four decades of Soviet domination that followed.

At the same time, practically enough, only a few iconic buildings were mimetically communist enough to be destroyed in the course of cultural landscape cleanings in Central Europe. Since it is far easier to redefine and reuse the buildings, only the most important ones had to be demolished. As late as 1999, the Mausoleum of Georgi Dimitrov, the Bulgarian communist leader, was torn down by the right wing royalist government in downtown Sofia (▶ 4). Many people also see Berlin's Palace of the Republic, which some vicious critics called the "Ballast of the Republic," as the victim of revenge. Its demolition began in 2006, officially due to the asbestos structure of the building. However, for most of the East Germans, the reason for eliminating this prominent symbol of the late German Democratic Republic was clearly a political one.[37] In some cases, the process of removing and/or demolishing icons became a fiesta and a symbolic gesture of liberation. The Berlin Wall had been the most popular icon, reflecting the division of Europe as well as communist supremacy and isolation. Its destruction clearly became the most illustrious symbol for the fall of a communist state in Europe (▶ 5).

Empty pedestals and the former sites of monuments such as the one left after the removal of the world's largest Stalin Monument in Prague, the empty spaces left where memorial plaques have been removed, or the vast squares and broad avenues designed for grand

4

4 Formerly meaningful, now empty: location of the Georgi Dimitrov Mausoleum, Sofia, Bulgaria, 2005.

5

marches and meetings, all silently speak of "the recent past." The message of these landscapes of silence can only be understood by those who still remember. Generally, many of the icons transformed in the early days have been completely forgotten. Fewer and fewer people can remember the former socialist street names, the exact locations of the monuments or the sites of former communist party buildings, let alone the meanings and texts officially attached to these icons.

The Re-Appreciation of Old Icons

Due to its limited contact with the outside world, the socialist landscape to some extent resisted the flow of globalization until the early nineteen-nineties. The functioning of collective memory is always deeply anchored in the practices of everyday life, more and more often focusing on the commercialization of the past in the process of market economy development. In many local communities, people have been seeking and articulating things related to the local past and then "merchandising" them by transforming them into products with certain market values.[38] There is a growing demand for grandeur and symbolism in the postmodern world, which can be found in many features of the socialist cultural landscape. Growing tourist demands, often combined with limited local attractions, have forced local societies to reinterpret old icons to meet the requirements and pressures of competitive markets.

5   Rebuilding history: illegally reconstructed part of the Berlin Wall near Checkpoint Charlie, Berlin, Germany, 2004.

This reinterpretation is based on "museumification," i.e., the preservation of features mainly from the nineteen-fifties as symbolic, museum-like objects, ignoring and stripping off their negative meanings. Historical patina turns the pompous landscape and Stalinist heritage into quite an attraction, which appeals to many tourists. Some of the grand designs have been preserved as architectural and cultural representations of past times. While some of the features have been quite widely recognized and appreciated, others are waiting for their moment of rediscovery. Some of the most spectacular Stalinist urban arrangements include the nineteen-thirties All-Union Agricultural Exhibition, which has not yet been fully recognized (▶ 6), together with the "Seven Sisters" towers (▶ 7), and Kutuzov Avenue in Moscow or Khreshchatyk Avenue in Kiev. Others have already become tourist attractions. The nineteen-fifties new town of Nowa Huta in Cracow, designed in a neo-renaissance and classicistic style known as Socialist Realism, the triumphalist former Stalin Alley in East Berlin, the neo-gothic street Lange Strasse in Rostock (▶ 8), or the Poruba district in Ostrava, Czech Republic (▶ 9) all meet tourist demands, having distinctive features more than fifty years old. All of these urban establishments are listed and are an integral part of city sightseeing programs, included in guide books and tourist maps.

One of the recent trends in Central European countries is a growing recognition for modernist design from the nineteen-sixties and -seventies. For some of the participants in post-socialist landscape discourse, modernist structures were the very best of "their times" that cities had to offer: functional, modern, avant-garde. Many of the architects and designers of these buildings are now recognized as architectural gurus. Recognition is connected with the nurturing of the previous and recent past. The local and national media cry out in indignation over plans involving the destruction of modernist architectural achievements. There is growing protest against the plans for significant refurbishments to the classically brutalist train station in Katowice (▶ 10) and Warsaw Central Train Station. Some of the architecture from the nineteen-seventies can be seen as highly original or artistic, even though, together with the structures from the nineteen-fifties and -sixties, it carries the stigma of being "wrongly inspired" or bearing "socialist texts." Many of the nineteen-seventies East German department stores *Zentrum*, were decorated with rather interesting metal-work façades. In the nineteen-nineties, most of the centrally located stores were bought by West German retail chains, and the old but somehow arty buildings are being replaced by functional, bunker-like new constructions, frequently covered in sandstone. One of the last to remain is the "tin box" in Leipzig, since the one on Dresden's prestigious Prager Strasse was demolished in the spring of 2007 along with the innovative and modern structures of the *Supersam* store in Warsaw. A new contextualization of the functionalist landscape is a difficult task, especially since most late twentieth-century urbanism generally failed to create significant landmarks and landscape icons. Also, in the eyes of a substantial number of Central European societies, mediocre architecture and scarcely functional functionalism are deeply connected with the failures of communist planning and landscaping. Negative connotations and associations,

6 Liminal melange: Lenin Monument and/or donkey and SpongeBob SquarePants, entrance to the former All-Union Agricultural Exhibition, Moscow, Russia, 2008.
7 Stalinist model: residential tower, one of the "Seven Sisters," copied with some variations around the Eastern Bloc in the 1950s, Moscow, Russia, 2008.

7 8

6

9

8 National in form, socialist in meaning: the 1950s "neo-gothic" granary-shaped apartment tower, Rostock, Germany, 2008.

9 Grand aspiration, grand design: triumphalist crescent in the 1950s district of Poruba, Ostrava, Czech Republic, 2007.

together with the limited practicality of block design and social malfunction, leave blocks being strongly interpreted as a "socialist landscape."[39]

Sometimes the re-appreciation of the former communist icons represents a much deeper level of admiration than a mere formal respect for an interesting architectural feature. Important sections of post-socialist societies, especially people who are older, less educated, or from the peripheries, have to some extent been excluded from the benefits of the free market, and consider democracy as leading to chaos, anarchy, and disorder. The pauperized, hopeless, disappointed, and/or neglected see the communism of the past in a different light, as an era of stability, order, together with social and economic justice. Icons such as memorials, red stars, or hammers and sickles are seen as an important part of personal, class, and sometimes national identities.

New Representations of Old Icons

Changing the social construction and the context of the icon does not completely transform all aspects of the landscape, but it definitely symbolizes political and cultural transformation of the liminal societies. The complexity of the practices of reinterpretation is mirrored in various attitudes and the contextualization of different social groups. Constructivism in a social sense emphasizes the shared character of language and landscape and is based on the assumption that things don't mean anything on their own; people do construct meanings, using systems of representation with their concepts and signs. Meanings are not conveyed

10   Disputed heritage: brutalist train station in Katowice, Poland, 2009.

by any feature of the material world, but by the system we use to represent our concepts. It must be remembered that one object or feature can have different constructivist meanings, allocated to it by different social groups. Frequently, groups of young people use a distinctly different system of representation from that of the older generation, so places and urban features might have separate constructivist meanings for them. Reconstruction is usually related to the reincorporation of deconstructed features and icons. According to Turner, reincorporation is the final rite by which the division between the "old" and the "new" becomes insignificant and eventually disappears or is used in new social roles.[40] This phase may have just begun in Central Europe, and it will most likely be implemented by the next generation. Numerous cultural groups create their own systems of representation, based on distinctive constructions resulting from specific experiences and expectations.

The former icons of the communist era landscape can be repacked and reinterpreted to meet contemporary place marketing demands. The new social context of nationalist pride has been attached to the Civic Center of Bucharest, especially to the Palace of the Parliament (▶ 11). Travel guides and brochures proudly concentrate on the magnificence and opulence of the building, constructed by Romanians alone using Romanian raw materials, while its infamous initiator is practically ignored in local texts or contexts. One of the most popular examples of the reconstruction of cultural codification and renegotiation is a statue depicting the head of Karl Marx in Chemnitz (formerly Karl-Marx-Stadt) in Germany. The huge head stands on a pedestal in front of a tall administration building at one of the central

11   The pride of the nation: former Palace of the People, now the Palace of the Parliament, Bucharest, Romania, 2005.

12 Looking for new identities: Stalin's gift to the Polish nation—the Palace of Culture and Science, Warsaw, Poland, 2008.

crossroads in Chemnitz. According to Weiske, 70 percent of inhabitants questioned confirmed that they see it as a symbol of the city.[41] Similarly, Warsaw's Palace of Culture and Science, a Stalinist mega-structure at the heart of the city, became a historical monument in 2007 and is one of the major symbols of the fast-growing capital of Poland (▶ 12).[42]

A further new but stylish use of the old iconic features can be observed in dozens of post-communist theme pubs and bars located in many cities in the region. These bars, such as the Committee in Lublin (▶ 13), the Under Red Hog in Warsaw, or the Café Sybille in Berlin attract both local clientele and tourists, with a familiar and funky slant. Both the names and the interior design, full of communist propaganda and icons, recall the communist past, but only in a funny, amusing, odd, curious, or comical way. These places are being promoted as "the last secrets of the Communists," with stylized pictures of Marx, Engels, Lenin, and other iconic "saints" enhancing the interior design. Some of the exhibits are original communist features, while others are recent copies. Many of these places are not only full of tourists, but also often frequented by local students, for whom the quest for a post-socialist past is a means of self-identification in a globalizing and amalgamated world. For most of the young tourists visiting *socialist theme parks* or pubs, a trip to communist times is as exotic as a journey to another continent, if not even more so.

Landscape icons were often intentionally left as a warning, in keeping with particularly anti-communist historical policies. Paying tribute to the heroes of the anti-communist resistance was often more than a mark of respect for the victims; it was also used for contemporary political reasons by conservative and right wing parties. The new memorials are often located in significant places such as former prisons or police quarters. They have been part of an ongoing process of commemoration rather than static objects that, once erected, are gradually forgotten. Their construction has drawn communities into lively debates about the past and, as new axis mundi, serve as the focus points of new rituals of commemoration.[43] "When justice does not succeed in being a form of memory, memory itself can be a form of justice," said Ana Blandiana, the founder of the *International Center for Studies on Communism*, based in Bucharest. The policy of "reminding to remember" reflects the attitudes of local and national authorities, but also of many ordinary people. The most famous examples of the transition of meanings and functions in memorials include the former prison of Sighet, Romania, which was turned into the *Memorial of the Victims of Communism*, or those located in the buildings of former state security quarters, such as the Budapest *House of Terror* and Berlin's *Stasimuseum*.

Conclusions

The settings of Central European cities carry the prints or stigmas of at least half a century of socialism. The production of new layers of meaning and different interpretations of post-socialist landscapes is an ongoing process. After the rapid conversions of the early nineteen-nineties, the process of landscape reinterpretation has recently settled down or

entered a new phase. It seems that the chronological sequence of the three phases as defined by Turner[44] may not always take place, as shown above. Sometimes a number of the aspects of the pre-liminal structure are incorporated by certain social groups, while other features are simultaneously separated by other groups. De-communization and the transformation of meanings are always connected with the cultural background of society, as well as with hopes and aspirations. Cultural landscapes, as a mélange of forms, meanings, and functions, project and represent the powers, needs, and values of society. People's attitudes towards post-socialist landscapes mirror previous humiliation and dictatorship as well as their present acceptance and reconciliation with their own history, and can be seen as an explicit indicator of political and cultural transformations. At the same time, the fate of old communist symbols represents attitudes towards the "recent past" and can be seen as a litmus paper, indicating positions in the liminal transformation.

Cultural coding does not remain stable; it is subject to change in time and space. It can or must be continuously reflected upon and negotiated. A society without memory, which banishes past evil to the realms of oblivion, somehow legitimizes it. Such a society is built upon the gratitude and loyalty of people who have denounced their neighbors, and often seized the property of their victims. On the other hand, a society that continues to live in the specific dictatorship of the past, upholding its memories, becomes a specific form of public cult. Incessantly creating new wrongs, it is condemned to stagnation. Not only the

13   Fun and laughter: murals in the post-communist thematic pub "Committee," Lublin, Poland, 2006.

terror of obliviousness, but also the terror of memory is used to achieve temporary social, political, or economic goals.[45] Memory, as the representation of the past, is an important political resource.[46]

The past, manifested in the memory practices of commemoration and rejection, influences contemporary identities and, to a further extent, future opportunities and developments.[47]

Endnotes

1 Denis E. Cosgrove, *Social Formation and Symbolic Landscape* (London/Sydney: Croon Helm, 1984); John B. Jackson, *"The World Itself." Discovering Vernacular Landscape* (New Haven, Connecticut: Yale University Press, 1984).

2 Denis E. Cosgrove and Stephen Daniels, "Introduction: Iconography and Landscape," in *The Iconography of Landscape. Essays on the Symbolic Representation, Design and Use of Past Environments*, ed. Denis E. Cosgrove and Stephen Daniels (Cambridge, Mass.: Cambridge University Press 2004), 1–10; Iain S. Black, "(Re)reading Architectural Landscapes," in *Studying Cultural Landscapes*, ed. Iain Robertson and Penny Richards (London: Arnold, 2003), 19–46.

3 Sharon Zukin, *Landscapes of Power. From Detroit to Disney World* (Berkeley, Ca./Los Angeles/London: University of California Press, 1993).

4 Mariusz Czepczyński, *Cultural Landscape of Post-Socialist Cities. Representation of Powers and Needs* (Aldershot, Hampshire: Ashgate, 2008).

5 Jean Gottmann and Robert A. Harper, *Since Megalopolis: The Urban Writings of Jean Gottmann* (Baltimore, Maryland: John Hopkins University Press, 1990).

6 Stuart Hall, "The Work of Representation," in *Representation. Cultural Representation and Signifying Practices*, ed. Stuart Hall (London/Thousand Oaks/New Delhi: Sage Publications, 2002).

7 Denis E. Cosgrove, *Social Formation and Symbolic Landscape* (Madison, Wisconsin: The University of Wisconsin Press, 1998).

8 Cosgrove, (see note 7), 1.

9 Joel Bonnemaison, *Culture and Space. Conceiving a New Cultural Geography* (London/New York: I. B. Tauris, 2005); Mariusz Czepczyński, "Understanding Cultural Landscapes: Approaches and Practices," *Past Place: Newsletter of the Historical Geography Specialty Group. The Association of American Geographers* 15 (2006:1): 5–6.

10 Gregory J. Ashworth, "The Conserved European City as Cultural Symbol: The Meaning of the Text," in *Modern Europe. Place. Culture. Identity*, ed. Brian Graham (London: Arnold, 1998), 261–286.

11 Victor Turner, *Dramas, Fields, and Metaphors: Symbolic Action in Human Society (Symbol, Myth, & Ritual)* (New York: Cornell University Press, 1975).

12 Arnold van Gennep, *The Rites of Passages* (Chicago: University of Chicago Press, 1960).

13 See: Neil Leach, "Architecture or Revolution?" in *Architecture and Revolution. Contemporary Perspectives on Central and Eastern Europe*, ed. Neil Leach (London/New York: Routledge, 1999); Ilona Sármány-Parsons, "Aesthetic Aspects of Change in Urban Space in Prague and Budapest during the Transition," in *Social Change and Urban Restructuring in Central Europe*, ed. György Enyedi (Budapest: Akadémiai Kiadó, 1998), 209–31.

14 *Studying Cultural Landscapes*, ed. Iain Robertson and Penny Richards (London: Arnold, 2003).

15 Zukin, (see note 3).

16 Czepczyński, (see note 4).

17 Michel Foucault, *Discipline and Punish: The Birth of the Prison* (New York: Random House, 1975), 25.

18 Czepczyński, (see note 4).

19 Ernest Renan, "What is a Nation" in *The Nationalism Reader*, ed. Omar Dahbour and Micheline R. Ishay (New York: Humanity Books, 1995).

20 Christopher Tilly, *A Phenomenology of Landscape: Places, Paths and Movements* (Oxford: Berg, 1994), 19.

21 George Orwell, *Nineteen Eighty-Four. A Novel* (London: Secker & Warburg, 1949).

22 Alan R. H. Baker, *Geography and History: Bridging the Divide* (Cambridge, Mass.: Press Syndicate of the University of Cambridge, 2003).

23 Baker, (see note 22); Czepczyński, (see note 4).

24 Czepczyński, (see note 4).

25 Orwell, (see note 21).

26 Brian Graham, "The Past in Europe's Present: Diversity, Identity and the Construction of Place" in Graham, (see note 10), 19–52.

27 Simon Schama, *Landscape and Memory* (New York: Alfred A. Knopf, 1995), 9.

28 Joseph Rykwert, *The Seduction of Place. The History and Future of the City* (Oxford: Oxford University Press, 2000), 9.

29 Turner, (see note 11).

30 See: Kenneth E. Foote, Attila Tóth, Anett Arvay, "Hungary after 1989: Inscribing a New Past on Place," *The Geographical Review* 90 (2000:3): 301–34; Czepczyński, (see note 4).

31 Grzegorz Węcławowicz, "The Changing Socio-Spatial Patterns in Polish Cities," in *Prozesse und Perspektiven der Stadtentwicklung in Ostmitteleuropa, Münchener Geographische Hefte* 76, ed. Zoltan Kovács and Reinhard Wiessner (Passau: L.i.s. Verlag, 1997).

32 Foote/Tóth/Arvay, (see note 30).

33 Szobor Park Homepage, 2007, http://www.szoborpark.hu (last accessed April 28, 2010).

34 "Przytułek dla pomników PRL," [Shelter for the PRL Monuments] *Polityka* June 9 (2007:23): 17.

35 Foote/Tóth/Arvay, (see note 30).

36 "Tallinn Erupts in Deadly Riot, Bronze Soldier Removed," *The Baltic Times* April 28 (2007), http://www.baltictimes.com/news/articles/17774/ (last accessed January 3, 2009).

37 Czepczyński, (see note 4).

38 See: Piotr T. Kwiatkowski, *Pamięć zbiorowa społeczeństwa polskiego w okresie transformacji* [The Collective Memory of Polish Society during the Period of Transformation] (Warsaw: Scholar, 2008).

39 Czepczyński, (see note 4).

40 Turner, (see note 11).

41 Christine Weiske, "Stadt und Welt. Fiktive Verortungen als die Images der Stadt Chemnitz," in *Neue Länder—Neue Sitten? Transformationsprozesse in Städten und Regionen Ostdeutschlands*, ed. Christine Hannemann, Sigrun Kabisch, Christine Weiske (Berlin: Verlag Hans Schiler, 2002).

42 Agata Passent, *Pałac wiecznie żywy* [The Palace is Still Alive] (Warsaw: Spis Treści, 2004).

43 Foote/Tóth/Arvay, (see note 30).

44 Turner, (see note 11).

45 Karl-Markus Gauss, *Das europäische Alphabet* (Vienna: Paul Zsolnay Verlag, 1997).

46 Michel Foucault, *Power/Knowledge: Selected Interviews and Other Writings, 1972–1977* (New York: Random House, 1980); Czepczyński, (see note 4).

47 Czepczyński, (see note 4).

TOWARDS BANALIZA-TION?

Trans-Forming the Legacies of the Post-Socialist City

Lydia Coudroy de Lille
Miléna Guest

The schism is devoid of sense out of reference to
any previous state:
the absolutely New is unintelligible,
even as a novelty.
Paul Ricoeur, *Temps et récit*, 1984[1]

Introduction

The city of Berlin has recently proposed a new attraction for tourists: an audio-guide allows them to follow the tracks of the former Berlin Wall, which no longer stands. Indeed, with the need for new plots in the inner city, reconstruction quickly swallowed up all traces of its former site, leaving no scar behind, and utterly confusing most tourists. The disappearance of material elements in this way is part of the ordinary evolution of the urban morphology. But sometimes, it raises basic questions about the relationship between a society and its territory. This is exactly what has been happening in post-socialist cities for the last twenty years. Indeed in these cities, and above all in the capital cities, there are emblematic, relevant monuments or buildings whose purpose was to exalt the regime's grandeur. These were "monuments such as our enemies could not imagine, even in their dreams" as Sergei Kirov said.[2]

This paper aims to question the transformation of socialist places. In the literature, the transformation of former socialist cities has mostly been analyzed in the light of globalization, social polarization, or the privatization of housing.[3] Here, we aim to observe the transformation of post-socialist cities according to the etymology of the word. To trans-form means to give a new form to an object, or to change it. This can be done in terms of its material morphology, but also by means of an action altering its signification, its social, cultural, use. The urban objects we will analyze are the most relevant witnesses of the socialist period in Warsaw and Sofia. During the construction that took place in the period 1945–90, some buildings, monuments, and houses were designed in order to express the magnificence and the power of the political order and the values of the new society: they were elements of the "symbolic policies" of the socialist regimes, such as hymns, flags, or political celebrations and parades.[4] They were in a sense exceptional. Our purpose is to analyze a trend in the transformation of these urban places that we will call banalization.

The banalization of a place is a kind of transformation, which can be material and/or functional. Our hypothesis is that banalization occurs through a double process of loss and gain: on the one hand, there is the loss of an ideological value (the socialist one), of monumentalism, of visibility, and a "loss of tragedy," and on the other hand, these urban objects also gain other functions, other values, a greater social acceptance, a kind of lightness. Of course, the meaning of banalization we are proposing is subjective. But we do not give it an axiological dimension, considering it to be bad or good. We will try to show the process by which, in post-socialist countries, the urban landscape is becoming less and less "socialist." We will also raise the question of the cultural and political debates surrounding this process. The comparison between two capital cities, Warsaw and Sofia, allows us to investigate the question of whether the trends of banalization or "counter-banalization" are general processes or if they still depend on a national context.[5]

From the Socialist to the Post-Socialist City

The political, social, and economic processes that are going on in former socialist countries are leading to a kind of "normalization" of the structure of the state and of society. The fall of the socialist regimes has also resulted in the erosion of certain social practices. Before analyzing these, we should recapitulate on what the components of the socialist identity of cities actually were.

When speaking of the socialist city we refer to two categories, not exactly identical but overlapping in some aspects: the first is the ideal city, whose characteristics were defined in ideological and political literature; and the second is the city of real socialism, whose material shapes and sociological and economical characteristics have been widely analyzed in the field of social sciences. In this paper we will focus on the second one. As outlined in Richard French and Ian Hamilton's famous book,[6] but also in György Enyedy's works on the socialist city, the main features of socialist urbanization led to the following elements[7]:

> On a macro-scale, the cycle of urbanization in socialist Europe differed from the developments in Western Europe. The fastest cycle of urban growth began after World War Two and was related to the needs of industrialization. Thus not only the tempo, but also the location of urbanization was in keeping with the demands of the largest national plants.

> On a micro-scale, we observe a specific organization of urban density in the socialist city: on the one hand, urban density is lower than in West European cities, thanks to the numerous parks and the high occupation of space by industrial zones or transport infrastructures on state-owned land. On the other hand, the highest population densities occur in the first periphery, where large housing estates are situated.

> Urban segregation did not totally disappear, despite the promise of an end to the class struggle in the city. But the social building and allocation of dwellings produced another feature of the social division of space, with older people in the inner city and families with young children in the new housing estates.

> The visual identity of the socialist city was also composed of a range of monuments and buildings that gave an ideological significance to the landscape. Most of them were erected during the first decade of the socialist period, especially under the reign of socialist realism in the culture of Central Europe, i.e., 1949–55.

The transition to the market economy had a large impact on the urban landscape. Whether it occurred in a quick process (shock therapy) or gradually, this shift considerably increased the need for services, especially in the capital cities. Furthermore, the competition for space occurred at a time when land regained a price. This led to a densification of the inner city and sometimes to the formation of central business districts, such as in Warsaw. These economic and urban transformations took place within a context of political decentralization.[8] The municipalities, entirely self-governing since 1990, could not always stand up to the pressure of private investors and their urgent need for land, offices, or infrastructures. In the nineteen-nineties, the adaptation of the city to the demands of the market economy proved to be a main concern, with priority over other topics such as the destiny of socialist legacies. A new legal framework was set up through the privatization of the economy, with the architectural evolution of cities partially owed to foreign investors. Although this adaptation did not take place exactly in the same way in each post-socialist country,[9] the fact is that it has led to what can be defined as a process of banalization.

Desacralization of Communist Legacies: Some Features of Banalization

The founding myths of communist regimes were built on a problematic reinterpretation of history, which is still now the cause of heavy ideological conflicts. This is why most political monuments and representational statues were soon destroyed; they had simply become intolerable. But many pieces of socialist architecture remained after 1990, passing through a process of neutralization, or banalization. This process sometimes affects the architectural shape itself, and sometimes only the way in which it is used. The banalization of a monument or an urban site may be the result of a clear political and social decision, or merely the outcome of several dissociated actions: post-socialist societies dealt with their urban legacies in many different ways. Are these a transgression, a kind of desacralization of inherited forms, or should they be seen as a mere "digression?" Some concrete cases of the transformation of communist heritages in Warsaw and Sofia will be considered, and treated as different modalities of banalization. Some of these case studies are emblematic places that might be considered "exceptional," whereas others are more "ordinary" because they were reproduced in urban spaces on a massive scale for the purposes of everyday life and common use.

"Minimal" Banalization

During or just after the fall of the Iron Curtain, the most symbolic elements (Lenin statues, red stars) on the front or roofs of public buildings were generally destroyed or removed in public demonstrations. But the official and administrative buildings remained untouched and are still used for administrative purposes, having lost their symbolic attributes. Those which were built in the era of Socialist Realism still have an easily recognizable visual identity, but their symbolism has gradually faded, and they have become more acceptable.

Designed to become the architectural model of a new political order, the House of the Party in Sofia (1948–54) represented the ambitions of new political power. It is not simply an emblematic building, but a symbolic estate that transformed the organization of the whole city under the plan of Luben Tonev. It was built after several architectural competitions. The first of these was held in November 1944, with the participation of Aleksei Shchusev, the architect of the Lenin Mausoleum in Moscow, and Nikolai Baranov, the chief architect of Leningrad. The second took place in 1945, under the guidance of the *Direction of Architecture and Urbanism in Sofia* (DAU) with the consultation of Soviet members of the *Academy of Architecture of the USSR*, and the final one in 1947. After this third competition, the House of the Party was erected, approved by Georgi Dimitrov, who was then the Prime Minister.[10]

This occurred in a particularly historic moment: the proclamation of the People's Republic of Bulgaria in September 1946 and the adoption of a new Constitution in 1947. The construction of the House of the Party represented an official celebration of the new system and participated in the legitimization of the new political power. The project of the architect Petso Zlatev was ultimately adopted. The architecture of the Party House is totalitarian in character—both in its form, its symbols, and its relationship with its surroundings, overlooking the walls of the ancient Roman city Serdica on the west side. The location is central, adjacent to the House of Commons and the Saint Sofia and Aleksander Nevski churches. Its front overlooks one of the oldest squares of the city, Largoto Square (named Lenin Square at that time). In 1990, it was surrounded by the tents of the "City of Truth," a movement protesting against the first so-called "free elections" in Bulgaria, won by the Socialist Party (▶ 1).

Social pressure demanded the demolition of the mausoleum and people removed the Red Star from the Party House. The building was set on fire, and parts of the archives were destroyed. François Maspero recounts: "Close to the subway building site, which was closed *sine die*, the tower of the disused building in the Stalinist style—albeit a particularly massive, low-built, rustic construction—had lost its red star. A helicopter had brought it to an unknown destination, waiting for better days."[11] The building was also vandalized and partially burned during demonstrations in 1990. Currently it accommodates various committees and working groups of the National Assembly.

The square is now undergoing further transformations: preparations for the construction of two office buildings on Largoto Square are underway. Furthermore, at the occidental extremity of the square, the statue of Sophia has been erected in exactly the same position as where the Lenin Monument used to stand. The new Master Plan for Sofia 2007–20 makes a breach in the occidental direction into the Old Town of Sofia, offering space for the development of a new *Central Business District* (CBD) (▶ 2).

1   The City of Truth in front of the House of the Party, Sofia, Bulgaria, 1990.
2   The Largoto Square, Sofia, Bulgaria, 2002.

Post-Socialist Chaos Producing Banalization

In many cases, banalization does not concern the buildings themselves, but their surroundings. As mentioned above, the lack of urban planning, political decentralization at the benefit of the communes, and the need for space for offices and commercial activities created a high demand for land in the city core. As a result, a new feature of space has appeared in the inner city, often seen as spatial disorder, or even chaos. A large number of functional buildings appeared—offices, hotels, shops, with advertising banners covering the entire façades of buildings and also, especially at the beginning of the nineteen-nineties, numerous kiosks and stalls for individual businesses. The liberalization and privatization of urban space did not exactly produce central business districts, but something resembling both a central business district and uncontrolled urbanization, not much different to what might happen in non-developed countries.[12]

This is what happened to one of the largest open spaces in Warsaw, Defilad Square (Parades Square), in front of the Palace of Culture and Science. Planned in 1955, this 250-meter-long square was the most important public space in the capital of the People's Republic of Poland: not only military and political marches, but also other major political events took place here. It was the scene of military repression during martial law in December 1981, and also of the mass celebrated by John Paul II in 1987. But starting in 1990, this empty space was suddenly invaded by hundreds of market salesmen, who installed themselves first on the square and then in numerous kiosks (▶ 3, 4).

This "bazaar" economy was partially transferred to two big metallic warehouses that temporarily occupied the square. Meanwhile, one of them accommodated a supermarket, whose owner is now a very wealthy businessman in Poland. Moratoriums followed one after another, and these two unsightly hangars continued to stand on the square until the beginning of 2009. The erection of kiosks, provisory commercial buildings and large

3

4

3　The supermarket on the Defilad Square, Warsaw, Poland, 2009.
4　The kiosks on the Defilad Square, Warsaw, Poland, 1997.

5

advertising banners on the roof of the warehouses undoubtedly transformed the landscape surrounding the Palace of Culture and Science, whose basement was hidden; the open space itself disappeared under this profusion of commercial activity. It lost its ideological signification and took on entirely new functions, and the landscape plainly reflected this new land use (▶ 5).

The accumulation of advertisements—much less controlled than in West European cities—in the urban landscape in the areas directly surrounding former politically symbolic places enhances the process of banalization. These banners and posters aim to sell goods and films using the same words, signs, slogans, and pictures as in any other metropolis. This banalization is an effect of what the French architect David Mangin calls "corporatization" or "brandization"[13]: the shape of the contemporary city tends to be designed, directly or in a roundabout way, for the needs of corporate firms. In addition to this process of privatization stricto sensu there are the effects of globalization, which find new markets for the international networks of shops, restaurants, et cetera in cities such as Warsaw or Sofia.

How Does the Market Economy "Digest" the Socialist Architecture?

More often than not, however, public buildings inherited from the former regime are recycled, either partly or in full, to take over other functions. Significant expanses of floor space in the core of capital cities had been devoted to administrative, cultural, or political

5   Advertising on the Constitution Square, Warsaw, Poland, 2009.

uses. In the early nineteen-nineties the budget for these areas was greatly reduced, and at the same time private corporations were in search of offices to let. These square meters downtown were a precious resource before the boom of the real estate market, and some public buildings became partly occupied by private firms, which increased their profitability. Thus, the needs of the market economy led to the loss of the ideological dimension of the most symbolic socialist or Stalinist buildings in the capital cities.

The Palace of Culture opened in Sofia in 1981 for the 1300th anniversary of Bulgaria. It consists of thirteen halls, over eight floors (plus three underground levels), accommodating 5,000 seats altogether. Until 1990, it was named after its initiator Ludmila Jivkova, Todor Jivkov's daughter. After 1990, one part was converted into shopping malls, with the higher levels continuing to host major cultural and economic events. In 2005, the Palace was even distinguished as the best conference center in the Balkans.

The Palace of Culture and Science in Warsaw, 230 meters high, was built between 1952 and 1955 under the direction of the Soviet architect Lev Rudnev. It was designed to house several public institutions such as the *Academy of Sciences*, the *Institute of Marxism and Leninism*, a cinema, theaters, the *Youth Palace*, a swimming pool, and a large congress hall. Faced with the enormous costs of maintenance, the city of Warsaw decided to lease part of the office space to private institutions such as banks and a private university (1997).

The same applies to the building named the House of the Party in Warsaw, constructed in 1951 (architects: Wacław Kłyszewski, Jerzy Morzyński, Eugeniusz Wierzbiecki), which became the seat of the *Polish Stock Exchange* in 1991.

These examples show how income derived from the commercial exploitation of the buildings allows their maintenance costs to be met. Furthermore, the emblematic sites of communism have acquired a new identity through this shift in function. Can a silent ideological victory of capitalism be observed here? The communist experience and the places that should have represented it have lost their tragic dimension. The material legacies of the communist regime, which were supposed to embody the promise of a radical political change, have now been desacralized, recycled.

After Banalization: Patrimonialization?

Every day in any given town, some houses or old factories are torn down because of their material condition, their low economic value, or because social use legitimates it. This is an ordinary process of reconstructing, made possible when a system of economical, social, cultural, and political agents agree on a common set of values and needs. In the early nineteen-nineties this allowed for the destruction of buildings from the nineteen-forties or -fifties. But in the late nineteen-nineties, it seems that some opinions began to turn towards a more patrimonial attitude.

The question of the political use of the past often refers to a restorative action and to the importance that we attach to the setting up of a consensual, indeed universal memory, which is questioned by Maurice Halbwachs.[14] Nevertheless, our intention is not to challenge the foundations of this memory, but to shed light on the relations between different forces that institute the changing means of post-communist places. Behind the desire to develop and maintain some legacy and some places, the social and political issues of capturing symbolic and economic resources and the appropriation of space have to be studied.

Tabula Rasa: The Political and Economic Foundations of Demolition in the Post-Socialist City

The context of systemic transformation is underpinned not only by a reversal of values, but also by the destruction of representative places. The removal of statues was a part of the dismantling of a political system, and can be treated as a historical turn. But some years later, buildings from the communist period were destroyed for technical, mostly economic reasons. Sometimes, they simply no longer fit in with the symbolic and cultural values of the new elite, and are thus destroyed.[15] Some of them occupied central locations, and had to make room for new investments. This occurred in the early stages, in an atmosphere of great indifference.

The Moskwa cinema, built in Warsaw in 1948, was an imposing object due to the modernity of its design, the large square in front of it, and two lion statues at the bottom of the steps leading to the entrance. It was closed in the nineteen-nineties and demolished. In place of the square and the cinema, a new investment was made. The new building, which is rather banal, occupies the whole area, with no open space remaining. It contains offices, a shopping mall, and a multiplex cinema. The only relics of the former building are the two lions; however, standing close to such an ordinary object, these are now hardly visible, having been deprived of any perspective and monumentality. The comments of Polish architects were very caustic, and this is understandable. They were intensified by the fact that the Moskwa cinema had been famous thanks to a political photo taken of it on December 13, 1981, the day martial law was introduced. On this day, Chris Niedenthal shot a photo of a tank standing in front of the Moskwa cinema, on snow-covered ground; a large poster hangs on the front of the cinema, showing the title of a film, "Apocalypse now." This photo, very famous at the time, was published in Newsweek, and contributed to the tragic dimension of the Moskwa cinema, which was recalled when it was demolished (▶ 6, 7, 8).

But the group of specialists participating in this debate was rather a small one. In the nineteen-nineties, the Polish public was not overly worried by the removal of pieces of the "ordinary" city. Nevertheless, this situation has been evolving since the end of this decade, clearly indicated by a larger debate arising in the case of a supermarket.

The first supermarket in Poland opened in 1962 in Warsaw; its name is "Supersam" (architects: Ewa and Maciej Krasiński, Jerzy Hryniewiecki). Its architecture is an example of modernism, and when it was built, not only was the concept of self-service entirely new in the country, but also the building's design; a very high and suspended roof provided an

6

6   Moskwa cinema, Warsaw, Poland, 1981.

7   The Silver Screen building, instead of the Moskwa cinema, Warsaw, Poland, 2009.
8   The statues of lions, remaining of the Moskwa cinema, Warsaw, Poland, 2009.

imposing volume and much light. The supermarket was closed for technical reasons related to security and its last owner, an investment fund, did not try to restore it. The building was demolished in 2007 in order to build a shopping mall (▶ 9, 10).

The Dimitrov Mausoleum was built in one week in 1949, according to the designs of Georgi Ovtcharov, Ratcho Ribarov and Ivan Dantchov. It was used as a tribune for major political events. In 1990, the "City of Truth," i.e., a group of tents and political posters, was set up around the mausoleum and the Party House by political activists and citizens as a sign of protest against the falsification and the manipulations of the first "free" Bulgarian elections for nearly half a century. The elections of autumn 1989, lost by the opposition and won by the *Bulgarian Socialist Party* (PSB), provoked a genuine social uprising oriented against two targets: the mausoleum and the red star on the Party House. The PSB was forced to appoint a special commission to decide its fate.[16] The mausoleum was emptied in September 1990 after a lengthy public debate, presented by the media as "a civil war of symbolic interpretations." This "war" affected other monuments such as the one dedicated to Lenin, the Monument of the Soviet Army, and others. Some people wished to overcome a legacy built on death or traumatic moments of national history. Others, quoting the example of the Pantheon in Paris or even the Mausoleum of Franco in Spain—which is rather ironic from a historical point of view—proposed that the empty mausoleum should be preserved. Finally, Dimitrov's body was given back to his family. Just one day later, the inhabitants of the "City of Truth" organized a "waste-party" (*sic*), gathering various objects (books, statuettes, flags) from their common past at the front of the tribune (▶ 11).

9   The Supersam, Warsaw, Poland, 1973.

10

11

What, then, was to happen to the mausoleum? In a competition, architects suggested transforming it into a modern ruin, partially destroyed, in a park displaying the best achievements of Socialist Realist art, thus becoming a pantheon of all victims of oppression (Turkish yoke, fascism, totalitarianism), or a National Museum warehouse. Finally, the mausoleum was dynamited in September 1999, before the official visit of U.S. President Bill Clinton. For some, the disappearance of the mausoleum meant a great step forwards; for others, it was seen as a mistake, a denial of history, the loss of a means of helping Bulgarians in the construction of their history and common memory. One part of Welow Square (the former Square of September 9, 1944) was transformed into a parking area. In 2000, large posters

10   The Lublin Union Square without Supersam, Warsaw, Poland, 2009.
11   The "waste party" in front of the Georgi Dimitrov Mausoleum, Sofia, Bulgaria, 1990.

advertising whisky took the place of the mausoleum. Recently, a stage has been erected where a world festival of folklore dance is held in the summertime (▶ 12).

This cathartic destruction of the mausoleum can be interpreted as a release of this central open space, and thus as a possibility for a better acceptance. The fact is that the destruction was accomplished quite late, in 1999, at a time when strong feelings had already subsided. In the two cases presented in Warsaw, the objects were more neutral and strongly related to the memory of everyday life. But their destruction also gave rise to an intense debate.

Building a Contemporary Patrimony

Socialist legacies, under political and above all economic pressure, are fragile. But since the beginning of this century, it seems that we are facing a turn: after a blatant lack of concern for this architecture, a consciousness has emerged for the idea that it can be considered a common patrimony, and that part of this patrimony is disappearing. A dynamic of patrimonialization is now following the processes of banalization. Socialist legacies are no longer degraded to the rank of objects standing on a plot with a value, but are considered as witnesses of a period of the history of architecture and of the country.

This reaction, particularly relevant in Poland, first came from urban planners and architects. But very soon, thanks to the media, it affected political and more general public opinions. In Bulgaria, the debate did not focus on specific objects of socialist architecture, but on a fragment of the territory with a great symbolic meaning, due to the heavy transformations of its buildings during the socialist period.

In Poland, such a debate focused on the most representative legacy of the Stalinist period of Polish history: the Palace of Culture and Science in Warsaw, which was a special gift from the Soviet Union to the People's Republic of Poland. The debate also concerns most "socialist" towns in Poland (except for the new towns built in the nineteen-fifties). Warsaw was almost entirely destroyed during the war, thus its landscape mainly reflects the different styles of socialist urban planning and architecture, with the exception of the Old Town, which was reconstructed according to its historical features. This is why the capital city of

12   New symbols, Sofia, Bulgaria, 2000.

Poland was always considered "nonpatrimonial" in comparison to such towns as Cracow, for instance. This also explains why the debate about socialist legacies began here. In 2001, the *Polish Association of Architects* (SARP) requested a commission to be formed in order to survey the destiny of Polish architecture from the period 1945–65. In 2003, the SARP gave the government a list of seventy-seven objects deserving protection, among which was the Palace of Culture and Science. In 2004, an exhibition was organized on this subject, which widened the scope of the debate. As a result, the Palace of Culture and Science was declared a historical monument on February 2, 2007. Political reactions were very unfavorable— indeed, the new President of Republic Lech Kaczyński was elected in 2005 on the basis of an election program of "decommunization." The debate took on a rather acrimonious tone: seventy public personalities sent a letter to the President, saying they were against the formal protection of a monument that symbolized the alienation of the Polish nation. Public opinion is still much divided on this question. Architects are now even more concerned about the fate of "ordinary" objects of the socialist period, and some cinemas, administrative buildings, and housing estates have been placed on the SARP list, to avoid what happened to the Moskwa cinema or to the Supersam supermarket.

In Sofia, the example of the Rila Hotel (built in 1964 by the architect Georgi Stoilov) crystallizes the social tensions relating to a far larger territory and issues far exceeding private interests. A project, launched in June 2008 by an investor, involves the demolition of the hotel and the construction of a twenty-two-floor business center and a multistory underground car park. But as it is located in the city center, the hotel is situated within the boundaries of the protected area—the architectural reservation of the "Serdica-Sofia," bound by the new master plan organization and planning of the capital in 2007, and its destruction is a problematic issue. First, it implies a revision of part of the plan (concerning the construction of the neighborhood), a revision that has not occurred since 1969. On the other hand, it requires the approval of the *National Institute of Monuments of Culture and City Council* expert planning. The mayor of Sofia supports the destruction of the hotel as an expression of "unsightly socialist architecture," but the borough mayor Sredetz, the Democrats for Free Bulgaria (DBL) town councilors, and the Bulgarian Metropolitan are mobilized against the project. The religious monuments located in its proximity, including the Saint Nicholas of Myra church, will also be affected. Its opponents refer to the project as "vandalism" and accuse the *Ministry of Regional Development and Spatial Planning* and the *Municipality of Sofia* of giving their support to the private investor before anything has been decided.

When architecture is considered valuable, it becomes an interest and a potential resource for attracting tourism. In Berlin, only a virtual visit to the Wall is possible. But in some cases, monuments have recently been promoted as tourist attractions not because of their aesthetic value, but because they represent a fragment of national history. This was the case in Romania in 2004, when the *Museum of Contemporary Art* in Bucharest was set up in the former Presidential Palace of Ceaușescu, and an exhibition held showing a collection of paintings created for the Romanian dictator. In Latvia and Lithuania, former military Soviet bases are now open as an experience for tourists, including the enactment of interrogation, spending a night in a cell, et cetera.

The tourist and cultural aspect also includes places of everyday life: in Nowa Huta (Cracow, Poland), a tourist agency offers a visit to a flat furnished and decorated in the Stalinist style of the nineteen-fifties. We can also quote the unexpected success of the German film *Good Bye, Lenin*.[17] The interpretation of what Germans call *Ostalgia* is not easy. On the one hand, we can see in this process of marketing a hyper-banalization of the socialist experience and a cynical exploitation of the past, even its tragic dimension. The fact is that we should differentiate between the uses of the socialist legacy for tourism, according to the original function of these places. On the one hand, the conversion of a former military base into an entertainment park is possible when a society considers that only the present matters. On the other hand, we can consider that the celebration of places of everyday life, such as housing estates, allows the "post-socialist" citizen to feel that his everyday life, his individual experience, was in fact a part of History as a whole; thus, it gives status to every member of the former "popular masses."[18]

Conclusion

The transformation of socialist legacies in Warsaw and Sofia reflects new needs, new practices, new representations, and thus new political attitudes toward socialist architecture. The comparison between Poland and Bulgaria shows the importance of the national context. There is now a legal framework defining a socialist "patrimony" in Poland, but not in Bulgaria. This is not simply because Poland has a stronger culture of architecture and urbanism. It is maybe also because the process of banalization went further in Poland during the nineteen-nineties, under economic pressure and rapid socioeconomic transformations.

From demolition to patrimonialization of socialist legacies—the question of deciding how a society should deal with the collective representations of its past is not exclusive to post-socialist countries. But the radical and sudden shift that took place in 1990 made it a more sensitive issue. Part of today's intellectual elite wishes to wipe out some parts of its memory because it does not fit in with today's opinions. But others consider that society has to face its past via the material structures of the city. The two case studies presented in this paper show that a turn has taken place. At the beginning of the nineteen-nineties, a French publication led by several historicists dealt with East European societies and their memory. It was written at a time when these societies were perceived to be haunted by past memories: "The particular is coming back in force, against the universal and dissolvent abstraction of communism.... In this disrupted mental landscape, sanctuaries of memory, of patrimony, these numerous places of aggregation and of the crystallization of identity codes and signs, play a strategic role."[19] This book was concerned both with abstract and material *memo-*

rial places.[20] As far as the material ones are concerned, we should conclude by pointing out the new trends emerging today in Eastern Europe. First, several memories compete as far as socialist legacies are concerned, and the issue of their political legitimacy has not yet been concluded. Second, since 1990, national or local particularities have been overtaken by another universality, i.e., globalization and the market, which is the main cause of the banalization of places.

Adam Michnik once said about Poland: "I am really very very glad to live in this country which does not interest journalists any more."[21] Does this statement also refer to the urban landscape? In a sense, yes, since most relevant signs of the communist period, urban facilities, have been disappearing for almost twenty years now, which is "normal." Post-socialist cities are continually losing their common identity, and looking more and more like other "Western" cities. However, we may wonder how the next generations can form an opinion of the communist period in countries such as Poland and Bulgaria if a part of its material legacy in the city disappears, replaced by shopping malls built in an international style, or transformed into entertainment parks. Some regret this, seeing "the sad lesson of spatial liberalism" in the evolution of Polish urban planning.[22] Two conclusions are quite certain. First, it is a hard political issue, to which public opinion reacts passionately when it has the opportunity to do so, as the example of the Palace of Culture and Science in Warsaw shows. Second, it has thus to be treated in a democratic way, and not just to the benefit of private economic interests.

Endnotes

1 "Le schisme est dénué de sens hors de toute référence à quelque état antérieur: l'absolument Nouveau est simplement inintelligible, même à titre de nouveauté." Paul Ricoeur, *Temps et récit, vol. 2: La configuration dans le récit de fiction* (Paris: Éditions du Seuil, 1984), 44.

2 Sergei Kirov, speach for the first Soviet Congress, 1922, quoted in: Anatole Kopp, *Ville et revolution* (Paris: Point Seuil, 1975), 293.

3 See: *Social Change and Urban Restructuring in Eastern and Central Europe*, ed. György Enyedi (Budapest: Akadémiai Kiadó, 1998); *Transformation of Cities in Central and Eastern Europe. Towards Globalisation*, ed. Ian Hamilton, Kaliopa Dimitrovska Andrews and Natasa Pichler-Milanovic (Tokyo: United Nations University Press, 2005); Sasha Tsenkova, *Urban Mosaic of Post-Socialist Europe: Space, Institution, Policy* (Heidelberg/New York: Physica-Verlag, 2006).

4 Pascal Ory, "Politiques symboliques: à l'est du nouveau," *Nouvelle Alternative* 20 (2006:66/67): 7–10.

5 The authors have been studying these two cities as geographers for a long period of time. The material used for this paper combines bibliographical and a several years of empirical knowledge on Sofia and Warsaw.

6 Ian Hamilton and Richard French, *The Socialist City* (Chichester: John Wiley & Sons, 1979).

7 György Enyedi, "Urbanization under Socialism," in *Cities After Socialism. Urban and Regional Change and Conflicts in Post-Socialist Societies*, ed. Gregory Andrusz, Michael Harloe and Ivan Szelényi (London: Blackwell, 1996), 100–18.

8 Lydia Coudroy de Lille "Métropolisation et démocratie locale à Varsovie," in *L'élargissement de l'Union Européenne: réformes territoriales en Europe centrale et orientale*, ed. Violette Rey, Lydia Coudroy de Lille and Emmanuelle Boulineau (Paris: L'Harmattan, 2004), 133–49.

9 Milena Alexandrova-Guest, *Habiter Sofia au tournant du XXIème siècle. Essai sur l'aménagement des espaces urbains post-socialiste* (PhD dissertation, ENS-LSH, 2006).

10 Diana Palazova-Lebleu, "La maison du Parti à Sofia: un prototype d'architecture totalitaire," *Livraisons d'histoire de l'architecture* 10 (2005:2): 137–46.

11 François Maspero, *Balkans-Transit* (Paris: Éditions du Seuil, 1997).

12 Stanisław Cieśla, "Globalizacja i metropolizacja. Niektóre aspekty badań polskiej przestrzeni," [Globalization and Metropolization. Some Aspects from Studies of Polish Space] *Studia Regionalne i Lokalne* 4 (2000:4): 23–36; Bohdan Jałowiecki, *Globalny świat metropolii* [The Global World of the Metropolis] (Warsaw: Scholar, 2007).

13 David Mangin, *La ville franchisée. Formes et structures de la ville contemporaine* (Paris: Éditions de la Villette, 2004).

14 Maurice Halbwachs, *Les cadres sociaux de la mémoire* (Paris: Albin Michel, 1994 [1925]); Maurice Halbwachs, *La mémoire collective* (Paris: Albin Michel, 1997 [1950]).

15 See the destruction of the Rossiya Hotel in Moscow in 2008, considered as "anachronistic" by the mayor Iuri Luzhkov. Cf: Anne Abitbol, "L'hôtel fantôme de la place Rouge," *Vingt-et-un* 2 (2009:1): 124–35.

16 Vladimir Gradev, "Le mausolée de Dimitrov," *Communications* 55 (1992:2): 77–88.

17 Wolfgang Becker, 2003.

18 David Crowley and Susan E. Reid, ed., *Socialist Spaces. Sites of Everyday Lifes in the Eastern Bloc* (Oxford: Berg, 2002).

19 Alain Brossat, Sonia Combe, Jean-Yves Potel and Jean-Charles Szurek, *A l'est, la mémoire retrouvée* (Paris: La Découverte, 1990).

20 Pierre Nora, *Les lieux de mémoire* (Paris: Gallimard, 1984).

21 *Le Monde*, November 11, 1997.

22 Magdalena Staniszkis, "Lekcja z ulicy Puławskiej," [Lesson from the Puławska Street] in *Krajobraz architektoniczny Warszawy końca XX wieku* [The Urban Landscape of Warsaw at the End of the 20th Century], ed. Sławomir Gzell (Warsaw: Akapit-DTP, 2002), 173–208.

A CUMBERSOME HERITAGE

Political Monuments and Buildings of the GDR in Reunited Germany

Arnold Bartetzky

Reunited Germany has inherited countless political buildings and monuments from the GDR era. This legacy of socialism has been significantly decimated during the last two decades, a development that can also be observed in the other countries belonging to the former Eastern Bloc. The first statues of communist heroes were destroyed in spontaneous actions accompanying the collapse of the system in 1989/90. A few years later, the demolition of political edifices from the GDR era began. However, despite this record of destruction, physical annihilation has not been the only approach towards the visual remains of the GDR regime, and not even the most predominant one. Indeed, most of the political monuments and buildings have survived, to be marginalized or simply forgotten, semantically redefined, redesigned, and reused or, in several cases, even carefully restored.

State Buildings between Demolition and Reuse

The post-1989 fates of GDR state buildings have not depended primarily on their original political function and symbolism, but rather on the degree of acceptance of their architectural design, on their location within the city and their suitability for profitable reuse and integration within future urban developments. It is undoubtedly true that the motivations for the demolition of Berlin's Palace of the Republic during the years 2006–2008 (▶ 1) were not least political ones, as has been pointed out endlessly in the passionate debates on this decision. In the long term, however, any other building of such a pure late modernist design

1   Demolition of the Palace of the Republic, Berlin, Germany, 2007.

would not have had good chances of survival on this site, where the historic center of Berlin is being redeveloped according to traditional, pre-modernist patterns.

Hence, the neighboring State Council Building (▶ 2), formerly the main center of power of the GDR, has survived due to the fact that its more moderate architecture, involving some traditional features, is somewhat more compatible with current trends. Furthermore, unlike the Palace of the Republic, it does not stand in the way of the envisaged reconstruction of the Prussian Royal Palace, due to its location at the edge of the square. After Germany's reunification, the State Council Building even served as the Federal Chancellor's interim office for a short time, until the new Chancellery was completed in 2001. Then, in 2002, it became the permanent seat of an elite business school. The ironic connotations of both usages are blatantly obvious—and certainly not unwelcome.

Outside the capital, numerous buildings formerly occupied by the GDR authorities have also survived, and are now reused for various purposes. One example of this is a huge complex in Leipzig, which formerly served as the seat of the notorious State Security Service. Its older part, originating from the early twentieth century, now hosts a museum dedicated to the Security Service's practices of oppression. The newer sections, added in the nineteen-sixties, are partially used as offices and a night club in a folksy Bavarian style, the latter being a bizarre example of reuse with an unintentional touch of irony (▶ 3). Sooner or later, this part of the complex will most probably be dismantled—not because of its demonic past, however, but due to its crude functionalist architecture, which is currently despised for aesthetic reasons.

2   The former State Council Building, seen from the site of the demolished Palace of the Republic, Berlin, Germany, 2007.

Many GDR buildings have already fallen into serious decay due to a lack of occupancy. An example of this is the State Guest House of the GDR government, also situated in Leipzig. Formerly an important representational building, it has now been more or less forgotten and subject to acts of vandalism in recent years (▸ 4). However, there is no reason to see the decline of the building as a sort of symbolic punishment for the role it played for the GDR regime. Indeed, the city would have appreciated its renovation, but up to now all attempts to find a willing developer have failed. Presently, the building is being offered for sale. Its future depends on the decision of the next owner. It may be preserved and renovated, or pulled down and replaced by a new building.

3

4

3   Entrance to the night club "Alpenmax," located in the former building of the State Security Service, Leipzig, Germany, 2009.
4   The former State Guest House of the GDR government, Leipzig, Germany, 2009.

Unwieldy Monuments

The reasons for the various fates and future prospects of the sculpted monuments and memorials are more multifaceted, with much stronger political implications. Lenin Monuments have had the worst chances of survival, as the hero of the Russian revolution is associated solely with the disastrous history of communism and, from the German perspective, he is perceived as an alien. Statues of Karl Marx and Friedrich Engels have had much better prospects, as both are seen not only as ancestors of the communist ideology but also as substantial representatives of German philosophy. In their latter function, they are commemorated even in present-day Germany by street names in several cities, not only in the Eastern part of the country. Thus the Marx Engels Monument at the former Marx Engels Forum in Berlin has survived all controversies on the future of the site up until now.

A more complicated case is Ernst Thälmann. He was the leader of the German Communist Party in the interwar period, and thereby a representative of a totalitarian force of the Weimar Republic that contributed to the failure of the first democratic state in Germany. In this function, he is hardly compatible with the official culture of remembrance in present-day Germany. Thus, some Thälmann memorials have been dismantled. However, at the same time, the communist party leader was an opponent and a victim of the Nazi regime. After over ten years of imprisonment, he was murdered in the concentration camp at Buchenwald in 1944. Respect for Thälmann—not as a politician but as a Nazi victim— seems to prevent his remaining monuments from being destroyed. The Thälmann Statue in Weimar, the city near Buchenwald, was even carefully restored in the late nineteen-nineties.

5

5   Ernst Thälmann Monument, Berlin, Germany, 2009.

6

The Thälmann Memorial in Berlin (▶ 5) also still exists, despite plans to dismantle it in the early nineteen-nineties. Only the propagandistic inscriptions have been removed. However, as the monument was not maintained for several years, it regularly attracted graffiti spray-ers. A group of local residents protested against these violations by displaying the slogan "Imprisoned, Murdered, Besmirched" ("Eingekerkert, Ermordet, Beschmiert") on the monument, thereby invoking Thälmann's status of a Nazi victim as an apodictic argument against the neglect of the monument. In 2000, several left-wing organizations founded an action committee that took on the task of regularly cleaning the site. Since 2006, the clean-ing has been taken over by the city again.

The decisions concerning whether to preserve or to remove a monument often depend not only on its subject matter but also, as in the case of buildings, on its location and compat-ibility with current projects. Especially in the case of works of art connected with architec-ture, which generally played a significant role in the visual propaganda of the GDR, the attitudes of the owners are crucial. Works in public ownership seem to have better future prospects than those in private hands.

Thus, the monumental wall mosaic on the present building of the *Federal Ministry of Finance* in Berlin, showing a Stalinist vision of a prospering socialist society, has been preserved and restored on its original site. In 2000, however, a semantically antithetic counterpart was displayed on the pavement in front of the mosaic. It is a historic photograph of similar di-mensions, showing a scene of the workers' uprising in 1953, which was bloodily suppressed by the GDR regime. In this way, the propaganda mosaic is confronted with a memorial displaying the failure of the socialist vision.

6   Reliefs from the façade of a department store in Leipzig, now at the driveway entrance to the under-ground car park of the building, Leipzig, Germany, 2009.

Despite this example of preservation and re-contextualization, most of the propaganda works on buildings, as far as they still exist, are under threat. Particularly when it comes to the dismantling or remodeling of the building, they are often destroyed, or at least marginalized by means of relocation to less prominent sites. An example of the latter practice are the reliefs showing scenes of post-war reconstruction that formerly decorated a department store in Leipzig. When the building was renovated, the reliefs were removed from the façade. Now they are displayed in a rather prosaic place at the driveway entrance to the underground car park (▸ 6).

The Banishment of Karl Marx from Leipzig, and his Revival in Chemnitz

Most of the decisions regarding the fate of state-generated GDR architecture and imagery have largely been made without the involvement of the public. A few projects, however, have become the focal point of debates on how to deal with the visual heritage of socialism and the conflicts related to this—reflecting a profound clash in competing concepts of collective memory, historical identity, and urban image-building. The most prominent case was the above-mentioned never-ending debate on the demolition of the Palace of the Republic and its planned replacement by the reconstructed Prussian Palace. This controversy was inevitable, as the project touches on one of the most symbolically meaningful sites in reunited Germany.

Rather unexpected, however, was the recent bitter dispute that arose surrounding a much lesser known piece of work in Leipzig's city center—the so-called Marx relief, which was on display on the main building of the university from 1974 to 2006 (▸ 7). In order to

7 Marx relief on the main building of the university, Leipzig, Germany, 1994.

8

understand why this debate became so heated, it is necessary to take a look back at the history of the building site.

Until 1968, the grounds were occupied by the St. Paul's University Church. This late gothic building, one of Leipzig's major historic monuments, had survived the war undamaged. However, it did not comply with the GDR regime's plans to create a modernist square of "socialist character" on this site. Therefore, despite some courageous protests, the church was blown up, together with the neighboring classicist university building, to make way for a new campus (▶ 8).

8   Demolition of the University Church in 1968 and the main building of the university on the same site mid-1990s, Leipzig, Germany.

9

The huge bronze relief, over fourteen meters in length, bearing the official title "Karl Marx and the Revolutionary, World-changing Essence of his Teachings," was conceived to visualize the ideological foundation of the University of Leipzig, which had been renamed Karl Marx University in 1953. It shows scenes of the "struggle for progress" under the spiritual rule of Marx, represented by an oversized head dominating the work. As the relief was located exactly at the section of the façade where the prominent frontage of the University Church used to stand, it could be interpreted not only as an icon of Marxism but also as a symbol of triumph over the university's Christian tradition.

The barbarous destruction of the University Church played a significant role in the culture of memory in post-1989 Leipzig. The main organizer of the remembrance activities was an extremely aggressive citizens' initiative, fighting for the re-erection of the church. In 1998, on the occasion of the thirtieth anniversary of its being blown up, the Marx relief was framed by a construction of steel beams in a shape recalling the contour of the former church gable (▶ 9). This artistic installation commemorated the act of socialist iconoclasm, thereby highlighting the symbolic connection between the Marx relief and the fate of the church. Although this link was obvious to everyone in Leipzig, the existence of the relief has not really been a bone of contention for very long, despite a few occasional voices demanding its removal. It only became the subject of a sharp controversy in recent years, during the course of the extensive remodeling of the campus, which involved the demolition of large parts of the building complex from the GDR era.

In 2007, the main building was pulled down (▶ 10) to make way for a new premises designed in somewhat gothic-like forms (▶ 11), ostentatiously paying tribute to the destroyed church that had once stood on the site. Before the building was dismantled, the relief had been carefully removed from the façade and put into storage. Yet it was obvious that it could not return to this site again, for aesthetic as well as ideological reasons. Thus, from this point onwards, a delicate question arose—what should be done with this unwieldy work of art? One of the possible solutions initially discussed was to install the relief in the courtyard of the remodeled campus, as an eloquent visual document of the university's history. The university rejected this idea, mainly using technical arguments related to the problems presented by the colossal size and weight of the bronze relief. However, the university evidently

9   Marx relief, framed by an installation commemorating the demolition of the University Church, Leipzig, Germany, 2001.

10   Demolition of the main building of the university, Leipzig, Germany, 2007.
11   Construction of the new main building of the university, Leipzig, Germany, 2009.

12

also had political reasons for this decision, wishing to avoid being accused of a symbolic continuation of GDR traditions on its campus.

Following lengthy debates, the university designated a more peripheral and rather unspectacular site for the permanent location of the relief—on the grounds of the Department of Physical Education, situated about three kilometers away from the city center. The decision to restore the monument using public money and reinstall it on a semi-public site caused the most heated dispute on GDR heritage experienced in Leipzig since 1989. The local newspaper published a flood of readers' letters, most of them protesting strongly against the university's plans. Several prominent figures from city life came up with various alternative proposals. Throughout this debate, voices demanding that the relief be displayed in a more conspicuous position were the exception. On the contrary, most of the participants indicated more or less explicitly that they had always felt insulted by the mere existence of the relief—although hardly any of them had demanded it be removed while it was still attached to the university building. In a poll carried out by the newspaper at the peak of the debate, more than 50 percent of the readers taking part voted for melting the work down or storing it away. Another proposal, favored by some local politicians, envisaged the installation of the relief on a hill at the outskirts of the city, where the rubble of the demolished University Church had been buried. The idea behind this proposal was to visualize the connection between the Marxist ideology represented by the relief and the act of cultural vandalism carried out by the GDR regime. Leipzig's mayor, who tried to mediate in the dispute, rightly drew attention to the fatal symbolism of this option—ultimately the relief would stand in a position where it would appear triumphant over the church.

12   Installation of the Marx relief on the grounds of the university's Department of Physical Education, Leipzig, Germany, 2008.

In February 2008, caving in to the pressure of public outrage, Saxony's *Ministry of Finance*—the provincial authority responsible for the university's building activities—put a halt to the ongoing preparations for the relief to be erected at the Department of Physical Education for a period of several days. After a crisis meeting with the university's rector and the mayor of Leipzig, the then Saxon Minister of Science finally decided to adhere to the choice of location, despite the protests. In order to appease the critics, a commission was charged with the formulation of an extended inscription to commemorate the destruction of the church and explain the intention behind the installation of the relief on its new site. To avoid misconceptions concerning this intention, the inscription emphasizes the fact that, after 1989, the university had renounced its former name of Karl Marx University, as well as the socialist ideology behind it. The decision for the reinstallation of the relief away from its original site is interpreted in the text—somewhat sophistically—as an expression of the university's accepting responsibility for its history, at the same time as distancing itself from the past. This explanation was hardly convincing to those who had demanded the annihilation of the relief. Nevertheless, after its installation in the late summer of 2008 (▶ 12), the outrage passed as suddenly as it had broken out. It seems that no one feels insulted any longer, and most people in Leipzig are not even aware of the exact location of the reinstalled relief.

An example of a totally different attitude towards a Marx Monument is found in Chemnitz, a formerly significant industrial city in the south of Saxony. After 1945, Chemnitz—which had suffered extensive destruction in the war—was designated to become a model of socialist urbanism. As a sign of this privileged status within the GDR, it was renamed Karl-Marx-Stadt in 1953. In 1971, the city's spiritual patron was honored with an imposing

13

13   Marx Monument, Chemnitz, Germany, 2009.

monument in the town center—a bronze sculpture portraying the head of the philosopher, seven meters high, placed on a base of almost the same height (▶ 13). Aptly, the portrait bust, allegedly the largest in the world, was situated in front of the extensive administration building, in which Marx's ideas were to be put into practice. Its façade is dominated by an inscription plate, eight floors high, with the slogan "Working Men of all Countries, Unite!" in several languages.

In 1990, Karl-Marx-Stadt was again renamed Chemnitz, in accordance with a referendum decision made by the vast majority of the citizens. In their view, the mammoth sculpture of Marx's head might have had at least as negative connotations as the Marx relief in Leipzig. It represented the imposition of socialism, the destruction of tradition, and—as it was designed by a Russian sculptor—even an enforced adoption of Soviet art. Thus, in the years following 1989, many citizens demanded the dismantling of the monument. In the course of time, however, another attitude has prevailed—the idea of preserving the monument as a unique historical document, at the same staging it somewhat ironically as a bizarre attraction of the city.

Meanwhile, the Marx head is being marketed as one of the major sightseeing attractions on the city's tourist trail. The former sense of shame surrounding the monument has turned into pride. In 2007, when a Lithuanian artist came up with the idea of temporarily relocating the head to the internationally renowned exhibition of sculpture in the Western German city of Münster, a storm of indignation broke out in Chemnitz. Even the request for permission to produce a replica of the head for this purpose was refused by the municipal authorities, in keeping with the general attitude of the population. "The head is a unique thing, and it should remain unique," said the mayor of Chemnitz.

However, the municipal authorities support artistic activities taking place in Chemnitz that serve the cause of promoting the monument. In the summer of 2008, a group of Austrian and Saxon art students joined forces with local art initiatives to organize a project entitled "Temporary Museum of Modern Marx." Their idea was to present the head in a new way by temporarily separating it from its urban context, thereby allowing new approaches to Marxist philosophy to arise. To this end, the head was enclosed in scaffoldings covered with white fabric (▶ 14). Visitors to the "Temporary Museum" could take a close look at the sculpture from the interior platforms of the construction (▶ 15). They were also encouraged to study the works of Marx that were on display, listen to an audio feature, and even record their own comments. The project, though intellectually somewhat half-baked, gained the support of the city and several local companies.

While Leipzig removed its Marx relief from the city center in embarrassment, Chemnitz openly presents the philosopher's head as an iconic, somewhat curious emblem of the city. The diverging destinies of these two monuments demonstrate once more that the original meaning and historical context of the visual relics of GDR ideology are not the only determinant affecting attitudes towards them. Their fates depend on various factors, not least

14

15

arbitrary local constellations such as the impact of contemporary political groups, social and cultural initiatives, the influence of prominent individuals, and the opinion-forming viewpoint of the media. Therefore, it is hardly possible to make a general forecast concerning the future prospects of GDR monuments in reunited Germany. As the development in Chemnitz indicates, a temporal distance to the experience of socialism can open up a wide range of new, creative approaches to these cultural relics. However, as the Leipzig example shows, this distance has not necessarily diminished the potential for iconoclastic hostility.

This article is based on a paper delivered at the session "'Damnatio Memoriae': Ideological Ruins and Political Memories," which was organized by the *International Association of World and Image Studies for the College Art Association Annual Conference* (Los Angeles, February 25–28, 2009). Many thanks to Maria Elena Versari for the invitation to speak at this conference, and to Louise Bromby, Christian Dietz, Roman Grabolle, Harald Liehr, Paul Sigel, and Thomas Topfstedt for suggestions and advice. A modified Czech version of the text has been published in the architectural periodical: *Stavba* 15 (2009:2): 76–81.

14   "Temporary Museum of Modern Marx," Chemnitz, Germany, 2008.
15   "Temporary Museum of Modern Marx," interior view, Chemnitz, Germany, 2008.

2

ARTISTIC REALIZATIONS

URBAN "TRUTHS"

Artistic Intervention in Post-Socialist Space

Cynthia Imogen Hammond

This essay seeks to consider the "urban intervention" in the context of the post-socialist city. Creative, sometimes anonymous, often illegal, urban interventions are oppositional acts that take place in the public realm. Neither strictly art, nor vandalism, nor yet protest— but having characteristics of all three—such acts engage cities physically: clinging to walls, occupying streets, creating visual disturbances, surprises, and annoyances. In short, they defamiliarize the city's surfaces and spaces, challenging the norms of order, ownership, and even the disarray that reinforces the feeling that the city is not ours, that it is under someone else's control. Interventions, by their nature, show that cities belong to a larger public, by bringing the question of ownership into representation. In so doing, interventions have the potential to articulate the deeply contested nature of civic space, and can thus frame a given space for reconsideration about what matters in the city, what has been forgotten, what is changing, and what might be reclaimed.

Interventions thus belong to what Ella Chmielewska has described as the "immersive nature of the visual [urban] landscape … uncertain in its material vulnerability, and precariously positioned between the discourses of art, architecture and increasingly, media and advertising."[1] What might a critical, art historical analysis contribute to understanding such interventions, particularly in the context of the post-socialist city? Given their tendency to be applied, added on, and supplemental, is it possible that urban interventions relate to their sites in the way that, traditionally, ornaments related to and expressed something about the building to which it was attached? If so, what are the implications of this relationship?

Krystian Czaplicki is a young Polish artist and designer who goes by the street name of TRUTH. Since 2003, he has been developing lightweight sculptural objects out of polystyrene, which he then attaches to buildings, signposts, ruins, and urban furniture such as seating, curbs, and outdoor stairways. He has recently become involved in gallery exhibitions and public art fairs, working at a large scale. The objects I will focus on in this essay—called "truthtags"—demonstrate an investment in the visual and design heritage of Constructivism, de Stjil, and the utopian architectural modernism of the nineteen-twenties and -thirties, particularly New Objectivity (▶ 1).

At the same time, the placement of the objects on city surfaces invokes obvious parallels with the practice of graffiti; indeed, of the growing commentary around this artist's work, writers tend to associate the pieces to graffiti rather than to sculpture. "Isn't it about time," one impressed blogger writes, "graffiti became 3-dimensional?"[2]

Czaplicki seems to invite the interpretation of his work as spatial graffiti by virtue of the name he has given to his works; a "tag" in English is generally the most banal and ubiquitous form of graffiti—a stylized signature hastily applied to walls, windows, and other surfaces. Czaplicki's works are certainly recognizable as signatures, but this is where any simple link to tagging ends. Unlike tagging, which is done opportunistically and in haste, Czaplicki's interventions are considered additions to the buildings to which they adhere, inviting viewers to make visual relationships between the truthtags and urban signage, ar-

1

chitecture, even with the decay of the built environment. At the same time they suggest, as Thomas F. Gieryn argues, that "truth," while it may sound universal, is a site-specific notion in that truths are produced in particular places, at specific moments in history, with resonance (perhaps only) for the participants in that place and time.[3] Truth becomes, in this sense, located and emplaced. In "Growing—Overgrowing" (Lodz, Poland, 2007), a work developed as part of an art exhibition, the installation emerges from the cracked, gray wall and leafy vines as if it were the most natural thing in the world (▶ 2).

The forms appear to have sprung into existence out of the cement like a strange urban mushroom, growing in a diminutive, parallel, but perpendicular universe. We seem to observe this little city from above, like gods of urban planning, but in fact we encounter this pristine construction from beside or below, troubling the habitual relationship between the planner's gaze and the architect's model. The arrangement, however, is neither as accidental nor as organic as it might initially appear—the artist has considered such elements as the damaged surface of the wall, the overall form of the building, even the moss and vines that have begun to grow over the cement. The aesthetic arrangement of the intervention transforms such elements into the dry riverbeds, the leafy forests, and the parkland of a tiny city.

1   Krystian Czaplicki/TRUTH, documentation of urban intervention, Wroclaw, Poland, 2006.

2

3

2 Krystian Czaplicki/TRUTH, documentation of "Growing—Overgrowing," urban intervention, exhibition "Beautiful Losers," Lodz, Poland, 2007.
3 Krystian Czaplicki/TRUTH, documentation of urban intervention, Pulawy, Poland, 2006.

Significantly, Czaplicki makes use of the viewer's architectural visual literacy, bringing established, professionalized ways of seeing the twentieth-century city—the bird's-eye view, the plan, elevation and most importantly, the architectural model—to the passer-by. In so doing, the artist subtly invokes the idealism or utopianism associated with each of these methods of urban or architectural representation, placing special emphasis on the early twentieth-century embrace of pure form, asymmetry, minimalism, and geometric rigor, and by extension, the particular hopes and ideals of that era. At the same time, the works sidestep their own potential nostalgia by making visual games of the existing street or architectural setting. In an untitled work from 2006 (▶ 3), the visual impact of the perfect, crimson forms contrast dramatically with the irregular patterns of decay; the perfection and newness of the intervention actually draws greater attention to the decay and neglect of the wall on which it sits.

Through his combination of distinct architectural references and graffiti "tagging" strategies, Czaplicki creates powerful resonances within the spatial and architectural conditions of the cities in which he works. My goal is to demonstrate through these particular interventions how alternative semantic possibilities can occur within urban space, like visual and spatial speech acts, which bring cities to articulate themselves differently. The urban intervention can, I argue, harness the potential of the built environment's potential to act as architecture parlante, a speaking architecture that communicates in surprising and subversive ways. As a kind of renegade ornament, these interventions are a new kind of public art, public because what they do is rehearse the potential of their spatial context to be public, that is, shared, communal, and open to singular or collective reinterpretation.

I am making a distinction here between public art, in the sense of public sculpture, and art or creative practices that take up space and insist that they be public, if only for the duration of its existence, before they are removed, washed away, or are overtaken by some other form of urban visual culture. Any understanding of such creative practices needs to consider the urban as the primary context, in addition to the history of art, although visual analysis is of course central to this research. As a text for a recent installation by Czaplicki in London, England, explains:

> Rather than merely existing as an isolated piece, "TRUTHTAG" exists only within its context of the place it's attached to. Without the place, the project would have no meaning. It is a multi-layered urban experiment which discretely sabotages and plays with the uncontrollable: degradation and urban accumulation … In some places, "TRUTHTAG" is a virus, a geometrical fungus, a wild mushroom spreading over the façades of empty buildings, industrial complexes and dilapidated walls. In others, "TRUTHTAG" puzzles like a mysterious code, like a sculpture that seems to have been designed as a firm part of the building's architecture and design.[4]

4

On one hand, the truthtags are sensitive to site, to the extent that they are meaningless without their context. On the other, they are virus-like in character, indiscriminately colonizing the spaces they occupy. Are there general characteristics of urban space at the beginning of the new millennium that make this amorphous position tenable? And are there specific characteristics of post-socialist urban space that make this position necessary?

Since the early nineteen-fifties in East Central Europe and since the nineteen-seventies in Western Europe and North America, there has been a growing dedication of local, regional, national, and supra-national resources to protecting, preserving, and reconstructing architectural heritage, even though the emergence of such initiatives differs vastly.[5] The fruits of such preservation have, ironically, become part of the "global city" phenomenon, as the growth of architectural tourism has coincided with the rise of global capital and cosmopolitanism.[6] Within the same time frame, a general, if not scholarly, concurrence has developed that the modern era in architecture and planning was fundamentally inhumane, either by virtue of its design or by association with patrons and regimes, and that it was aesthetically inferior to architectural cultures prior to World War One.[7] The heritage city has risen to challenge the modernist city, purportedly combating the arid anonymity of modernist visions with selective historic preservation. Private and commercial architecture take up the sideline opportunities offered by the heritage craze and the fashion for the vaguely historic: architectural styles that rarely explore their colonial roots or links with regimes of power.[8]

4   Złote Tarasy, completed in 2007, Jerde Partnership, Warsaw, Poland, 2008.

Since the fall of the Berlin Wall, a new generation of architecture has emerged, which is neither exactly modern nor historicist. This "iconic architecture" is closely tethered to civic aspirations and often to the signatures of the architects who design it, such as Jerde Partnership's massive Złote Tarasy, or the "Golden Terraces" shopping center and entertainment complex in downtown Warsaw, which boasts the country's first Burger King (▶ 4).

This new iconic architecture is, according to Leslie Sklair, different from the famous or recognizable buildings of the past. Iconicity in architecture and cities today, he writes, is mobilized "to facilitate the assimilation of the general public into the culture-ideology of consumerism, to keep people spending."[9]

These factors, which bring questions of architectural history into the discussion of the commercialization of post-socialist space, contribute to a third concern of this paper: the growing practice of intervening, visually and spatially within urban environments on the part of non-specialists, that is, people and groups whose work or actions are not intended to be read as civic sculpture, sanctioned design, or top-down planning. These interventions remake the city from below, enacting the simultaneous possibility that representational space may also be a space of representation, to use Henri Lefèbvre's terminology. But of course, the capacity to "intervene" is not the territory of artists or renegades alone. It would be equally possible to speak of the "interventions" of major corporations or urban developments, which take up precious space in the visual urban field with logos, signature architecture, and their often-bombastic scale (the Złote Tarasy exceeds, in square meters, all shopping centers in Warsaw in 1989 put together). These, too, are urban agents.

Ella Chmielewska, by way of Mieczysław Porębski, has identified the "iconosphere" of the city, that is, the combination of the visual landscape, the signscape, and the spatial immersivity of the city. The iconosphere is a way of thinking about the urban realm that makes equal various "acts of erasure and overwriting" in the city, whether these are the work of centralized government or a handful of spatial dissidents.[10] Warsaw, for Chmielewska, exemplifies such acts, for historically, the city—in its visible language, signs, symbols, street and business names, posters, advertisements, inscriptions, and decorations—recorded as well as telegraphed various shifts and conflicts (political, linguistic, and cultural) that were played out against the larger forces of history, the modernists' visions for urban development, and political and economic pressures. The surfaces of Warsaw reflected the vulnerable self-consciousness of the city's precarious geopolitical position on the quicksand of history, and the palpable margins of European identity.[11]

These charged surfaces are, however, lost to all but the most dedicated researcher, submerged under multiple political and urban regimes as well as the dramatic changes that have recast post-socialist cities as players in the European Union, as tourist destinations, and as renewed regional centers. Chmielewska concludes that today, "the iconosphere of Warsaw looks eerily similar to that of any North American city, its local markers, big and small, disappear from the walls of the city."[12]

5

The confluence of the rise of the global heritage city, the fall of (Soviet) modernism, and the example of the purged iconosphere of Warsaw together form a fraught context for Czaplicki's interventions in this and other Polish urban sites. His little, self-contained cities and puzzling additions to urban surfaces appear to be fragments of a very specific aesthetic language, the idealistic period in European modernism. Czaplicki performs a fascinating trick on the buildings, walls and signposts with which he collaborates: the era to which his work refers, aesthetically, is the era that abhorred the very thing that his work is: ornament.

Ornament in architecture has traditionally been something that is applied to a basic structure for the purpose of creating visual delight, but also—crucially—for the purpose of suggesting meanings of a space. A well-known example will aid in demonstrating this point. Just before ornament was banished from the modern movement in architecture and design, American architect Louis Sullivan (1856–1924) used a profusion of applied ornament to express, exuberantly, the entrance to his otherwise proto-modern department store in Chicago (▶ 5).

Sullivan's wrought-iron, extravagant door dealt directly with the practical issue of how to lead the customer inside. Importantly, however this lavish portal also suggested the con-

5   Louis Sullivan, Carson Pirie Scott Department Store, designed 1903, Chicago, Illinois, USA, 2006.

sumer treasures and the tactile pleasures that lay beyond its threshold. In this way, ornament could add a kind of language or a layer of signification to the surface of existing spaces, an addition that helped those spaces to communicate directly and powerfully to their users. Architectural history is full of examples of this type of communication. From the metaphorical journeys articulated on the west fronts of Christian cathedrals to the symbolic, ornamental gardens of the Taj Mahal, architectural embellishment has played a crucial role in how people approach and use architecture.

Only five years after Sullivan completed his store in Chicago, the Austrian architect and polemicist, Adolf Loos would proclaim ornament to be "criminal," a sign of cultural degeneracy, and the mark of epistemological backwardness.[13] This dramatic statement found an enthusiastic audience in Swiss architect, Le Corbusier, who reprinted Loos' essay in *L'Esprit Nouveau*, and established him as a father figure to the functionalist era, using Loos' moralist rhetoric to fire his own anti-ornament sentiments. The history of the purported "break" between pre-modern and modern architecture pivots as much around the stripping of ornament from the surface of buildings as well as the new approaches to materials, construction, and site. Even beyond architecture, the disavowal of ornament is a primary narrative of twentieth-century culture.[14] But Loos, still considered the spiritual forebear of the modern movement, could not himself resist a little ornament here and there. A devoté of fashion, Loos liked to select his second wife's decidedly un-modern clothing and jewelry.[15] Loos's buildings, particularly the interiors, are likewise surprisingly vivacious with the "unnecessary" adornment that modern architecture fervently disowned.

Given the denigrated place of ornament in much architectural theory and practice of the twentieth century, it is not surprising that the publication of several books championing the communicative nature of applied decoration was met with controversy. Architect Robert Venturi published *Complexity and Contradiction in Modern Architecture* in 1966,[16] then co-wrote *Learning from Las Vegas* with architects Denise Scott Brown and Steven Izenour in 1972.[17]

The thesis of these books was that architecture had lost its signifying potential during the modernist purges and needed to "learn" from the decorative strategies of kitsch and vernacular buildings. These ideas rose to the forefront of architectural discourse, and the question of ornament returned, if in a limited fashion, to the table (although perhaps these books and debates suggest that in fact, ornament had never really left the room).

The feisty debates that followed upon these publications found a support of sorts in the rise of the worldwide heritage movement. This movement, too, had its origins in the backlash against destructive modernist city planning, which disposed of many beloved architectural landmarks and historic neighborhoods. Grass-roots initiatives to protect historic architecture sprung up all over the world in the late nineteen-sixties and early -seventies, coming somewhat later than the initiatives in socialist countries to document and, in some cases, preserve their respective architectural heritage.[18] One consequence of the outpouring of energy towards the salvage and protection of endangered historic architecture was the rearticulation of the importance of heavily ornamented and decorative styles, particularly those of the nineteenth century.

Western preservation initiatives, which germinated in the waning of post-war affluence and consumption, were paralleled by a new kind of artwork, which took the rapidly changing cityscapes as its locus. Gordon Matta Clark's well-known work, *Conical Intersect* (1975) was, in the words of critic Nancy Spector, a "critique of urban gentrification in the form of a radical incision through two adjacent seventeenth-century buildings designated for demolition near the much-contested Centre Georges Pompidou, which was then under construction."[19] Matta-Clark's "antimonument" to the loss of the historic block is a clear link between new artistic practices of the nineteen-sixties and -seventies, the contemporaneous, burgeoning heritage movement, and the rejection of the sweeping gestures and incongruous designs of much modernist architecture and city planning. To put it another way, the dramatic changes taking place in Paris provided Matta-Clark with the opportunity to engage in a new kind of art.

Urban geographer, Rob Shields argues that any given city—by virtue of its histories, urban designs, geographic location, architectural and social specificities—has affordances, that is, opportunities or potentialities for reflection and action within the city that emerge from the cultural, spatial and architectural characteristics of that place. Likewise, all cities possess virtual or intangible qualities that make them resistant to simple categorization or ranking within overly optimistic "global city" or "creative city" clichés.[20] Something as simple and ubiquitous as a park or green space, designated as a place to exercise, relax or socialize, can also afford, that is to say, invite and support other uses such as sleeping, informal or illegal exchange, or as a symbolic site for collective identity or resistance. Urban interventions confound the more conventional expectations and disappointments of the urban realm, translating or inverting them. The city thus affords certain visual and spatial conditions, which in turn can be defamiliarized, brought into relief or emphasized, by the intervention of an artist, an anonymous individual, an individual architect, or even an entire community. These affordances summon, unexpectedly perhaps, the art historical concept of site-specificity, which understands "sites" to be particular both in their physical or material conditions, but also particular in terms of the social and cultural relationships that occur within them.[21] The mutuality of site and action become apparent, and thus Matta-Clark's powerful intervention in Paris was afforded, in a sense, by the very changes he hoped to critique.

Now that an historic link has been suggested here between the fall of modernism, the rise of heritage, the return of ornament and the collective affordance or condition that all three create for the urban intervention, I would like to turn to the cities in which Czaplicki has made his interventions, to see whether this link has any value within the context of post-socialist urban space. A graduate-level study of Polish tourism identifies, among others, the cities of Warsaw, Cracow, Wroclaw, and Lodz as "the most popular towns" in Poland.[22] These towns are the sites that Czaplicki uses most consistently in his work.[23] While these cities have distinct urban histories, all share traces of the Soviet effort to create a unified culture, and all share as well a sharp rise in visitor interest and spending in the new millennium. Monika A. Murzyn describes the present "extraordinary fashion" for the city of Cracow, which attracted over seven million tourists in 2005, and which is the site of a new "heritage trail" and various tours that simplify "the complex socialist experience into one digestible by foreign tourists."[24] At the same time, however, Cracow has capitalized on its status as a *European City of Culture* (2000), "westernizing" its urban identity.[25] Lodz, Poland's second largest city, is described by Padraic Kenney as the country's "preeminent worker city in the twentieth century."[26] Also home to some of the country's most sophisticated Art Nouveau architecture,[27] Lodz depended historically, like Wroclaw, upon a booming textile industry. Today, the city's post-socialist identity is shaped by a dominant image that sutures present-day Lodz to "a nineteenth-century industrial and multicultural 'Golden Age' ... [which obscures] the socialist past and the importance of Russia and the Soviet Union in the development of the city."[28]

The city of Wroclaw, where Czaplicki works most frequently, lost nearly half its architecture during World War Two. While traces of the city's baroque past remain, it also has a strong history of association with the idealist phase in modern architecture. Local architects such as Hans Poelzig, Marlene Poelzig, and Max Berg, who designed the city's World Heritage Site, Centennial Hall (1911–13), were key members of the New Objectivity movement within modern architecture in the nineteen-twenties. For its practitioners, New Objectivity meant the transcendence of stylistic demarcations, and the end of the use of ornament. In the post-1989 years, Wroclaw became an important financial and educational center in Poland. The city's official website extols Wroclaw's multiculturalism and opportunities for investment, making no mention of the recent socialist past.[29]

David Crowley describes Warsaw as being a city "perpetually in crisis."[30] After World War Two, which saw the destruction of 85 percent of the city's architectural fabric, massive urbanization programs traded in adequate housing for a series of public architectural visions in the socialist era, including "parade grounds, public artworks, and 'people's palaces,'"[31] as well as "libraries, cultural centers, schools and theaters."[32] Crowley suggests that in Warsaw, such projects were hoped to provide a dramatic counterbalance to the housing shortage in the post-war era, which was followed by another era of extreme overcrowding in the newly built housing estates. Crowley and Susan E. Reid describe the monumental parade grounds of socialist cities, including Plac Defilad in Warsaw, where "marchers were arranged to animate the city and to embody the inexorable force of history."[33] These displays helped to characterize what Karina Kreja calls Warsaw's "unique image." She writes, "the socialist character of Warsaw's rebuilt urban structure and the concentration of wealth there" combined powerfully in what became a "city of extremes."[34]

6

Since the end of the socialist era, the extremes of Warsaw have taken a new turn. Kreja explains that the "marginalization of retail and marketing under the socialist authorities was replaced during the nineteen-nineties by extreme praise of their value and importance," a change that is mirrored in the dramatic increase in spaces devoted to consumption.[35] While new commercial projects have been an important aspect of the changes since 1989, the historic side of Warsaw has likewise been a focus, through increased tourism. Warsaw's Old Town, completely destroyed in 1944, was a very early historic reconstruction project in the city. In 1953, the process of rebuilding the Old Town's eighteenth-century fabric began (▶ 6).[36]

Since the Old Town's designation as a *UNESCO World Heritage Site* in 1980, tourism has been noted as a "threat," as the preservation or "musealization" of the Old Town has subordinated the needs of citizens to those of tourists.[37] The nearby proliferation of high-rise office towers, advertisements and banking institutions points to other changes. "The area has been transformed," writes Czepczyński, "into the landscape of a typical American city in just a few years."[38]

Thus, the cities in which Czaplicki works have a number of factors in common: the westernization or internationalization of what was, formerly, visibly socialist space; the provision of reductive, tourist-friendly communist narratives, and the celebration of the pre-Soviet aspects, particularly the architecture of the city. In addition to these commonalities, these cities also share a memory of the recent socialist past, despite the fact that this memory has been reconstituted and manufactured for tourist consumption on one hand, and diminished within idealized city narratives and images on the other. What are the visual and spatial qualities of this memory? Gregory Andrusz explains:

6   Royal Castle Square, Old Town, Warsaw, Poland, 2005.

The general image of the socialist city, consisting of modern, high-rise housing of different heights and of schools, hospitals, research centers, and factories built according to a standard design, conformed to an ideal of socialist reality ... Alongside the range of monotonous multistory tower blocks that are part of the spatial legacy of the socialist city stand the workers' palaces of culture, the ornately decorated railway stations built during the Stalin era and the large squares with their statues of political actors, artistic prodigies and military heroes.[39]

In addition to these architectural and spatial characteristics, Mariusz Czepczyński argues that in socialist cities, the conflict between the "humanist" (such as housing) and "aggressive" (such as parade grounds) aspects of socialist space was mediated spatially as well. "Communication with vast, agitated crowds," Czepczyński writes, "required a language that could be broken into segments, articulated in bold, abstract bursts, great stress on single words. ... The language also had to be familiar." Iconic images and powerful words thus "appeared in the cultural landscape of ... Central Europe to emphasize the significance of the new powers in popularly [understood] spatial language."[40] Thus the post-socialist city recalls both the monumental architectural programs of these spaces, and the negotiation of dissent through the embedding of propaganda in collective, social space. Because of this domination of the social structure, the built environment, and the iconosphere of the socialist city, the very notion of "public" is itself a historically vexed and contested terrain.

Katerina Gerasimova has demonstrated that western concepts of public and private do not easily translate to East Central European contexts, noting in particular that the western gloss of liberation and democracy, often associated with publicness, is incommensurate with the ways in which the Soviet era regimented collective space.[41] Accordingly, I use the word public in this essay carefully, to refer to places, buildings, and spaces in the cities of Cracow, Wroclaw, Lodz, and Warsaw that belong in a collective sense to either residents or to other kinds of stakeholders in the city. This usage means the inclusion of architectural or urban elements that are shared visually, even if they are not public in the sense of providing bodily entry. Façades as well as public squares, or platz are thus potentially public; likewise the details of streetscapes, such as the specific details of a given building, the names of streets, or the language or text used to name a place are also, subtly, "public."

But space becomes public in another important way. In such places as the street and the platz, protesters, for example, insist by their presence that the space they are temporarily occupying is indeed public. In this way, the publicness of space is not a given; rather, it is something to be continually rehearsed and negotiated, exercised, and sometimes lost. The occupation of space, whether by authority, advertising, tourists, or citizens, inflects the degree to which it may be said to be public. Thus, I see the publicness of space not in a binary mode, whereby it is either public or not, but rather as one characteristic of space whose intensity is strengthened or lessened by a variety of other factors. Fundamentally, however, I believe—as I would suspect many urban interventionist artists do—that art has a particular capacity to act upon the urban realm, to engage this charged dynamic by which inhabitants must continually assert their agency, spatially, within cities.

Just as Louis Sullivan's ornate entranceway signified clearly to the users of his department store, so too do Czaplicki's interventions indicate a kind of conceptual access to the buildings to which they are attached. Either in sympathy with the modernist legacy of their host buildings, or in contrast to the historic ornament with which they compete, the truthtags comment directly upon the history of design and architecture of the twentieth century; further, they ask, what has been privileged; what has been forgotten? And how can those who are not architects, planners, members of the political or military elite, shape the city?

In 2006, on a battered and neglected building in Warsaw, five brilliant orange horizontal bands hugged the corner of a chipped, tiled column, just within arm's reach (▶ 7). The context of shuttered storefronts and flaking cement drew attention, by contrast, to the robust color and precise linearity of the forms. Out of place, yet responding to—indeed, built for this place—this truthtag framed the building like a parergon. Neither belonging to nor divorced from the architecture, the work enabled the building to speak of its sorry state, and its potential for beautification. At the same time, the work was not, nor did it pretend

7   Krystian Czaplicki/TRUTH, documentation of urban intervention, Warsaw, Poland, 2006.

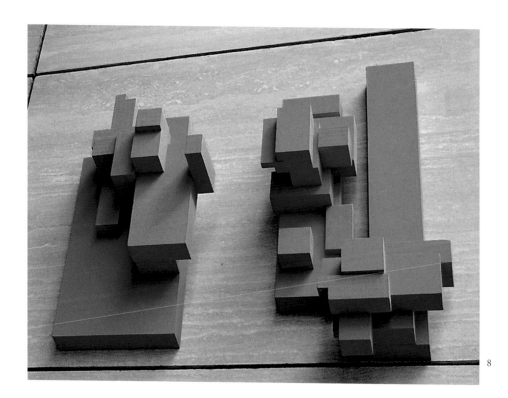

to be, that beautification; it sat, like a little parasite, ready to be stolen or rearranged at any moment. Passersby were free to regard, remove, or rearrange the forms to their liking, take them to other locations entirely or ignore them as they saw fit.

While the artist does sometimes have permission to install his pieces, sometimes he does not; the audience, or participants do not always know. Czaplicki's three-dimensional, spatial gestures provide the possibility for others to continue with the intervention themselves, testing the freedoms of the post-socialist city. As discussed above, this freedom is not without its limits, controls, and amnesia, as the image of the post-socialist city is a profitable concern. Czaplicki's interventions in Polish cities demonstrate skill and irony. At the same time that they make reference to an era that disowned history and the signifying capacity of ornament, the works themselves are also a kind of ornament, which observe in turn the present sidelining of modern architecture to new-build corporate projects and pre-communist architecture. Further, the works make a subtle comment on the loss of this modern heritage under communism, and the gentrifying, historicizing, and rapidly developing twenty-first-century city. In this way, they expose the paradox of the contemporary post-socialist city—bound to competing versions of the past as it reaches towards the future.

The truthtags, however, do something more. They raise the question of the "city from below," but also the city beside. As many of the interventions resemble cities in miniature,

8 Krystian Czaplicki/TRUTH, detail of Figure 1: documentation of urban intervention, Wroclaw, Poland, 2006.

taking up vertical walls as if they were horizontal planes, they recall to viewers and participants the language and power of architecture from above, translating the monumental, megalomaniac urban visions of the twentieth century into something small in scale, fragile in nature, and fundamentally mutable in nature (▶ 8). As the passerby pulls one polystyrene form off the wall, and moves or pockets it, an urban planner of a different sort is born, sharing the privilege of vision and destruction on a minor scale, but always in relation to the surface that has just been touched, seen, encountered, and thus, known differently for a moment.

A city is a multifaceted entity, whose historical, economic, social, and cultural dimensions can hardly be summed up in a map or an image. But a city is nevertheless a sort of map of its own past, its future desires, and most of all, its internal contradictions and struggles. It is a place of what Ernst Bloch calls "contemporaneous non-contemporaneity,"[42] whereby bits of the past lurch into our present, and vice versa. As theorist Rosi Braidotti writes, the city is "one huge map that requires special decoding and interpreting skills; in the hands of … artists the city also becomes text, a signifying artifact."[43] In the context of East Central Europe, this map has special characteristics that distinguish it from western models of urban development. As the essays in this volume collectively demonstrate, the socialist city lives on within the post-socialist city, its limits and possibilities, but in unexpected ways. Near the beginning of this chapter, I asked whether there are general characteristics of urban space at the beginning of the new millennium that make Czaplicki's amorphous position tenable? And are there specific characteristics of post-socialist urban space that make his position necessary? If, as I have argued above, the iconospheres of post-socialist cities offer site-specific "truths" of spatial and visual control, of layers of historic and architectural erasure and selective, tourist-friendly memories, then the "tagging" of such places through an elegant and incongruous, renegade ornament is a freighted gesture. As urban interventions, the truthtags are the quizzical interlocutors of the cities in which they appear, engaging the situated knowledge of the occupants of the post-socialist city.

Acknowledgements

The author would like to thank Marina Dmitrieva, Arnold Bartetzky, and Alfrun Kliems for their encouragement with this text, particularly in the context of her residency at the *Center for the History and Culture of East Central Europe* (Geisteswissenschaftliches Zentrum Geschichte und Kultur Ostmitteleuropas) in July 2008, Leipzig. Special thanks also to Thomas Strickland for reading multiple versions of this essay, and to the students and scholars who commented on a public presentation of these ideas at the University of Leipzig. Appreciation also goes to Dominik Art Projects, Cracow, for their help in supplying images, and to Johnny Nawracaj, for assistance with translation and communication.

Endnotes

1   Ella Chmielewska, "Signs of Place: A Close Reading of the Iconosphere of Warsaw," in *Neue Staaten—Neue Bilder? Visuelle Kultur im Dienst staatlicher Selbstdarstellung in Zentral- und Osteuropa seit 1918*, ed. Arnold Bartetzky, Marina Dmitrieva and Stefan Troebst (Cologne/Vienna/Weimar: Böhlau, 2005), 243–255, here 243.

2   Philip Wood, "Truthtags," Scrapbook Citizen: Exploring Life Through Objects, (September 29, 2006), http://scrapbook.citizen-citizen.com/subjectivity/truthtag/ (last accessed January 3, 2010).

3   Thomas F. Gieryn, "Three Truth-Spots," *Journal of the History of the Behavioral Sciences* 38 (2002): 113–32.

4   Truthtag, "Art, London: Truthtag," Polish Cultural Institute, (July 2008), http://www.culture.pl/en/culture/artykuly/wy_in_truthtag_london_2008 (last accessed February 24, 2010).

5   While preservation movements in the United States and England found their initial energy in citizens' groups and grass-roots movements, Christopher Long explains that preservation was part of many socialist countries' agendas as early as the nineteen-fifties. See: Christopher Long, "East Central Europe: National Identity and International Perspective. Teaching the History of Architecture: A Global Inquiry II (Special issue)," *Journal of the Society of Architectural Historians* 61 (2002:4): 519–29.

6   Leslie Sklair, "Iconic Architecture and Capitalist Globalization," *City* 10 (2006:1): 21–47.

7   There is a substantial literature on this topic. Key texts include Jane Jacobs, *The Death and Life of Great American Cities* (New York: Random House, 1961); Denise Scott Brown, Robert Venturi and Steven Izenour, *Learning from Las Vegas* (Cambridge, Mass.: MIT Press, 1977) and Charles Jencks, *The Language of Post-Modern Architecture* (New York: Rizzoli, 1984). Popular literature has reinforced the notion that architectural modernism was a mistake of epic proportions, divorcing architecture from its humanist legacy; see: Herbert Bangs, *The Return of Sacred Architecture: The Golden Ratio and the End of Modernism* (Rochester, Vermont: Inner Traditions, 2006). Scholarly work that explores the implications and effects of this widespread disavowal includes Kathleen Bristol, "The Pruit-Igoe Myth," *Journal of Architectural Education* 44 (1991:3): 163–71 and France Vanlaethem, "The difficulté d'être of the Modern Age," *The Journal of Architecture* 9 (2004): 157–71. The threat to the socialist fabric of many East-Central European cities has been the subject of recent academic concern. See Richard Anderson, "Taking Stock: Russia's Modern Heritage," *Future Anterior* 5 (2008:1): 81–86, also *Heritage at Risk: The Soviet Heritage and European Modernism*, ed. Jörg Haspel, Michael Petzet, Anke Zalivako and John Ziesemer (Berlin: Hendrik Basser Verlag, 2007).

8   Antony D. King, *Spaces of Global Cultures: Architecture, Urbanism, Identity* (London/New York: Routledge, 2004), 107.

9   Sklair, (see note 6), 36.

10 Chmielewska, (see note 1), 247.

11 Chmielewska, (see note 1), 247.

12 Chmielewska, (see note 1), 254.

13 Adolf Loos, "Ornament and Crime," (1908) reprinted in: *Crime and Ornament: The Arts and Popular Culture in the Shadow of Adolf Loos*, ed. Bernie Miller and Melony Ward (Toronto: YYZ Books, 2002), 29–36.

14 Brent C. Brolin, *Architectural Ornament: Banishment and Return* (New York: W. W. Norton & Co., 2000).

15 Mary McLeod, "Undressing Architecture: Fashion, Gender and Modernity," in *Architecture: In Fashion*, ed. Deborah Fausch (New York: Princeton Architectural Press, 1994), 63.

16 Robert Venturi, *Complexity and Contradiction in Modern Architecture* (New York: Museum of Modern Art, 1966).

17 See note 7.

18 See note 5.

19 Nancy Spector, quoted in European Art Projects, "Gordon Matta-Clark: Biography," Megastructure Reloaded, http://www.megastructure-reloaded.org/en/321/ (last accessed January 3, 2010).

20 Rob Shields, "The Urban Question as Cargo Cult: Opportunities for a New Urban Pedagogy," *International Journal of Urban and Regional Research* 32 (2008:3): 716–17.

21 See Miwon Kwon for a full discussion of the term "site-specificity" in her chapter, "Genealogy of Site Specificity," in *Site, Space, Intervention*, ed. Erika Suderberg (Minneapolis, Minnesota: University of Michigan Press, 2000), 11–31.

22 Monika Borowa, "The Demand for Tourism Services in Poland, 1995-2005," (MA thesis, University of Kalmar, 2008), 5.

23 The artist has also frequently worked in Pulawy.

24 Monika A. Murzyn, "Heritage Transformation in Central and Eastern Europe," in *The Ashgate Research Companion to Heritage and Identity*, ed. Brian Graham and Peter Howard (Aldershot, Hampshire: Ashgate, 2008), 329, 337.

25 Craig Young and Sylvia Kaczmarek, "The Socialist Past and Postsocialist Urban Identity in Central and Eastern Europe," *European Urban and Regional Studies* 15 (2008:1): 54.

26 Padraic Kenney, *Rebuilding Poland: Workers and Communists*, 1945-1950 (Ithaca, NY: Cornell University Press, 1996), 15.

27 Ákos Moravánszky, *Competing Visions: Aesthetic Invention and Social Imagination in Central European Architecture, 1867-1918* (Cambridge, Mass.: MIT Press, 1998), 123.

28 Young/Kaczmarek, (see note 25), 66.

29 City of Wroclaw, "Information About the City," Tourist Information Center in Wroclaw, (August 23, 2008) http://www.wroclaw-info.pl/it/view/id/235/lang/EN (last accessed January 3, 2010).

30 David Crowley, "Warsaw Interiors: The Public Life of Private Spaces, 1949–1965," in *Socialist Spaces: Sites of Everyday Life in the Eastern Bloc*, ed. David Crowley and Susan Reid (New York: Berg, 2003), 181–82.

31 David Crowley and Susan E. Reid, "Socialist Spaces: Sites of Everyday Life in the Eastern Bloc," in Crowley/Reid, (see note 30), 4.

32 Crowley, (see note 30), 182.

33 Crowley/Reid, (see note 31), 2.

34 Karina Kreja, "Spatial Imprints of Urban Consumption: Large-Scale Retail Development in Warsaw," in *The Urban Mosaic of Post-Socialist Europe: Space, Institutions and Policy*, ed. Sasha Tsenkova and Zorica Nedovic-Budic (New York: Springer, 2006), 257.

35 Kreja, (see note 34), 256–57. Kreja shows that between 1989 and 2006, the amount of space devoted to shopping malls increased in Warsaw by nearly one million square meters.

36 Jacek Friedrich notes that this rebuilding was understood at the time to be a "creative reconstruction" or "resurrection," rather than slavish replication, which was "part of the process of legitimizing the new [Communist] rulers of Poland" as "communists with a national colouring." See: "Politics and Reconstruction: Rebuilding the Historical Towns of Eastern Europe after the Second World War: Gdańsk, Warsaw, Kaliningrad, Minsk," in Bartetzky/Dmitrieva/Troebst, (see note 1), 173.

37 UNESCO, "Poland: Historic Centre of Warsaw," Periodic Reporting: State of Conservation of World Heritage Properties in Europe, 2006, http://whc.unesco.org/archive/periodicreporting/EUR/cycle01/section2/30-summary.pdf (last accessed January 3, 2010), 3.

38 Mariusz Czepczyński, *Cultural Landscapes of Post-Socialist Cities: Representation of Powers and Needs* (Aldershot, Hampshire: Ashgate, 2008), 170.

39 Gregory Andrusz, "Wall and Mall: A Metaphor for Metamorphosis," in *The Urban Mosaic of Post-Socialist Europe: Space, Institutions and Policy*, ed. Sasha Tsenkova and Zorica Nedovic-Budic (New York: Springer, 2006), 73.

40 Czepczyński, (see note 38), 64.

41 Katerina Gerasimova, "Public Privacy in the Soviet Communal Apartment," in Crowley/Reid, (see note 30), 207–30.

42 Ernst Bloch, "Summary Transition: Non-Contemporaneity and Obligation to its Dialectic," in *Heritage of Our Times*, ed. Ernst Bloch (Berkeley, Ca.: University of California Press, 1990), 97–116.

43 Rosi Braidotti, *Nomadic Subjects: Embodiment and Sexual Difference in Contemporary Feminist Theory* (New York: Columbia University Press, 1994), 20.

SCREENING THE POST-SOVIET METROPOLIS

Representations of Urbanity in Contemporary Russian Cinema

Eva Binder

The modern metropolis and the cinema have always been closely connected. During the first decades of its existence, the cinema was an urban phenomenon, created for the urban masses. Both the metropolis and the cinema are intimately linked to our notions of modern life and forms of perception. While the cinema and the modern metropolis have clearly shaped one another, the city film has not emerged as a genre in its own right. The narratives are so varied and include such a broad range of styles and forms, film artists, and directors spanning more than hundred years of cinematic history. The relationship between modern cities and films is perhaps best explored through the lens of the "cinematic city," a concept that I would like to describe here in more detail.[1]

One can speak of a "cinematic city" when the urban environment forms an integral element of the production—it is not simply the location and setting for the cinematic narrative. The cinematic city is an important figure, both in "dramatic and dramaturgical terms," which performs multiple complex functions within a film's network of meanings and directly influences its potential impact. The concept of the cinematic city also highlights the fact that these images of the cityscape are media constructions integrated within the multiperspectival context of the cinematic narrative. As artistically designed images, these cinematic representations of the cityscape refer to the fields of the imaginary and the visionary, the symbolic and the ideal. These processes are not, however, completely disconnected from our concrete reality. Viewers will, in any case, compare the cinematic city to its actual counterpart and to the real circumstances, locations and atmosphere.

The cinematic cities of post-Soviet Russia will form the focal point of this study. Moscow and, to a lesser degree, St. Petersburg, are the primary film locations and cinematic representations of the modern mega-city. The images of the cityscape presented in films are preconfigured images, both in aesthetic and cultural terms, and the cinematic city lends itself to the exploration of diverse issues surrounding the origins, specifics, and shifts in social and cultural concepts of urbanity. Similarly, a study of the cinematic city can reveal the characteristic media representations and perceptions of a city in a particular period of its existence. In examining these cinematic representations of places, architecture and ways of life, we can identify the cultural and social concepts deployed in an artistic text and its narrative world, and see how film impacts on these ideas. The focus of this paper, therefore, will be on the cinematic city both as a space that is shaped by social, political, and economic discourses; and as a text capable of imparting meaning and creating a sense of collective identity.

Cinematic representations of cities and their forms of representation have changed significantly since the collapse of the Soviet Union. The present study will outline these changes by drawing on concrete examples. The post-Soviet cinematic city is shaped and perceived in contrast to its socialist predecessor, and therefore it seems necessary to trace its origins in Soviet film history and to outline the specific connections between the past and the present that shape (whether openly or latently) the themes and formats of contemporary films.

The Cinematic City in Post-Soviet Cinema

The end of the Soviet Union precipitated the decline of Soviet cultural institutions. The transition to a market economy had a more significant impact on Russian cinema than on many other fields of cultural endeavor, and the industry was dogged by financial crisis and confusion through to the late nineteen-nineties. The disorientation that marked the first decade after the collapse of the Soviet Union was preceded by the comprehensive deconstruction of the Soviet social utopia. The Soviet utopia envisaged the social body as a moral and political unity centered on nodes of meaning tied to specific urban sites including Red Square, the Lenin Mausoleum, and the Moscow Metro. In contrast to this practice, the cinema of the Perestroika era explores a variety of urban spaces that resist integration within the concept of a unified social body. Instead of normality and order, the cinema of the Perestroika era explores lifestyles that exist beyond the boundaries of social conventions, and focuses its cinematic gaze on previously marginalized figures and themes: prison inmates, criminals, prostitutes, drug addicts, the homeless, and visceral images of sex, violence, illness, and death. The dystopias of Perestroika-era cinema are situated in tenement courtyards, cemeteries, mortuaries, prisons, landfills, and abattoirs.

The cinema of the Perestroika era marked the succession of the collectivist social model by an individualist model. With this transition, the city, in particular the Russian capital of Moscow, was stripped of its sites of ideological and social meaning, and—transformed into a space of vagrancy and alienation—interiorized in the awkward and pessimistic films of the Perestroika era. The protagonists of the films produced in the Perestroika era and the first post-Soviet years are vagrants, unable to settle permanently. These homeless wanderers are strangers in their own land and at the mercy of their inhospitable urban environs. In that sense, the cinema of the Perestroika era explores a vision of the city and of metropolitan life with which Western audiences were already long familiar—the often criminal energies that are present, whether latently or openly, in all big cities. The crime, action, and mafia thriller genres are among the genres adopted by post-Soviet cinema and they significantly shaped post-Soviet perceptions of the city.

Post-Soviet Russian cinema adhered to the artistic conventions of the Perestroika era for some time before gradually adapting to the new social and economic situation. A significant innovation in the cinematic representation of the city, which emerged in the late nineteen-nineties, was the exploration of the more recently constituted centers of urban life. The emergence of these new sites of social exchange was marked by the appropriation of public and private urban spaces by capital. Money, as the new and dominant medium of social exchange, became the catalyst for processes of social differentiation, which had been held in check for decades by the Soviet social utopia resulting in an emphasis on material values (as opposed to the ideal values of the Soviet era), and the elevation of objects of monetary value to the status of fetish objects.

Irrespective of the moral appraisal of the material objects and new social spaces put forward in each individual film, these phenomena have shaped the emerging vision of the cinematic city in post-Soviet cinema. These new urban spaces are signs of the processes of social distinction and include fitness centers and luxuriously decorated apartments and clubs. Of all the various fetish objects held in such high regard by the newly constituted and predominantly materialistic social classes, penthouse apartments, and expensive western automobiles are perhaps the most highly prized signifiers of contemporary urbanity. Mobile telephones and notebooks are other noteworthy symbols within contemporary urban lifestyles. Genre films have transformed the cinematic city, in particular Moscow, into a site of social distinction and selection. In the course of this transformation, the city has been stripped of the characteristics that defined the city of Soviet films produced during the Thaw and the Brezhnev era: the intelligentsia milieu with its complex characters and "difficult" conversations; the cultural and artistic life of the city with its specific locations (including museums and various sites of academic life); and the principle of the equitable distribution of material wealth.

Valery Todorovskii's psychological drama *Liubovnik* (The Lover, 2002) offers an aesthetic and moral echo of the cinematic city of the Soviet-era intelligentsia. Both in terms of its visual aesthetics and the constellation of its characters, *Liubovnik* runs counter to popular cinema. The film, notable for the quiet tempo of its edit, explores the relationship of two men; a professor of linguistics and a retired officer, brought together by the sudden death of a female acquaintance. The film's locations—a university, a concert hall, a small city apartment packed with books, and a solitary tram—evoke the cinematic city that was such a formative influence in Soviet cinema since the Thaw. Indeed, the film's frame of reference is Soviet cinema in its entire historical dimension: the images of the tram and of the road sweeper draw on the clichéd imagery of city films from the nineteen-twenties, while the director's choice of Oleg Iankovskii for the main role is an explicit allusion to the intellectual auteur cinema of the nineteen-sixties to the nineteen-eighties and Iankovskii's roles in Andrei Tarkovskii's films *Zerkalo* (Mirror, 1975) and *Nostalghia* (1983).

The last decade has seen a veritable renaissance of the city film. The post-Soviet city and its characteristic locations, the movement of film protagonists through urban spaces and the upbeat attitude of the films' predominantly young protagonists are all vital narrative elements in a battery of comedies and melodramas that includes *Piter FM* (2006, director Oksana Bychkova), *Zhara* (The Heat, 2006, director Reso Gigineishvili), and *Rusalka* (Mermaid, 2007, director Anna Melikian). A common denominator of these works—besides the fact that the crew and actors represent a new generation of film makers—is their tendency to enhance the sensory experience by allowing movement and speed to dominate the creation of cinematic space and by employing a host of disjointed camera perspectives. In doing so, these films follow in the footsteps (if indirectly) of the city films of the nineteen-twenties and draw on Dziga Vertov's metropolitan symphony *Chelovek s kinoapparatom* (Man with a Movie Camera, 1929) as an aesthetic, if not a conceptual, inspiration. The characteristic aesthetic resources of these more recent films include fast-cut sequences and a heightened tempo that does not let up even when the film protagonists are simply strolling through the streets. These city films are also united in their tendency to fragment our visual and spatial perception through the use of camera shots that collapse conventional structures of space and time, coupled with the intrusion of street noise and soundtrack music in film dialogues. The use of hand-held camera shots and camera perspectives filmed through visual barriers such as fences, glass windows, and even through video and photographic cameras enhances the audience's subjective involvement and creates a diversity of perspectives.

Progulka (The Walk, 2003, director Aleksei Uchitel') was one of the first films to express this new metropolitan atmosphere and to showcase one of the two major Russian cities (in this case St. Petersburg), and it is certainly one of the most aesthetically innovative contemporary films. An active documentary filmmaker since the mid-nineteen-seventies, Uchitel' did notturn to fictional films until the mid-nineteen-nineties. In *Progulka*, Uchitel' adopted a format that was first popularized in the city films of the nineteen-twenties—a day in the life of a city—while practically reducing the film's narrative time to the actual running time of ninety minutes. At the film's outset, the female protagonist alights from a car on Nevskii Prospekt and embarks on a long trek—filmed with hand-held cameras—through the crowded city streets. As she makes her way down Nevskii Prospekt she flirts with a young man who is soon joined by a friend. Tensions mount between the men, culminating in shouting matches and fisticuffs as they vie for the confident young woman's favor. The protagonists' fast-paced journey ends in disappointment for the young men when the female protagonist reveals her ruse: her trek across the city was intended to prove to her fiancé that she was fit to embark on their honeymoon in the Himalayan Mountains. At the film's conclusion she meets her fiancé in a bowling club; the young men have served their purpose as witnesses to her stamina and as a passing amusement.

Parallels to Georgii Daneliia's comedy *Ia shagaiu po Moskve* (I'm walking through Moscow, 1963) are clearly evident in *Progulka*'s cinematic narrative and its constellation of characters. Daneliia's city film popularized the cinematic vision of the big city typical of films produced throughout the Thaw. As a genre the city films of the Thaw era introduced numerous narrative experiments and technical innovations, and the films are indicative of the social and political changes of the era. These tendencies are particularly evident in Marlen Khutsiev's Moscow films, which so vividly captured the spirit and thinking of the younger generations of the Thaw era.

Progulka differs starkly from Daneliia's Thaw-era production, however, both with regard to its underlying atmosphere and the film's vision of social reality. Daneliia's protagonists stroll through the streets of Moscow with an aura of resurgent freedom and are carried along by the attractions of the big city. Their carefree spirit is a product of the as yet intact Soviet social utopia. In contrast, Uchitel's narrative unfolds before the backdrop of a society based on struggle and competition. *Progulka* explores the struggle for individual well-being in the

face of rapidly changing social conditions and illustrates this struggle through its exposition of individual and collective patterns of behavior and conflicts including references in the film's dialogues to the animal kingdom, a running battle between football fans, and, in particular, the rivalry between the film's male protagonists. The film's final scene, featuring an increasingly violent altercation between two men following a minor road accident, is clearly intended to illustrate this theme. Uchitel's representation of social relations highlights the prevailing belief in post-Soviet society that "might is right" and the accompanying desire to make a profit in all transactions—whether they are of an emotional, social, or financial nature. Improvisation, self-dramatization, and deception are vital strategies in this bitter game.

The blurry line between reality and illusion, and the razor's edge that separates the fulfillment of desire from its mere illusion are the central themes of *Rusalka*, a contemporary urban fairy-tale that references Hans Christian Andersen's *The Little Mermaid*. *Rusalka*'s Moscow is a vibrant capitalist metropolis that has devoured the former socialist city. One of the most memorable scenes in this visually intense film focuses on a huge advertising banner mounted on an apartment block. The banner entirely blocks the inhabitants' view of the city, thus exposing the emptiness of its message—"It's nice to be at home."[2] The meaningless slogans of the countless advertising billboards and banners that are an almost omnipresent feature of contemporary cityscapes have long transcended their role as advertisements for individual products. Broadcasting images of an unattainable ideal of happiness, they achieve their effect through their ubiquitous presence in urban spaces. The film's protagonist occasionally takes their messages at face value and acts on their basis. Her naïve world view exposes the illusory character of the dreams produced by the capitalist economic system (▶ 1).

1 Moscow as a vibrant capitalist metropolis that has devoured the former socialist city; *Rusalka* (2007, director Anna Melikian).

The City Discourse in Genre Films

In the aftermath of the crises of the first post-Soviet years, genre films gradually gained a foothold in Russia and followed international trends. In the course of this appropriation of American genre cinema, the imported formal language has been adapted to the Russian context. The two *Brat* (Brother) films by Aleksei Balabanov (*Brat*, 1997, and *Brat 2*, 2000) and Petr Buslov's *Bumer* (2003) are illustrative examples of the appropriation and adaptation of genre elements for Russian cinema. Furthermore, both directors use the city as the backdrop for their explorations of contemporary social ambivalences and contradictions. Aleksei Balabanov, the director of the mafia thriller *Brat*, is widely regarded as the first director to have captured the lived realities of the young post-Soviet generation in an innovative cinematic format and to have expressed these collective experiences in the cinematic medium. Balabanov's *Brat* films anticipated the wave of blockbuster films that emerged in the Putin-era and established a patriotic discourse based on exclusion and ethnic prejudice. A comparison of the representations of urban space in the two *Brat* films reveals the tendency of the sequel to favor unambiguous messages and states of emotion. *Brat 2* is marked by the semiotic transformation of the signs of Soviet and pre-Soviet history, ultimately signaling their co-option for contemporary agendas.

The narrative of *Brat* follows the story of the Bagrov brothers. The elder brother is a mafia hit man in St. Petersburg; he introduces his younger brother to the profession but eventually betrays him to save his own skin. Unlike his elder brother, the younger of the two men emerges as a character with high identification potential as he evolves from his original role of social misfit and country-boy into a formidable figure in a city dominated by organized crime and populated by marginalized social figures. The second part of Balabanov's mafia duology depicts a trial of strength between Russia and the United States, in which Danila Bagrov (the younger brother) battles an international mafia network and fights for justice, truth, and brotherhood.

The city discourse of Balabanov's first *Brat* film references the deconstruction of the communist utopian society that accompanied Perestroika and heightened public awareness of criminals, alcoholics, drug addicts, the homeless, violent men, and abused women. The anti-utopian discourse underlying the first *Brat* film is clearly recognizable in the characterization of the protagonists and in the film's atmospheric and gloomy depiction of the post-Soviet metropolis. The arrival of the film's protagonist in St. Petersburg marks the beginning of a journey through a fragmented and disjointed metropolitan landscape that is incapable of instilling a sense of identity in any conventional sense of the term. Key stations in this journey—depicted in contrasting images of St. Petersburg's historical city and its faceless, ahistorical periphery and set to the powerful rhythms of the film's rock soundtrack—include a bustling market populated by predominantly non-ethnic Russian hawkers and stallholders, a Lutheran cemetery on St. Petersburg's Vasilii Island, and miscellaneous streets and squares throughout the city.

Brat not only reflects the anti-utopian city discourses of the Perestroika era and the first post-Soviet years, it also draws strongly on historical city discourses. In one scene, a homeless German character by the name of Gofman reproduces a historical city discourse in which the city figures as a "den of moral corruption, luxury and debauchery … a breeding ground of misery, fraught with disease and mortality."[3] In this troubled vision of urbanity the city is little more than a grave for its population: unable to provide for itself, the city survives thanks only to the regular influx of strong and healthy migrants from the country-side. Gofman's characterization of the city and its "terrible power" frames the protagonist's journeys through this urban space. At their first and last encounter, the homeless drifter describes the city as a place where the law of the jungle prevails: "The city—the city is a terrible power. And the bigger the city, the stronger it is. It devours you. Only the strong survive."[4] The film's protagonist proves Gofman wrong by surviving the challenges of the city. He leaves St. Petersburg an unbroken man and heads for Moscow, the site of unbridled power. "Moscow is the place to be. Moscow is where the power lies,"[5] summarizes Danila's older brother.

Superiority, strength, a simplistic and almost childlike moral sense, combined with his brutality, disregard for the law and capacity for decisive action earned Balabanov's protagonist the epithet of "a hero for our times." In the first *Brat* film this new "hero" was a relatively ambivalent figure—a brutal killer, who sought to aid "the good people," defend the weak, give to the poor, and judge the wicked. In the sequel, however, Balabanov resorted to more obvious means of directing audience identification. This is quite evident in the film's patchwork of contemporary issues, national-patriotic sloganeering and mythologizing motifs. *Brat 2*'s national-patriotic, perhaps even right-wing, discourse is foreshadowed in *Brat* by Balabanov's particular interpretation of urban social politics and the film's ethnic agenda with its references to the dominant role of Caucasian (in particular Chechen) traders on the city's markets. This aspect is excellently illustrated in one brief scene in which the protagonist argues with two Caucasian men, culminating in the insult: "I'm no brother of yours, you black-arsed maggot!"[6]

Unlike the first *Brat* movie, which focused on the dilapidated cityscape and largely ignored St. Petersburg's historic city, *Brat 2* foregrounds notions of the center as the head of a hierarchical culture. The first part of *Brat 2* (the second part is situated in the US) depicts a vision of Moscow that is both anchored in diachronic time and resurgent in the radiant splendor of post-Soviet capital. This image of Moscow draws on a collage of various historical texts and symbols, and projects them into the simultaneity of the present. In *Brat 2*, the visual presence of Moscow is expressed in an array of pre-Soviet, Soviet and post-Soviet signs. The palace of a mafia boss resonates with echoes of aristocratic Russia. The Red Square, Lenin's Mausoleum, and the former Lenin Museum represent Soviet Russia, while the homes of the "new Russians" mark the post-Soviet era. The film images of Moscow city, captured in footage shot from moving cars and apartment windows, are focused primarily on the

historical center. The massive apartment blocks on the city's periphery, for example, are deliberately hidden from view. In contrast, the city's Stalinist-era high-rise buildings are presented as eye-catching landmarks and denote the city's resurgence. The camera switches from glimpses of run-down courtyards, to freshly renovated pre-revolution building façades and attractive views across the Moskva River from the Embankment. The urban landscape never threatens to dominate the images and the film offers few panoramic views of the city. In spite of this fact, Moscow has a very tangible presence and connotes power, might, and history (in the sense of a historically evolved space) (▶ 2).

The transformation of historical meanings and the appropriation of historical symbolic forms for contemporary agendas is illustrated clearly in one particular scene that transforms a Soviet artifact into the catalyst for a new form of Russian patriotism dividing the world into "nashi" ("us") and "ne nashi" ("them" or "our enemies"). The scene features a gun battle between the two brothers and members of the mafia. A machine gun taken from the collection of the Lenin Museum decides the battle. The Civil War-era machine gun draws its symbolic meaning from the tales of the heroism of Red Army soldiers, such as the popular Chapaev myth. The role of this weapon in the Bagrov brothers' victory over the Mafiosi catapults the gun from its historical origins into the contemporary context of the national Russian struggle against capital. Besides these shifts in semiotic meaning and appropriation of historic symbols, the scene also illustrates the film's populist tenor. The gun fight vividly illustrates the relocation of national history from the dusty archives—exemplified here by the machine gun stored in Lenin Museum—to the streets, and the energy that historic symbols can unleash through the performative act of combat. Here, history is wrenched from its intellectual guardians and "managers" and handed back to the "ordinary people," as represented by the film's protagonists. The occupation of the symbolic center by these

2   Against the backdrop of an American-style city, the protagonist Danila Bagrov is caught up in a struggle against the power of money; *Brat 2* (2000, director Aleksei Balabanov).

new "national heroes," demonstrated here by Balabanov, is yet another sign of the paradigm change mentioned above: the disappearance of the cinematic city of the intelligentsia in post-Soviet cinema.

Like the Brat movies, *Bumer* was produced by the successful St. Petersburg production company STV and there are numerous ideological and aesthetic parallels between the film and Balabanov's thrillers. The film's protagonists are characterized by their male perspectives and forms of behavior, in particular their willingness to use excessive force. In aesthetic terms, the most obvious similarity between Balabonov's action thrillers and director Petr Buslov's debut film lies in their soundtracks, which both feature Russian rock music. The soundtrack to *Bumer* was written by Sergei Shnurov, the lead singer of the famous rock band *Leningrad*. Likewise, Buslov's film is also situated in the urban criminal milieu of the nineteen-nineties. The film sees four youngsters from Moscow with a passion for fast Western cars forced to flee from the city after they become embroiled in a conflict with a rival mafia gang. In the course of their aimless wanderings in a stolen black BMW 750 (also known as a "Bumer" in the gangster milieu), the city dwellers travel to a Russian village and, later, to a provincial town, where an attempted heist results in the death of two of the young men.

Buslov's film includes a number of significant elements from the road movie genre, which emerged in US filmmaking in the late nineteen-sixties. One dominant feature of the road movie genre is the contrast it draws between the city and the countryside—the outward journey is presented as an escape from the highly regulated life of the city dweller and as a quest to rediscover personal freedom in the infinite vastness of the open landscape. In some films these journeys are an attempt to flee from the scene of a desperate crime or state prosecution. Whatever their motivation, these journeys enable the protagonists to transcend conventional social norms and figure as a liberating experience based on mobility and speed.[7] The semantic attributions of the road movies' city-country dualism differ fundamentally from modernist visions of the city. In the road movie genre, the automobile—as the genre's constitutive means of transportation—is associated not with the city and its connotations of industry and progress, but with the countryside. Similarly, in the road movie, the promise of freedom can only be fulfilled beyond the city borders.

Buslov's *Bumer* film semanticizes the quintessential stylistic and ideological theme of the original US model—the promise of freedom through the journey from the city into the countryside—in a completely different manner. The film's four protagonists carry the specific post-Soviet urban versus rural conflict described in the film with them on their travels and accordingly fail to find freedom in the open countryside. The encounter of these two poles of Russian society is the central focus of the narrative, which associates the city with the dynamic processes of globalization and the free market economy, and the village with guardianship and constancy. In Buslov's narrative the city and the village do not meet as equals; instead the city's relationship to the countryside is one of exploitation and parasitism.

The urban-rural dualism, which the film draws on, ties together a number of historical discourses and explores them in the light of contemporary issues. In the film's narrative the four protagonists, clad in black leather jackets, are cast as representatives of the capitalist metropolis of Moscow. They appear to be young, dynamic, and strong young men at first glance. But confronted with the realities of life in the Russian provinces, they prove consistently to be inferior to the situation. Both of the heists that they attempt to carry out on their travels fail miserably. In their encounter with the countryside, the city is exposed as a foreign body that does not produce anything of worth and preys on the countryside like a parasite. The city consumes the produce of the land and its honest inhabitants. This subtext is highlighted in particular in those scenes that depict the four protagonists consuming food; whether at a roadside diner, a farmhouse, or at their accommodation in a provincial town. The most obvious example of this portrayal of the city's parasitic hunger is the scene in which the protagonists enter an herbalist's farmhouse, where they have fled after one of them is seriously injured. Finding the herbalist in a waking sleep inside the farmhouse, they rush to devour the leftover food in her kitchen, waking her in the process. She comments on their behavior: " … what do you want? Have you come here to steal?"[8]

Parallel to this vision of the city, the film develops an image of the Russian village anchored in historical discourses. In *Bumer*, the village is imbued with a feminine identity: it appears devoted, patient, old and infirm, poor and lonely, yet also steadfast, unwavering, and stable—a place of warmth and salvation. The film's discursive background spans the urban-rural dualism of pre-modern Europe, the Slavophile discourses of the nineteenth century, and patriotic Soviet discourses; the latter are communicated by heavily inscribed objects such as the Soviet-era tractor that comes to the rescue when the elegantly urban BMW is stranded in snow on a rural road. Similarly, the protagonists are repeatedly forced to fall back on outdated Soviet landline telephones when their mobile phones prove too unreliable, and the sole survivor of the film's showdown makes his escape in a rickety Soviet bus after abandoning the Western car in the forest. The film celebrates the loyalty and self-sacrificing character of the only girl in the village, who has returned from the city to nurse her paralyzed mother; whereas her urban counterpart, one of the gangsters' girlfriends, emigrates to France in her partner's absence.

Although the film's semantic oppositions invite comparisons to the relationship between Russia and the West, they are embedded within a more complex set of references that center on the post-Soviet, blood-sucking, metropolitan capitalism of the Yeltsin era. The clichés employed in the film point to an indirectly articulated, latent state of fear and unease in the face of global changes. In that sense, the film's urban-rural dualism hints at the unconscious fear of post-industrial urbanization, which, according to Henri Lefèbvre, transforms the countryside into little more than an urban "periphery," a feature on the urban horizon, a border, and impacts on the entirety of our social relations.[9] Significantly, a number of minor themes in the film's narrative heighten its negative characterization of the city. The militia is one of the protagonists in this subplot and represents the old principles of municipal power, law, and order. In the film's specific cinematic context, these guardians of the law are clearly imbued with negative connotations: they are slaves to the alluring power of (Western) money and attempt to elicit bribes whenever the opportunity presents itself. The truck drivers, from whom the four gangsters attempt to extort protection money, are far more ambivalent characters. They are depicted as the real losers of contemporary political and social change in Russia and have borne the brunt of the transition from the Soviet system to capitalism in the nineteen-nineties. And it is a truck driver who expresses the metaphor of capitalism as a blood-sucking entity: "They have sucked out so much of our blood!"[10] he remarks about his extortionists. The truck drivers, however, seem degenerated and perverted in their own way.

On a conceptual level *Bumer* conveys a fatalistic sense of inevitability with regard to post-Soviet urbanization. The film portrays its protagonists as the victims of an array of global forces and social circumstances that have conspired to defile and corrupt Russian youth. The herbalist in the farmhouse recognizes this fact and comments on their impending doom: "All of you will be killed sooner or later. And for nothing … your car is horrible, too—it's like a hearse."[11] Neither the old Soviet system, represented in the film by the truck drivers, nor the Russian village, which is reduced to the passivity of enduring the new circumstances, provides a feasible alternative to the parasitic capitalist city.

Socialist Moscow as a Cinematic Effect in Genre Cinema

Timur Bekmambetov's fantasy film *Nochnoi dozor* (Night Watch, 2004) is widely regarded as the first post-Soviet blockbuster and the first Russian film since the collapse of the Warsaw Bloc to achieve success in US and European markets, including the key French and German markets. Like the genre films *Brat*, *Brat 2*, and *Bumer*, *Nochnoi dozor* and its sequel *Dnevnoi dozor* (Day Watch, 2005) set imported forms in relation to specifically Russian material. In the present context, however, the films' ideological dimensions are less interesting than their successful use of imagery of Soviet cities and everyday life as a cinematic effect in a blockbuster film.

The two films are based on a tetralogy of novels written by Sergei Luk'ianenko (published 1998–2005), which depict the battle between the forces of light and darkness. The "Light Others," a group of beings with supernatural powers, constitute the so-called Night Watch. The "Dark Others," a group of vampires, witches, and masters of black magic, form the Day Watch. The films' diegetic universe draws viewers into a parallel world that is only accessible to the so-called "Others," but exists alongside everyday life in Moscow. The balance of power between the forces of light and darkness is guaranteed by a complex agreement, which has secured a truce between the powers for many centuries. When this fragile peace is once again put to the test in modern Moscow, the hostilities escalate into an open confrontation.

Aesthetically, both films are effect-oriented spectacles featuring scenes of horror, action, and graphic violence. The films' breathtaking editing, coupled with the extensive use of dazzling special effects, computer-generated scenes, unusual camera angles, and elaborate costumes make the films a mesmerizing experience. While the plot is obscure and confusing, particularly for viewers unfamiliar with the films' literary basis, the visual effects are captivating and, no doubt, the main draw card for most cinema-goers.

The remarkable effect of Bekmambetov's fantasy films is rooted in the contrast between the films' setting and the conventions of its genre. Films such as *The Matrix, Underworld, Blade,* and *The Lord of the Rings* are among the more obvious aesthetic and narrative intertextual references. In that sense, Bekmambetov's films may well be regarded as an experiment. The films' focus on everyday activities and locations is not only unusual for the genre, they focus viewers' attention on realities that have become symbols of backwardness and indignity since the Perestroika era, such as the overcrowded trains of the Moscow Metro with their cursing and jostling masses, supermarkets staffed by hostile and frustrated workers, the unromantic reality of the kolkhoz markets with their bloodied cuts of meat, and the entrance to a prefab apartment block with its tiled walls and tin mailboxes. The films' particular aesthetic achievement is their aestheticization of urban spaces and objects previously considered unfit for inclusion in the beautified urban landscapes of Russian cinema; hence, the focus in Bekmambetov's films on the metro's speeding trains rather than the aestheticization of the automobile commonly employed in mafia-action films (▶ 3).

The desire of the films' creators to expand and enhance the quality of the cinematic experience provides a remarkably vivid rendering of the city of Moscow. On the one hand, the film captures the everyday manifestations of life in a Soviet city: standardized apartments

3

3   Prefabricated buildings from the Soviet era provide the cinematic scenery of a fantasy film in two parts; *Nočnoj dozor* (2004, director Timur Bekmambetov).

4

with large-print wallpaper and the obligatory living room cabinet filled with crystal glasses, dilapidated stairwells with typical Soviet-style doors, buzzers and lampshades, and semi-rural figures such as the elderly Russian grandmother who tries to strike up a conversation in the stairwell with her neighbors. But the films also visit the Moscow city center and include striking images of the Kremlin, the Bolshoi Theater, and a Stalinist skyscraper. The films contrast a modern furnished apartment with the protagonist's modest domicile, while the extensive use of aerial footage of Moscow is juxtaposed with the cramped scenes shot inside the metro tunnels. Besides their obvious visual function, the films' many and varied panoramic views of Moscow serve to cement Moscow's position in the ranks of the world's leading cities and lend the city a distinctive, individual flair.

But the socialist metropolis and its realities also play a more meaningful role in the films than this aestheticization of surfaces (Bekmambetov is a veteran of the advertising industry) would perhaps suggest. The narrative's dualism of good versus evil draws on the same ideological judgment that underlies Luk'ianenko's literary work. The struggle between the "Light Others" and "Dark Others" can be read as the struggle between two social models: the "Dark Others" are motivated solely by self-interest and place an absolute value on individual freedom, while the "Light Others" have a more progressive social agenda and base their decisions and actions on the good of the many. This polarization is rooted and reflected not least of all in the attributes and territories assigned to these two forces. There is something typically "Soviet" about the apartments and office rooms used by the forces of light and their organization "Gorsvet": the floors of their dingy offices are covered with threadbare rugs and bare cables run along the poorly painted green walls. Not only does

4   The ruler of the "Dark Others" stops the vehicle belonging to the "Light Others," a van of Soviet design; *Nočnoj dozor* (2004, director Timur Bekmambetov).

the Night Watch use a claptrap Soviet-era van for transport, their headquarters are located in one of Moscow's most famous examples of Soviet constructivist architecture—an office block designed by Aleksei Shchusev and constructed in the late nineteen-twenties to house *Narkomzem* (Narodnyi commissariat zemledeliia/People's Commissariat for Agriculture). In contrast to the forces of light, the forces of darkness draw their ranks from the profiteers of the political and social transformation and resemble figures drawn from the post-Soviet media scene. Many of them inhabit lavishly furnished modern apartments, drive expensive Western cars, and cultivate a post-Soviet-style celebrity cult (▶ 4).

The good-evil dualism in Bekmambetov's films is characteristically ambivalent. At the plot level, this ambivalence is registered in the licenses that the "Light Others" issue to their dark counterparts, allowing them to pursue their ends. The vision of a functioning world presented (indirectly) in the novel and its film adaptation is based on a balance of power between antagonistic forces that was characteristic of the Cold War. Irrespective of the ideological subtext, which the international film audience would largely fail to decipher in any case, the socialist city of Bekmambetov's films is primarily a cinematic effect, comparable with Eisenstein's *Attractions*—edited without recourse to their semantic context, they speak directly to our senses.

Fragments of the Metropolis in Documentary Cinema

Like all fictional texts, films—and in particular genre films—construct their own worlds. With the support of their viewers, who contribute to the process of construction, these worlds are totalities—closed systems in which particular aspects are subordinated to the rationale of the fictional text as a whole. By comparison, documentary films tend to be more open and present a less complete totality. Freed from the obligation to integrate the concrete within the totality of their narratives, documentary films can focus on momentary experiences. It is not just their stronger focus on reality that enables documentary films to more readily capture the practices and experiences that comprise everyday life; it is also their fragmentary nature. Siegfried Kracauer noted that cinematic perception focused on the material world and the "flow of material life"[12] in a manner that no other form of art had previously achieved. Subscribing to Kracauer's principle, documentary filmmaker Viktor Kossakovskii created a different vision of the city in his film *Tishe!* (Quiet!, 2002) by recording the various events that occurred over one year outside his apartment window.

Not much happens in the quiet side street which Kossakovskii observes through his camera lens, and yet contemporary urban life has a tangible presence in this film: elderly pedestrians pass through the street, some sit down to rest on a bench and others walk their dogs. A couple of lovers splash about in the puddles following a torrential downpour. In one scene, two detainees attempt to escape from a police car that has halted at the intersection; in another scene, three young men emerge from the opposite building and glance up and down the street nervously—their clothing and hairstyles identify them as Jews. In addition to these unique events, the documentary also records rituals, reoccurring events and familiar clichés. A construction crew returns to tear up the street several times; they cut away a section of the asphalt, dig a hole, inspect and replace sections of underground pipe, before filling the hole and resealing the road surface. These road maintenance sequences are edited in a slapstick fashion—like scenes from old silent movies, they are accompanied by stereotypical silent film music and the figures move unnaturally fast (▶ 5).

Kossakovskii's nuanced observations contrast with the complex urban text that has emerged in the course of cinematic history. Kossakovskii's gaze is anything but voyeuristic. Unlike Alfred Hitchcock's *Rear Window*, the focus of this film lies on freely observable phenomena within the public domain, rather than what might be occurring behind the curtained windows of other apartments. Kossakovskii even goes so far as to undermine the materiality of the cinematic image by inserting abstract images into the edit. These images are actually extreme close-ups of the material world—snowflakes, beads of water on the asphalt surface of the road and the coarse gravel that lies behind the surface. These magnified images reveal complex surface structures and highlight the specific nature of Kossakovskii's method of observation, which does not seek to penetrate the surfaces and façades.

In contrast to contemporary action films, Kossakovskii's documentary focuses on non-events and imbues them with the qualities of the spectacular. Nevertheless, the film's refusal to contextualize the individual non-events makes them seem fragmentary and mysterious.

5

5   Documentary study of city life in a side street in St. Petersburg; *Tishe!* (2002, director Viktor Kossakovskii).

This underlying principle distinguishes Kossakovskii's film from the observations of Dziga Vertov. While Vertov's works also drew on documentary material, their visual montage was dictated by the broader ideological context. The slapstick antics of the road workers with their jerky and unnaturally fast movements lead viewers back to the earliest days of the cinematic medium: to the city as the birthplace of the cinema and to urbanism as a sensory phenomenon that brought forth and was simultaneously shaped by film.

With his highly self-reflective documentary, Kossakovskii not least demonstrates that the "cinematic city" has remained a central cinematic topos up to the present day, and that the cinematic possibilities and forms of representation of the metropolis have not been exhausted in the course of more than a hundred years of cinematic history. In the Russian fiction films of the first two post-Soviet decades, the cinematic city can be regarded as a focal point for the changes society has undergone since the collapse of the Soviet Union. The cinematic representations of the city and of urban life, as well as the various discourses connected to the city, reveal a shift in values closely linked to the supersession of society's elites. The intellectual, immaterial values of the intelligentsia that had had a formative influence on Soviet cinema since the Thaw were replaced by the topos of the criminal city, predominant in the media in the nineteen-nineties, and subsequently by the urban manifestations of a consumer society, oriented on materialistic values and more and more subject to the influence of globalization. Aesthetically, this change finds its most obvious expression in a tendency to enhance the sensory experience by means of movement and speed. By placing the emphasis on the creation of a glamorous surface, which is certainly one of the characteristics of the globalized consumer culture and entertainment industry, cinema and the modern metropolis merge once more.

Endnotes

1   For an extensive study of the relationships between the city and the cinema in Germany, see: Guntram Vogt, *Die Stadt im Kino: Deutsche Spielfilme 1900–2000* (Marburg: Schüren-Verlag, 2001).

2   Russian original: "Khorosho byt' doma."

3   Rolf Peter Sieferle and Clemens Zimmermann, "Die Stadt als Rassengrab," in *Die Grossstadt als "Text,"* ed. Manfred Smuda (Munich: Wilhelm Fink, 1992), 53–71.

4   Russian original: "Gorod, gorod—strashnaia sila. A chem bol'she gorod, tem on sil'nee. On zasasyvaet. Tol'ko sil'nyi mozhet vykarabkat'sia."

5   Russian original: "V Moskvu ekhat' nado. V Moskve vsia sila."

6   Russian original: "Ne brat ia tebe, gnida chernozhopaia!"

7   Christine Engel's comments on road movies and her interpretation of Bumer in: "Reisen durch die russische Gegenwart als Road Movie," in *Flüchtige Blicke. Relektüren russischer Reisetexte des 20. Jahrhunderts*, ed. Wolfgang Stephan Kissel (Bielefeld: Aisthesis-Verlag, 2009), 645–63. For an extensive study of the iconography and narrative structures of this genre, see: David Laderman, *Driving Visions: Exploring the Roadmovie* (Austin, Texas: University of Texas Press, 2002).

8   Russian original: "… a chego vam nuzhno? Grabit' prishli?"

9   Henri Lefèbvre, *Die Revolution der Städte* (Dresden: Postplatz, 2003), 23.

10 Russian original: "Skol'ko oni nashei krovi popili!"

11 Russian original: "Poubivaiut vas vsekh kogda-nibud'. Ne za chto. … I mashina u vas strashnaia—katafalk kakaia-to [sic!]."

12 Siegfried Kracauer, *Theorie des Films: Die Errettung der äusseren Wirklichkeit* (Frankfurt a. M.: Suhrkamp, 1964), 389.

THE GOLDEN CITY AND THE GOLDEN SHOT

Images from Prague
after the Velvet Revolution

Alfrun Kliems

Standing here at the intersection again. One of the most commonplace ones, one of those intersections civilization makes carbon copies of everywhere. Trams, busses, cars, mommies, bums, crowds coming out of the subway and crowds going back in, winos and bawling children, old-timers, gypsies, Chinks, beggars and snitches, baby carriages with brand-new members, smog.

Jáchym Topol, *Angel*, 1995[1]

This is the Prague of Jatek, the hero of Jáchym Topol's novel *Angel*. Not much is left in the mid-nineteen-nineties of the old Czech-Jewish-German myth of Prague, which has been replaced by a post-socialist confusion of physiognomies and roles: Laotians and Vietnamese, Ukrainians and Poles, Gypsies and Slovaks—the foot soldiers of globalization.

But Topol's portrait of this blend of multiple provenances is more than a timely reflection on the phenomena of globalization. Rather, his Prague novels *Angel* (1995) and *City Sister Silver* (1994) take up the theme of diversity in order to tell stories of the underground. In these works, Topol describes a divided city that functions as the ideal city of the underground in that the categories "rich," "established," and "official" are only there for contrast: "under," after all, presupposes a "ground." The emphasis in these novels is on the sociocultural fissures in the urban space after the collapse of communism and is utterly removed from the dominant trend of reviving the multicultural legacy of the Central European cities by casting a romanticized look back at the Czech-German-Jewish Tripolis Praga and its store of memories.

Topol presents Prague as a multicultural place of memory as well, but turns the convention in another direction. In the following, I will examine his novels *Angel* and *City Sister Silver*, along with Vladimír Michálek's film adaptation of *Angel*, in terms of a shift from the Tripolis Praga to the global city of and for the underground.

Prague's multicultural legacy in the twentieth century encompasses at least three topoi. First there is the former Tripolis Praga, the German, Jewish, and Czech "city of three peoples." Second there is the Slavic topos of the "golden city"—a city that flourishes and thrives at the hands of its Czech population. Finally there is the topos of "magical Prague," whose architecture and history is connected to Rudolf II, his astronomers, and his passion for alchemy and mannerism.

These topoi have made Prague a multifarious projection surface for many writers since the turn of the twentieth century. To the Germans and the Jews, Prague was a ghetto, a linguistic enclave, and a frightening labyrinth; to the Czechs on the other hand it was a living capital city. It is primarily literature by authors from these three groups that continues to generate the myth of multicultural Prague to the present day—regardless of how much the groups actually had to do with each other and how contrived their cultural, national, and linguistic differences ultimately were.

The notion of Prague as the city of three peoples has been a classical *locus communis* since at least the second half of the twentieth century, a literary topos, and thus an element of speech passed on from one generation to the next. The topos of the city of three peoples seems to belong to Prague as much as the Prague Castle, Charles Bridge, and Wenceslas Square. It appears in many different contexts and functions as a condensed image as well as an ambivalent narrative. But there is something else at stake in its actualization or resurrection after the "Velvet Revolution"—the hidden ideal of a pure monoculture, albeit divided by three (and thus secretly multiplied). In other words, talk of Prague's multiculturalism functions as a narrative for which it is insignificant who actually lived here peacefully—or not so peacefully—with whom. The topos of the Tripolis Praga embodies a claim of multiculturalism that extends the ideal of a monoculture into an absolute by construing the German, the Jewish, and the Czech simultaneously as singularities and as a unity. By turning *multi* back into *mono*, the topos raises itself to a higher power.

Jáchym Topol's Prague novels contain hardly any of the traces or common connotations of German-Jewish-Czech Prague. In *Angel* and *City Sister Silver*, Topol not only replaces the groups but also realigns values: from the elitist Prague modernism shaped by written language he moves by way of gutter slang to the speakers of a post-Babylonian "Kanak language."

Another reading of this depiction of contemporary Prague might take into consideration its implied refutation of socialist internationalism, or perversion of former ideological standards. I will not pursue this line of argument at this point, though, but only suggest it for discussion.

Born in 1962, Topol was himself a well-known representative of the underground before the collapse of communism and today is an author with cult status. For Topol, the end of authoritarian state socialism also meant the end of the underground. Such an underground may continue to exist in China, in Vietnam, or in other totalitarian regimes, he argues, but no longer in Eastern Europe, and certainly not in Western Europe or the United States. He was able, however, to rescue the group phenomenon of the underground with his ego and declared: "I am the underground!"[2] In order to make this comprehensible, I will now give a rough sketch of what is meant by "the underground"—also because I, unlike Topol, consider the novels he published after 1989 and the subsequent film adaptations to participate in a poetics of the underground.

Taking a stance of negation and provocation, the underground rejected late socialist consumer society and called for lifestyles inspired by the American Beat Generation. The underground did not have a uniform style or dominant direction, but was rather characterized by its independence from any authorized form of expression. Under socialism, this meant that the underground was, quite literally and politically, underground: forbidden, kept under surveillance, and persecuted. Once it had positioned itself as a way of life, the underground's pursuit of overtly performative art was only consistent. Its adherents were interested in resistance, dissidence, and an all-embracing form of expression aimed at non-conformity. The key category was life in its totality. By means of self-stylization and auto-mystification, the underground created its own mythology, which embraced the banality, brutality, and vulgarity of the everyday. It was susceptible to mystical and religious scenarios and celebrated a Bohemianism opposed to every aspect of the bourgeois establishment.

Conditions for a countercultural public sphere changed after the collapse of communism. On the one hand, political censorship, surveillance, and bans on publications and performances disappeared; on the other, the controlling mechanisms of the market now came to bear on culture. Formally, however, the commercial sphere was now free and the government could be voted out of office. The underground no longer had the option of radically distinguishing itself from the (socialist) establishment.

It was in this period that Topol's Prague novels *Angel* and *City Sister Silver* were published. Both books were adapted as films a few years later in collaboration with the writer. *Angel* centers around an intersection in the Prague district of Smíchov called Anděl, Czech for "angel." A pharmacy called "Zum Engel" (German for "angel") was once located here, which is where the square supposedly got its name. The Smíchov district belongs to Prague V and was once an industrial suburb located on the left bank of the Vltava. Prior to the nineteenth century, it was full of gardens and villas, but by the turn of the century it had become nothing but a dismal factory landscape. Later, during socialist times, subway tunnels were built underneath the tramlines and the station was given the rather untraditional name of "Moscow Station."[3] Because of the office and shopping complex "Smíchov Gate," built here a few years ago, the area around Anděl Square is now referred to as Prague's West End. There is some disagreement on the origins of the name "Smíchov." It could refer to "smíchaný" (mixed) but it could also, as several legends would have it, derive from "smát se" (to laugh).

But now back to Topol's Prague and his novel. It is a drug novel; it is also, if you will, a *Wenderoman*, a novel at the crossroads and on the threshold of a new era, set just after the political changes. Jatek, the inventor of a miracle drug based on his own blood, is trying to get back on his feet in Prague and live a "normal" life with Ljuba. He fails. The story is interspersed with Jatek's visions at the Anděl intersection: hallucinatory images of flaming red over Prague and of its subterranean chasms.

When Topol describes urban landscapes in his novel, we hear the buzzing of neon lights, the screeching of sanding machines and circular saws, the clattering of trams, the creaking of cables in the wind, the gurgling of pipes, and the shrieking of sirens.[4] In the middle of this pool of urban sounds, the German-Jewish-Czech history of Prague makes an appearance:

> In front of the synagogue it smelled like piss. Who knows how many generations have pissed here since the war, onto the barricaded main entrance in the arcade. There were notices posted there. He followed the letters and learned that the Perun Club was looking for female members, that the Alliance for a More Beautiful and Glorious Prague

was building something, and that the Tatra Smíchov Boxing Association always kept its cool … He would rather look up. He knew that above the whole multifaceted, amoeba-like backdrop, let's call it of the everyday, there was a chiseled inscription in Hebrew and Czech: "Peace and salvation to those far and near."[5]

Topol's description of the synagogue evokes the Tripolis Praga, the former Jewish population of Prague, and its architectural legacy. Topol's Prague functions like a palimpsest, or rather: like an advertising column. New layers are pasted onto the past, onto the synagogue. Bills, posters, and proclamations bear witness to other times and inhabitants, to social, cultural, and political shifts, without completely effacing older layers. After all, closed and decaying buildings like the synagogue remain in the landscape, bearing traces of historical memory, even if for most passersby they serve as nothing more than a public urinal.

Jatek stands out from the crowd precisely because he "would rather look up" at the inscription, thus tearing his gaze away from the everyday notices on the walls and façades of the city. The lines written above in two languages refer back to the beginning of the novel where there is a description of a Christmas mass, and to its epigraph, a Psalm from the Bible. Smíchov thus spans many pages as a place where religions and languages commingle.

Jatek, however, does not pursue the traces of "old" multiculturalism. He leaves fresh marks instead, reading the city in a new way, from his own perspective—that of an outcast, an erstwhile underground artist who is now a paranoid drug addict. *Angel* presents Prague's current inhabitants in all of their facets. In their form is reflected the idea of the underground, of the mass of outcasts. They are outsiders: losers, drug addicts, homeless, dealers, whores, members of sects, and shady profiteers of the recent political changes: "The underground in its classic setting returned to one of its oldest focal points and became the underworld."[6]

The current inhabitants of the city are not really new, they have only become more visible, making evident its social fragmentation rather than demonstrating the diversity of the city as linguistic home. They turn Prague into a classic divided city: "There was snow on the hill and slush in the city. Down at the crossing it was swarming with whores and pimps, queers, junkies and slave drivers. It was teeming with the stuff like insects in a fresh wound."[7]

All of this is taken up by the film adaptation, which was released in 2000 with the title *Angel Exit*. More than any other film in the post-communist era, Vladimír Michálek's adaptation conveyed an underground image of the city. The film was controversial among the Velvet Generation, precisely because its unsettling images of Prague were ill suited to winning over "normal" audiences. Michálek's digital camera filmed Topol's drug novel like a drug trip. The result is an ingenious transposition of Topol's associative stream of language and its mixture of slang, vulgarity, and poetry.

The film blurs the novel's urban outlines. The hallucinatory stream of images includes hardly any topographical markers of Prague. The two-minute title sequence introduces the film by shattering the notion of Prague as the "golden city," as Tripolis, or magical place. The

1   Dying carp, scene from *Angel Exit* (2000, director Vladimír Michálek).
2   Eating dog, scene from *Angel Exit* (2000, director Vladimír Michálek).
3   Santa Claus under palm trees, scene from *Angel Exit* (2000, director Vladimír Michálek).

sequence is made up of images, voices, snatches of music, and sounds. The rhythm of the rapid cuts is determined acoustically, particularly by an ambulance siren and the sound of trams. Michálek's prologue superimposes Christmas kitsch, global commerce, and bloody slaughter. Close-ups guide the eye in seconds from a dying Christmas carp (▶ 1), its mouth gasping for air, to a dog eating the remains of the carp on the street (▶ 2), to an ambulance with flashing lights, to people rushing by. Again and again, similar details come into focus, until the concentration shifts from the holiday bustle to the slow suffocation of the carp. The image sequence creates a leitmotif between the fish blood, a plastic Santa Claus between palm trees (▶ 3), and the red dusk over Prague.

The way shots are edited together can make the establishment of spatial coherence either easier or more difficult for the viewer.[8] *Angel Exit* unambiguously frustrates the viewer's experience of space. For one, traditional symbols of Prague such as the Vltava, the Little Quarter, Old Town Square, or the Prague Castle are missing. It is thus unclear at first where the film is set. Second, the chronological sequence of events is constantly interrupted by hard cuts. Third, there are no gradual transitions between the shots, which has the effect of intensifying sequentiality. Fourth, the viewer has to keep up with a moving camera that is constantly panning and zooming through space. Not only that—the pans are whip pans, which means that they are very quick. Fifth, the aural repertoire of street noise, Christmas music, and sounds of slaughter destroys the illusion of a space visible in its totality. Spatial information gets lost in this web of references, correspondences, and contrasts.

The result of all of this is that Michálek's film turns holiday season Prague into a conglomeration of details, colors, faces, movements, and sounds. Michálek films Prague as a settlement of outcasts, where the street is a place to rip people off and kill—or be killed. His images, in any case, clash starkly with the notion of a peaceful Advent season, and the viewer only begins to relax once the camera settles on Anděl Square, drenched in red evening light, and Mikeš' (Jatek in the book) story begins.

These images hardly refer to the traditional multiculturalism of Prague. And yet they do—the opening sequence plays with the ruins of the Tripolis Praga myth more thoroughly than the novel by not even taking the myth into consideration. Michálek in his film creates a Prague with an incredible lure, putting forward an autonomous view of the city that has little to do with the "real" post-socialist city and all the more with the concept of the underground. By appearing as a parallel universe, Michálek's Prague comes across as inscrutable. Life is filmed from below. *Angel Exit* is about (sub)urban survival—which many of the characters fail to do in the belly of the city: they are murdered or give themselves the "golden shot." The death of the fish in the opening sequence is their symbolic representation. The cityscape portrayed in the film reflects the struggle for survival on the street and in the back alleys. The deep red and blue-gray hues of the spectacular images give the urban landscape an expressionist flavor (▶ 4), creating a new form of magic and mysticism—a mysticism of the underground (▶ 5).

4

5

4   Anděl Square, scene from *Angel Exit* (2000, director Vladimír Michálek).
5   Anděl Square, scene from *Angel Exit* (2000, director Vladimír Michálek).

It is almost as if Michálek's film conveys this mysticism more effectively than Topol's text. This is not due, however, to the different media, but to different closing images. In the film Mikeš rescues the gypsy girl Nadja and disappears with her into the tunnel of the Anděl metro station (▶ 6). The final image, in which the gray-blue maw of the Prague subway swallows the two figures, sentimentalizes the survival of the "right ones." The ones who survive in the film are, idealistically, those who are the least corrupted by either group—they have neither become well established nor have they alienated themselves from all order. The ending may come across as kitschy or melodramatic, but it allows for the continued existence of a "true" underground next to the Prague underworld.

In the book, Nadja does not survive, and only for Jatek does the maw close over the Anděl intersection. The expressive red tones of the abyss, which stands for more than the real urban topography, is also reminiscent of the marble of the metro station, red in honor of its socialist name: "Moscow Station."

In his novel *City Sister Silver*, Topol dissociates himself from the Tripolis Praga topos completely. The main character, Potok, is a former underground artist roaming through his hometown, post-socialist Prague, in search of his "sister"—an imaginary lover who remains vague throughout the story. Together with friends Potok founds an ORGANIZATION, which is actually more of a gang than an association of friends. The ORGANIZATION is a youth cult and is both family and business club for a group of former undergrounders, punks, self-appointed priests, businessmen, city and country folk. Eventually, Potok has to go into hiding. His travels take him first to Berlin and then on an odyssey ever deeper into Eastern Europe before finally bringing him back to Prague.

6   Underground, scene from *Angel Exit* (2000, director Vladimír Michálek).

Potok concocts his own version of Prague, making room not only for gypsies, who also figure in *Angel* as one of Prague's population groups, with the narrator giving them credit for shaping the city's history. They appear likewise in *City Sister Silver*: God, we read here, sent "these raggedy gypsy women with their deadened urchins out into the world,"[9] into the European cities, so that those living there can see how poverty dulls the senses. Here, too, gypsies are the Noble Savages of modern times; "barefoot brownies" Topol calls them, "Balkan-Ugro-Finnish-backwoods Romany types."[10] Their competitors for space in the city are Asians—to whom, Potok claims, the future belongs. The cultural hodgepodge in the cities—first and foremost Prague and Berlin (here referred to as Berlun) incorporates every variety of difference and plays with them to the point of unrecognizability or indifference.

Chinese, Laotians, Vietnamese, or Hmong mountain people—no matter where they come from, they remain on the margins. Spit onto the streets of Prague, they run straight into its gutters—and feed Potok's underground, where he welcomes them into his ORGANIZATION. The Asians who come to Prague are called Minh, Phu, or Vang and have one defect: they are infected with the virus of genocide—like the European peoples, like all peoples.

City Sister Silver nevertheless goes on for pages developing a new form of cosmopolitanism and putting forward a plea for nomadism. After all the war and murder, Potok finds one exception in the relentless circle dance of peoples: the gypsies.

> But there's another people here, trained in the art of survival, an this one doesn't write, its only chronicles are scars, occasionally on other peoples' skins … this people lives in rough coexistence with the state, an for them the state's always been a killer, they're the People of the Pack, who tend to the family an don't mind a bit that it's crawling with lice from time to time … an wages its miniature war with pockets an shivs …[11]

Potok considers the Roma a peace-loving people because they only wage miniature wars. He describes them as unbegrudging, family-oriented dreamers who do not submit to progress. While the ORGANIZATION does not succeed in emulating them, it does achieve a mixture of cultures, the globalization of Prague: "… our ground floors and cellars turned into a Laotian initiation camp … and bastard Bohemia's hardened arteries got hit with a fresh dose of Asia."[12]

Nothing is as it seems, which is why nothing needs to be overrated: no ethnicity, no culture, no language—with one exception, that of the "pure" gypsies. In the novel, destitute Romanians from the camp turn out to be Portuguese thieves, a Bulgarian theology student is actually an Indian witch, Armenians on the run prove to be feral Azerbaijanis, Serb dissidents to be Bosnian Muslims. Potok concludes: "We were all Kanaks. The megarace of the tunnel."[13] This insight is accompanied by a look at his own affiliation: the narrator is certified as having "yellow Slavic blotches," as being a "Celtic somnambulist, Germanic dummkopf, Jewish ganef, transitional AIDS, you stud, incipient raw graphomania."[14] If everyone's a Kanak, it doesn't matter who sleeps with whom, where people come from, or where they're going. It is only—and here is the connection to the underground—the attitude that counts, the mistrust of every authorized form of expression. "We are all Kanaks" does not unequivocally refer to anyone and everyone, but to the inhabitants of the other city, the underground city, which remains closed to people like tourists and Prague's "normal" residents, however they may be classified. But "we are all Kanaks" also means: we are one people, we come from the same tribe. Attitude is vested with the dignity of ethnicity, nation, or national affiliation.

"Prague is no longer a city of peaceful coexistence. But it is still a city with a living past," write the editors of the illustrated book *Prag—Einst Stadt der Tschechen, Juden und Deutschen* (Prague: Once the City of Czechs, Jews, and Germans).[15] There is no such thing as peaceful coexistence in Topol's work, not in *City Sister Silver* and not in *Angel*. It is simply not an option, even if it is always present as a kind of anti-vision. Topol's option is a subcultural, not a high-cultural one. He does present small-scale concepts, but refuses all coherence by sticking to a radical present. The synchronous and diachronic rifts, antagonisms, and "murders" remain inevitable. By burying sentimental memoria, Topol shows us ways in which to circumvent the amoeba-like nature of post-socialist daily life (or daily life anywhere) and to maintain an awareness of the historical layers in the memory of the city's inhabitants. Unlike the majority of Prague literature, Topol's novels create their own kind of symbiosis, a symbiosis of social conflict focused on but not limited to Prague—a megalomaniac urban vision.

"We are all Kanaks" is an offer of identification, a creation of collective identity. The very notion of affiliating oneself in this way goes beyond a statement like: "We are all Praguers." The point is no longer to inscribe oneself into certain Prague contexts, to take up and extend the myth of Tripolis Praga. What is going on here is on an entirely different level. While Jewish, Czech, and German writers still wanted to inscribe *themselves* into the legacy of the city of Prague, its current inhabitants become inscribed by virtue of their socially marginal position.

It is in this way that Topol casts Prague as the ideal city of the underground. The city was always a—no, is *the* existential condition for the way of life of the underground. It connected and connects the marginally (sub)urban with political dissent in the form of social nonconformity. Ironically, before the collapse of communism, the underground often took place in the countryside, where control of local venues tended to be porous. Nevertheless, the art that was created there was unequivocally urban. This is a basic aim of the underground—to subvert "official" claims about the city and to shift spatial hierarchies, including politically intended and socially motivated mappings of center and periphery. In order to do this, the underground must begin at the center, at the top of the hierarchy, and constantly turn other places into its centers: places that the general public does not consider privileged, but that are also not located outside of the inner city—but rather underneath it. The art of the underground targets the "*colonization* of urban space" (Henri Lefèbvre), which can mean consumerism, organization, or anything imposed from the outside. The underground is neither in search of a romantic agrarianism, nor does it propagate rural escapism. The underground does not flee: it stays and undermines.

Potok actually has all the ingredients that make up a "true" resident of the Tripolis: he has Slavic, Celtic, Germanic, and Jewish roots; he is also an aspiring artist and writer. He can thus be considered transcultural in Wolfgang Welsch's sense.[16] Welsch rejects homogenizing and separating ideas about ideal culture in favor of the notion of global cultural networks. What is unusual about his approach is that he also applies it to the micro-level. In other words, for Welsch the incessant mutual interpenetration of contemporary cultures does not begin at the macro-level. We must also be able to think the transcultural provenance of all individuals, the fact that we are all "cultural mongrels"[17]: "There is nothing that is absolutely foreign anymore. Everything is within inner or outer reach. Nor is there anything that is absolutely local anymore. Authenticity has become folklore, simulated local flavor for the others—a group to which the native has long belonged himself."[18]

Here we have the notion of "trans." Topol's novels make use of a "transitory poetics."[19] This concept refers in general to forms of transition, to the moment of risk, to that which endangers identity, to the difficulty of describing a self and its place. The adjective "transitory" refers to the provisional, the fleeting, the temporary, to characteristics of the transient. The transient as defined by Dorothea Löbbermann refers to "other" inhabitants of the city who produce "other" spaces.[20] As winos, junkies, vagabonds, bums, and tramps they do not connect cultural highlights like tourists on their tours through cities, but disrupt routes and form obstacles. In this sense, Topol's figures—especially Potok—are not ordinary users of the city.

But Topol's novels and the art of the underground in general can also be read as transgressive. A poetics of transgression means the refusal to acknowledge boundaries and restrictions. Here it is not a matter of going from A to B and back. It is also not a matter of arriving anywhere. It is rather about incessant rupture, about transgression as event, action, and performance—not as achievement. "Transgression," writes Michel Foucault, "incessantly crosses and recrosses a line which closes up behind it in a wave of extremely short duration, and thus it is made to return once more right to the horizon of the uncrossable."[21] This constant movement turns the boundaries themselves into spaces, into ever reemerging anti-spaces that can be extremely perilous to the body. Topol's characters envisage urban solitude, post-multicultural fissures in the (great) city of Prague, dying there, intentionally or unintentionally—without being able, or wanting, to give the city up. There is no alternative, for them, to the urban environment, to a life in (shifting) crevices.

This article is an excerpt from the book *Der Underground, die Wende und die Stadt*, forthcoming by the author.

Translated by Millay Hyatt

Endnotes

1 Czech original: "Zas stál na křižovatce. Tý nejobyčejnější, tý, co ji civilizace sází přes kopírák, tramvaje, autobusy, auta, mámy a pobudové, davy z metra ven a davy zase sem, ochmelkové i pokřikující drobotina, starousedlící, cigoši, žluťasové, žebrácí i fízláci, kočárky s úplně novejma účastníkama, smog." – Jáchym Topol, *Anděl* (Prague: Labyrint, 2000 [1995]), 66.

2 "Slalom mezi idejemi: Rozhovor se spisovatelem Jáchymem Topolem," *Respekt* 25 (1994): 10.

3 Fritz Böhm, *6 mal Prag* (Munich/Zurich: Piper, 1990 [1988]), 199–202.

4 Topol, (see note 1), 42.

5 Czech original: "U synagogy cítil moč. Od války tu chčije už kolikátá generace opilců. V podloubí na zatlučený hlavní dveře. Jsou tu vývěsky, sledoval písmena, aby se dozvěděl: Klub Perun prijímá členky, spolek Za Prahu krásnější a jasnější buduje a Boxerská Jednota Tatry Smíchov je v naprostým klidu. ... Radši zdvihl hlavu. Věděl, že nad vší touhle měňavou amébovitou kulisou, řekněme: všedního dne, uvidí hebrejsky i česky vytesaný nápis: 'Mír a zdar dalekému i blízkému'" – Topol, (see note 1), 107. The synagogue in Smíchov has since been restored and serves as an archive for the Jewish Museum.

6 Czech original: "A underground se ve svých nejstarších klasických kulisách vrátil k jednomu ze svých nejstarších ohnisek; stal se podsvětím" – Topol, (see note 1), 75.

7 Czech original: "Na kopci byl sníh, ve městě břečka. Dole na křižovatce se rojili kurvy a pasáci, úchylové, narkomani, násilníci, rojili se tam jak hmyz v čerstvé ráně" – Topol, (see note 1), 79.

8 Nicole Mahne, *Transmediale Erzähltheorie: Eine Einführung.* (Göttingen: Vandenhoeck und Ruprecht, 2007), 93.

9 Jáchym Topol, *City Sister Silver* (North Haven, Connecticut: Catbird Press, 2000), 470. Czech original: "tyhle votrhaný cigy" – Jáchym Topol, *Sestra* (Brno: Atlantis, 1994), 426.

10 Topol, *City Sister Silver* (see note 9), 51. Czech original: "takový balkánskougrofinskolesní romský typy" – Topol, *Sestra* (see note 9), 41.

11 Topol, *City Sister Silver* (see note 9), 214–15. Czech original: "Ale je tu ještě jeden lid, vycvičenej v umění přežívání, a ten nepíše, ten má

svý kroniky jen v jizvách, občas na cizí kůži … tenhle lid žije v těžký koexistenci se státem a stát mu byl vždycky vragem, je to Lid tlupy, kterej vošetřuje rodinu a nic mu nevadí, že je občas zavšivšená … a vede svou miniaturní válku kapsy a kudly, a co to je proti genocidě … " – Topol, *Sestra* (see note 9), 200.

12 Topol, *City Sister Silver* (see note 9), 53. Czech original: " … v našich přízemích a sklepech byl malej zasvěcovací laoskej tábor … a bastardí Bohemie dostávala do zkornatělejch tepen čerstvou asijskou dávku" – Topol, *Sestra* (see note 9), 43.

13 Topol, *City Sister Silver* (see note 9), 229. Czech original: "Všichni jsme Kanaci. Megarasa z tunelu" – Topol, *Sestra* (see note 9), 213.

14 Topol, *City Sister Silver* (see note 10), 57–58. Czech original: "žlutý slovanský skvrny … keltskej somnambul, germánskej trotl, židovskej ganef, přechozenej AIDS, ty frajírku, počínající surová grafománie" – Topol, *Sestra* (see note 9), 47.

15 *Prag: Einst Stadt der Tschechen, Deutschen und Juden*, ed. Jiří Gruša, Eda Kriseová and Petr Pithart (Munich: Langen Müller, 1993), 93.

16 Wolfgang Welsch, "Transkulturalität: Zwischen Globalisierung und Partikularisierung," *Jahrbuch Deutsch als Fremdsprache* 26 (2000): 327–51.

17 Welsch, (see note 16), 337.

18 Wolfgang Welsch, "Transkulturalität. Lebensformen nach der Auflösung der Kulturen," *Information Philosophie* 2 (1992): 5–20, here 11.

19 Rüdiger Görner, *Grenzen, Schwellen, Übergänge: Zur Poetik des Transitorischen* (Göttingen: Vandenhoeck und Ruprecht, 2001), 7–12.

20 Doris Löbbermann, "Weg(be)schreibungen: Transients in New York City," in *TopoGraphien der Moderne: Medien zur Repräsentation und Konstruktion von Räumen*, ed. Robert Stockhammer (Munich: Fink, 2005), 263–85.

21 Michel Foucault, "A Preface to Transgression," transl. by Donald F. Bouchard and Sherry Simon, in *Religion and Culture*, ed. Jeremy R. Carrette (Manchester: Manchester University Press, 1999), 60.

3

DISCURSIVE
RECODINGS

POST-TOTALITARIAN AND POST-COLONIAL EXPERIENCES

The Palace of Culture and Science and Defilad Square in Warsaw

Małgorzata Omilanowska

The history of architecture and urban planning in the twentieth century has convincingly demonstrated that totalitarian systems leave behind the grandest, most monumental and sumptuous architectural and urban projects. Obviously, the democratic world is not free from such ambitions, but as a rule it settles for much more modest and less impressive, yet far more practical and often much more avant-garde solutions. Large systems based on oppression and power gladly resort to grandiose spatial projects rooted in the classical tradition, which serve as a visible sign of the power of the authorities. Of particular importance in totalitarian systems were mighty complexes—designed with large public gatherings, parades, and rallies in mind—whose goal was to consolidate society, yet at the same time to indoctrinate it, oppress it, and subdue it to a specific ideology, inciting strong emotions readily released in gathered human masses. With the collapse of the totalitarian system, complexes such as these are deprived of their purpose and function, becoming an unwanted legacy of the past, a monument to tyranny, and, simply speaking, an urban challenge.

1   Draft design of the center of Warsaw, Maciej Nowicki, Poland, 1945.

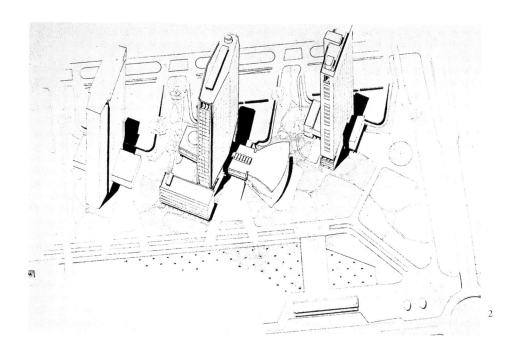

2

After World War Two, Poland found itself within the sphere of influence of the powerful machinery of the Stalinist totalitarian regime, and although it retained some of its sovereignty as far as decision-making was concerned—especially with regard to the reconstruction of its cities—it was forced to give in to the power of the monumental architectural solutions implemented in Soviet architecture. The limited number of such projects results merely from the fact that Polish architecture was in thrall to the Stalinist doctrine for only seven years, from 1949 to 1956. The major challenges of the time were war devastation, housing shortages, lack of economic infrastructure, and the need to rebuild towns. Thus, the resources that could be allocated to grandiose urban projects were extremely limited, which meant that the majority of them remained merely on paper.

However, one of the grandest projects designed for the center of Warsaw—and here the term "grandest" refers to every aspect of it—was actually implemented, what is more at the speed of lightning, within more or less three years. This included the construction of a giant skyscraper for the Palace of Culture and Science, 230 meters high, with a vast open space, the so-called Defilad Square. Its name, meaning "parade," implies its purpose: it was to be used to stage large parades and rallies. Both the Palace and the square have survived to this day, constituting one of the most daunting unresolved challenges to architecture and urban planning of the last twenty years.

What is more, and most importantly, this project is not merely the product of the Stalinist regime, but also the fruit of Soviet thoughts on architecture and urban planning. It was designed by Russian architects, constructed using Soviet materials supplied to Poland espe-

2   Competition design of skyscrapers in the center of Warsaw at the junction of Jerozolimskie Avenue and Marszałkowska Street, Zbigniew Ihnatowicz and Jerzy Romański, Poland, 1947.

cially for the purpose, and built by thousands of Soviet workers brought to Poland from distant Soviet republics. Thus it was a "gift from the Soviet people to the Polish people," a "gift" that has turned into a symbol not only of a totalitarian regime, but also of an alien culture.[1] The Soviet character of the building was, however, partially concealed by the ornamentation of both the elevation of the building and its interior, which makes reference to Polish architecture and Polish folk art; many Polish artists contributed to the Palace's furnishing.[2]

In the aftermath of the destruction of almost all the housing that made up the Warsaw Ghetto in 1943, followed by the bombardment of the city in the course of the Warsaw Uprising in August and September 1944, and subsequently by a planned, systematic demolition of Warsaw's buildings by special Nazi sapper troops between October and December of the same year, the center of Warsaw was almost totally annihilated. Paradoxically, the colossal destruction of the city center created a completely new urban potential. The layout of new communication routes or the planning of new urban elements was not subject to the limitations of existing structures. The oldest fragment of the city was to be reconstructed, but not the parts from the nineteenth century, so architects immediately seized the opportunity to erect a new city center. The first plans for its new development, already drawn up during World War Two (▶ 1), were published by Maciej Nowicki immediately after the war ended in 1945.[3] Applying the visionary urban concepts of Le Corbusier, these designs were to concentrate the new city center along its major commercial thoroughfare, Marszałkowska Street, with slender skyscrapers freely located within open city spaces.[4] Thus Nowicki was the first architect to propose the redefinition of the traditional pre-World War Two city structure concentrated along Krakowskie Przedmieście Street and the Old Town. A similar desire could be sensed in subsequent designs (▶ 2) produced throughout 1947, for the competition for the development of the city center.[5] In 1948, architects were still drawing visions of a modern city with daring flyovers and slender skyscrapers freely located within the open city spaces.[6]

The year 1949 was a turning point in Poland's post-war history, for the authorities had succeeded in "finally crushing" the opposition and suppressing the remnants of underground forces, finally proclaiming a single political ideology and the doctrine of Socialist Realism in the art it embraced.[7] Therefore, after 1949, work on the new city center was carried out under completely new political circumstances.

The six-year plan for the reconstruction of Warsaw presented at the party conference on July 3, 1949 revealed the great concepts of a city center that was to be transformed into a perfect homogenous Socialist Realist structure, in compliance with the new ideological directives redefining city space. Thus its past was also to be modified in order to conform to the favored and only accepted vision of history. The city needed a new center where the life of the capital could be focused. Several locations along the Saska Axis were initially taken into consideration as the new central square in Warsaw, thus pointing towards Victory Square (J. Piłsudskiego Square today), and later the vicinity of Żelazna Brama Square.[8] In

the final winning concept, the new center was located close to Marszałkowska Street, between Jerozolimskie Avenue and Świętokrzyska Street, more or less where Maciej Nowicki had initially suggested. The designs, drawn in late 1949 by Warsaw's Urban Planning Office (*Biuro Urbanistyczne Warszawy*) under Stanisław Rychłowski and published in 1950, planned to broaden Marszałkowska Street to twice its original size and arrange a chain of stately squares all along it, as well as create a large central square, more than a kilometer long, between the two thoroughfares mentioned above. This square was conceived as a "venue for large mass rallies and manifestations on important occasions for the whole of society."[9] Already at that stage, plans were made to erect a giant skyscraper housing the Central House of Culture (▸ 3) on the western side of the square and to develop its eastern frontage with a complex of monumental edifices.

The concept began to take on a more precise shape when, during a visit to Poland on July 2, 1951, Vyatscheslav Molotov made an official offer for the Russians to erect the skyscraper housing the Palace of Culture and Science in the city center. On August 12, 1951, the Party Politburo finally allotted the 36-hectare quarter consisting of some dozen pre-war buildings along Marszałkowska Street, between Jerozolimskie Avenue and Świętokrzyska Street, for the construction.[10] Designed by a Russian team of architects under Lev Rudniev, it was constructed between 1952 and 1955 as a gift from the Soviet people. The Palace was named

3   Central Palace of Culture in the sketches of Socialist Realist Warsaw, Stanisław Rychłowski and team, Poland, 1950.

4

4   Competition design for the development of the eastern frontage of Marszałkowska Street, Warsaw, Poland, 1953.

after Stalin, whose name was given to a vast square planned in front of its main eastern elevation.

Rudniev's skyscraper closely resembled other buildings of the type built in Moscow at the time. However, it had to comply with the requirements of Socialist Realism, so it was to be both socialist in content and national in form. For that purpose, a group of Soviet architects was invited for a two-week stay in Poland in September 1951, during which they were taken on a tour of Poland to view Polish towns. On their departure, they were given photo albums of the important historical buildings they had been unable to see during their stay.[11] As a result, the mass of a typical Soviet skyscraper in the form of a step pyramid was ornamented with attics modeled on the form of Polish Renaissance buildings. Construction work started in the summer of 1952, preceded by a land survey.

At the onset of the construction work in 1952, a competition was held for the outline development of the central square and the city center in the vicinity of the skyscraper. Thirty-one design teams participated in the competition and, although no prizes were awarded, the eight best designs (▶ 4) were rewarded with equal bonuses. Meanwhile, the competition jury session served as an excellent platform for broad discussions on the buildings that were to be erected around the square.[12] The assumption was that the main edifice of the eastern frontage along Marszałkowska Street was to hold municipal authorities, i.e., a town hall. The architects tried to outdo one another, suggesting monumental solutions based on expansive vista axes, multiplying grandiose constructions, or creating subsequent open spaces threaded one after another onto the main axis of the Palace.

The debate gave rise to further design work on the issues discussed, finally leading to the implementation concept for the development of the area surrounding the Palace.[13] The square in front of the eastern front elevation of the Palace was delineated as a large rectangle, 400 meters long and 80 meters wide, parallel to Marszałkowska Street and running into it at both ends with diagonal access lanes (▶ 5). At its center, a parade stand was designed for dignitaries receiving parades, with Stalin Monument at the back of it.[14] The surface of the square, which would have to withstand grand military parades with heavy armored vehicles, was to be especially hardened and covered with extremely thick cobblestones.

In this way Stalin Square, later renamed Defilad Square, has never been a proper square in terms of urban planning. It was actually built to fulfill two major purposes.

The first was to create an appropriate view of the Soviet giant, a kind of approach, so to speak, for the skyscraper. One of its main features, an ideological trait distinguishing Soviet skyscrapers from their American counterparts, was the generous, almost limitless space dedicated to the construction site and the vicinity of the building. According to Soviet propaganda, American skyscrapers were the result of capitalist land-profiteering, creating the necessity for extremely high buildings to be raised in order to fit precisely into small plots of land along relatively narrow streets. Soviet skyscrapers, on the other hand, were the response of Soviet technological thoughts to the American challenge. Their peculiar mass,

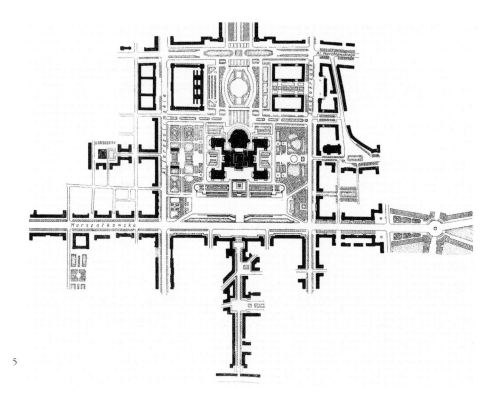

5

supported by a broad, in some cases ridiculously expansive horizontal "foot" and surrounded by incredibly vast empty spaces, especially in front of them, they were to demonstrate the superiority of the planned Socialist economy and the advantages of eliminating private land ownership.[15] Similarly, the Warsaw Palace was erected in the midst of a vast open space; a particularly large expanse of open, undeveloped land was left in front of its eastern front elevation so that visitors approaching the building would have to walk a large distance, thus additionally enhancing the grandiose impact of the whole project. The second purpose—strongly emphasized from the very beginning—was to create a special venue for holding mass events, mainly parades and marches, which in the Stalin era did not so much integrate society as help to indoctrinate it.[16]

The fact that the square accommodated these needs, while neglecting others, prevented it from ever becoming integrated into the urban tissue of Warsaw. Its outline was delineated on three sides by stretches of greenery, while the fourth line was formed by the stand, seen against the background of the Palace. Genetically, this vast rectangular space is rooted more than anything in the military tradition of the *Paradeplatz*, or even drill grounds. From the very onset, the square was not planned as a fragment to be integrated in the surrounding urban space. Furthermore, the results of competitions for the development of Marszałkowska Street's eastern frontage confirm that the majority of architects and urban planners never

5   Design of the Stalin Square, Warsaw, Poland, 1955.

6

7

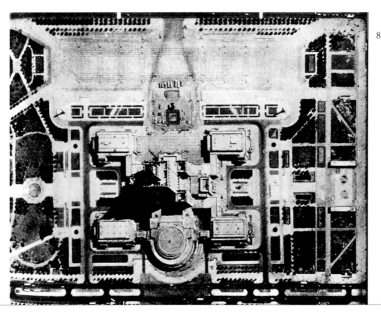

8

6   Design of the Stalin Square, Halina and Bolesław Kosecki, Warsaw, Poland, 1954.
7   Parade in Stalin Square on the inauguration of the Palace of Culture and Science on July 22, Warsaw, Poland, 1955.
8   Bird's eye view of Defilad Square, Warsaw, Poland, 1960.

9

dared to even slightly interfere with the surroundings of the Palace, in compliance with the directives formulated by the Party Politburo. The development of the so-called eastern wall in the spirit of Socialist Realism finally crystallized in 1954, when work on designs featuring ten variations of the development of the square began. The eastern frontage of Marszałkowska Street was to feature a compact block of residential housing with the large edifice of the Municipal Council building on the axis of the Palace.[17] However, these designs (▶ 6) remained unimplemented.

Defilad Square was first used as the venue for a May Day parade in 1955, and then for a large rally and a fair on July 22, 1955, the day when the Palace of Culture and Science was inaugurated (▶ 7). A month later, it was the central venue for the mass events accompanying the *World Festival of Youth and Students*. The following year, the Square witnessed the May Day and Independence Day parades, but as early as October 24, 1956, a great rally marking the end of the Stalinist era in Poland was held there. Władysław Gomułka addressed the crowds from the stand, trying to convince the people that the Socialist system could be reformed.

Political changes in Poland in 1956 prevented the completion of all the elements of Warsaw's central complex. The Stalin Monument was never erected, nor—as mentioned above—was the eastern frontage of Marszałkowska Street in the Socialist Realist style (▶ 8). The whole issue was tackled again in 1959, when a new competition was held. It is interesting that this competition already featured new designs suggesting that the greenery belts separating the

9   Unimplemented competition design for the development of the eastern frontage of Marszałkowska Street, Hanna Adamczewska and Kazimierz Wejchert, Warsaw, Poland, 1959.

square from Marszałkowska Street should be built up, thus closing up the square with its own frontage. This solution was proposed, for example, in the design submitted by Hanna Adamczewska and Kazimierz Wejchert, which was awarded one of the first prizes in the competition (▶ 9). However, the other of the two designs awarded (by Zbigniew Karpiński and Jan Klewin) was actually to be implemented; it planned to raise a sequence of low commercial pavilions alternating with residential tower blocks.[18]

The square, constructed especially to host grand parades and marches, was used only a few times a year in the late nineteen-fifties and -sixties. In the seventies, not even the May Day parades actually entered the square; instead, the crowds marched directly along Marszałkowska Street, cheering the officials who were situated on a temporary parade stand raised along its western side. On a regular basis, the square was to host only military parades celebrating the end of World War Two and July 22, the holiday commemorating the proclamation of Poland's communist manifesto. Slowly, however, Defilad Square was turning into the city's largest car park, used only sporadically for mass events, concerts, or a large Holy Mass celebrated by Pope John Paul II in June 1987.[19]

Yet the Palace of Culture and Science itself has become fully integrated into the life of the city. It has been the seat of the *Polish Academy of Science*; it houses several cinemas, three theaters, a spacious Youth Center with sports halls and swimming pools, and a few museums (e.g., the Museum of Technology). It also contains a giant Congress Hall, which is still Warsaw's largest auditorium, and the venue of communist Party congresses and concerts given by famous musicians such as Marlene Dietrich, Ella Fitzgerald, and the Rolling Stones (1967), as well as the excellent annual Jazz Jamboree festival, which has been held in Poland since 1956 and in the Palace of Culture since 1965. In total, more than 11,000 events have been held there.[20]

The large square in front of the Palace, which urban planners were so enthusiastic about in Stalinist times, lost its cachet even before the collapse of communism. In 1987, Edmund Goldzamt distanced himself from his rapturous opinion of it in the nineteen-fifties, writing the following about the space surrounding the Palace: "The current state of Warsaw's central complex is far from satisfactory. This is mainly due to the hypertrophy of open spaces around it, their large scale, totally 'out of proportion' with the network of city streets."[21] He postulated that the task for urban design was to develop this space.

The year 1989 and the transformation of the political system in Poland brought about essential changes in attitudes toward the legacy bearing the stigma of the past communist regime. The Palace of Culture and Science had become (both literally and metaphorically) the largest symbol of Soviet dominance, and the vast space consisting of Defilad Square and the surrounding stretches of greenery constituted a valuable plot for future development and potential new buildings. Under the new circumstances, a decision had to be made about what to do with the Palace and its surroundings. Since then, and actually until this day, Defilad Square has functioned as if on two completely different dimensions: the real and the virtual one, the latter of which is evoked by subsequent generations of architects and urban planners.

The Palace has survived as a large multifunctional building, now used commercially. It has become a controversial edifice, and elderly people who can still recall Stalinist indoctrination are so emotional about it that again and again suggestions have been made to thoroughly remodel the whole complex, although this proposal is completely unrealistic; some even call for its demolition. As a matter of fact, Warsaw can boast a wide experience in this respect. After World War One, when it had regained independence after the partitions, almost all the Orthodox churches in the city were demolished, including the largest one on Saski Square, which had been designed by the leading St. Petersburg architect Leontij Benois as a symbol of Russian domination over the rebellious city.[22]

For the generation of the middle-aged, Defilad Square and the Palace are first and foremost a venue for many interesting and important events: they are associated with the annual book fair and various theater and cinema events, but most importantly with the great Congress of Polish Culture, which was held there in 1981 and dramatically disrupted by the introduction of martial law.[23] For many youngsters, the Palace constitutes a sort of unique city attraction, a kind of a cult object, long "tamed" by different forms of popular culture.[24]

The final debate on the future of the Palace was held in 2007 among the circles involved in monument conservation and politics, as well as in the media. Then, finally, the *Provincial Office for Monument Conservation* decided to register the Palace of Culture as a listed building, thus ending the arguments concerning its future. However, the square and the land around the Palace are a different thing; because they are extremely tempting pieces of space, no registry will protect them.

On the dimension of reality, Defilad Square has been witnessing an amazingly dynamic development of free trade. In the early nineteen-nineties, in support of the free market in Poland, which was still in its initial stages, municipal authorities allowed people to place hundreds of metal stalls called "jaws" around it. Thus the trading that had been going on there spontaneously for some time, with people selling goods displayed either on blankets stretched on the ground or on folding camp beds, was officially sanctioned. Within a few weeks, Defilad Square was transformed into a large marketplace where anything and everything was sold. Appeals for the square to be returned to order and the stallholders driven away remained unheard. However, the municipality did grant some entrepreneurs permission to raise temporary metal market halls in the middle of the square. In time, small tradesmen with metal stalls either moved to other marketplaces or into the new market hall erected in the square in 2001. The remaining part of the square has functioned as a parking lot all along, very rarely used as a venue for celebrations or shows.

The deplorable reality of the square vividly contrasts with the visions of the new concept for the development of this part of the city and the impressive plans made by the subsequent political teams governing Warsaw for almost the last twenty years. The starting point of

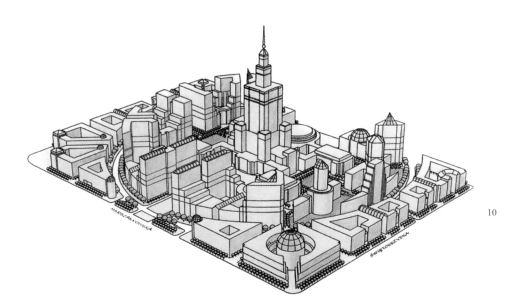

10

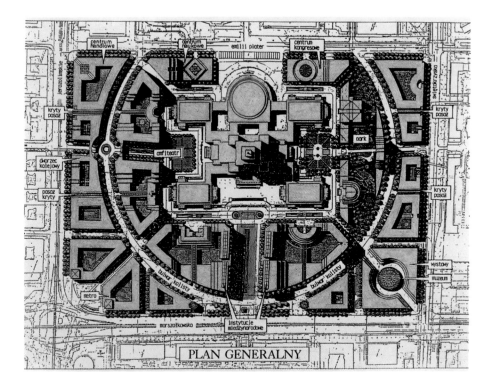

10   Design for the development of the vicinity of the Palace of Culture and Science, Andrzej Skopiński and Bartłomiej Biełyszew, Warsaw, Poland, 1992.

every proposal is to determine the future fate of the Palace itself and define its position within the urban tissue.

From the very beginning, it was clearly unrealistic to think about demolishing the Palace. Thus another option has been considered, namely to develop the areas surrounding the Palace in order to conceal it and thus reduce its spatial and symbolic dominance. It was also clear that the thousands of square meters of space around the Palace offered considerable financial potential, which the city found difficult to renounce under the new economic circumstances in Poland. As early as 1990, an international competition for the development of the area surrounding the Palace of Culture and Science was launched. The winning design (▶ 10) by two Polish architects, Andrzej Skopiński and Bartłomiej Biełyszew, was selected on April 4, 1992. It proposed marking out a circular boulevard around which a ring of skyscrapers of various shapes and sizes would be raised, forming a frayed skyline surrounding the Palace from all sides. At the same time, this would create a unique landmark unlike that found in any other city in the world.[25] Paradoxically, however, although the design was meant to eliminate the architectural dominance of the Palace, it actually underscored the overwhelming character of the Soviet skyscraper.

Despite protests from certain circles of architects and urban planners, politicians found the concept extremely attractive. Encouraged by the design's genuine character, they commissioned its implementation in 1994. Nonetheless, the design was never completed in its final version, though in subsequent years the surrounding buildings were raised higher and higher, sometimes reaching monstrous proportions. Architects and urban planners unanimously judged the 1998 version as the greatest possible disaster that could have happened to the city.[26]

The "crown" concept survived until 2003; by the end of this year the new head municipal architect, Michał Borowski, had commissioned the elaboration of an alternative design. This assumed a grid of low buildings around the Palace, leaving a limited amount of free space in the central part of the present Defilad Square, enclosed within two buildings forming an L shape: a department store and the Museum of Modern Art. The municipality approved the new design and on December 15, 2005 an international competition was launched for the design of the Museum building. As usual, a scandal ensued.[27] The first competition was cancelled on June 26, 2006 and the greatest world architectural celebrities who had been participating, such as Zaha Hadid, Zvi Hecker, and Dominique Perrault, took offense.[28] The Swiss architect Christian Kerez won the second competition, which was judged on February 18, 2007. The design chosen for implementation gave rise to a great deal of controversy, but a large exhibition displaying all the proposals put forward in the competition made many of the protesters realize that the jury had had very few alternatives to choose from.[29] Kerez's proposal, unquestionably very minimal and formally reserved, did not try to compete with the abundant detail of the monstrously large Palace of Culture, but constituted a well-balanced counterpoint to it.

Meanwhile, since autumn 2006, Warsaw has been run by a new mayor, Hanna Gron-
kiewicz-Waltz. Representing a different political platform, she promptly dismissed Michał
Borowski in December 2006, and at the same time dismissed the concept of a grid development. The vision of a circular boulevard with a crown of skyscrapers was resumed, and
work on this was begun by a new architectural team employed by the municipality and
headed by Skopiński and Biełyszew.[30] On February 14, 2008, a new design was presented
(▶ 11). Its essence clearly refers to the competition concept by Skopiński and Biełyszew
from 1992, but it also takes into account the elements of Borowski's plan that cannot be
rejected due to prior commitments made to the association of tradesmen involving the
design of the department store and decisions regarding the construction of the Museum
of Modern Art.[31]

However, the publication of the option representing a compromise for the development
of Defilad Square did not really conclude the debate on its future; rather, as the following
months were to show, it was merely rekindled anew (▶ 12). There was a flood of new proposals prepared by independent architectural offices. Zaha Hadid paid a visit to Warsaw,
and immediately put forward a proposal to build the skyscraper she had suggested for a different quarter of the city in the vicinity of the Palace of Culture. The wide range of proposed
variations also include some that plan to hide Marszałkowska Street in a tunnel, creating

11   Design for the development of Defilad Square and the vicinity of the Palace of Culture and Science,
Warsaw, Poland, 2008.

a space above it containing a maze of promenades and green spaces with freely dispersed edifices on various scales,[32] or to surround the Palace or even replace it with an artificial lake.[33] On November 24, 2008,[34] the media revealed the new development plan for this part of the city. The circular corso around the Palace had disappeared, and in its place giant skyscrapers, 300 meters high, and a densely built grid area appeared, plus a "boulevard" along Jerozolimskie Avenue. All that remained in Defilad Square were the Museum and the department store planned earlier. Subsequent proposals with a varied sequence of skyscrapers around the Palace have been published by the Warsaw media on a quarterly basis. Although each concept stirs up the emotions of the local population and journalists, so far not one of them has been considered satisfactory.

By 1956, Defilad Square had already become useless in both functional and ideological terms, yet fealty to the owner of the Palace effectively prevented any attempts to alter the urban structure of this part of the city. With the events of 1989, any restrictions on the new development of the area were lifted, clearing the way for the removal of Defilad Square, yet for the next twenty years nothing of any significance happened. Subsequent political teams and generations of architects have been demonstrating their helplessness in the face of the power of the building and the vast expanse of space surrounding it. One might even risk saying that the grandiose Palace standing amid the empty square overwhelms politicians.

Finally, the pragmatism of the simple tradesmen who have been swarming around the Palace for years, carrying out their small business transactions, offers the best protection against the

12 Design for the development of Defilad Square and the vicinity of the Palace of Culture and Science, Warsaw, Poland, 2008.

magic power of the giant.[35] The more grandiloquent the approach, the further-reaching the grandiose plans supported by the anti-communist ideology become, the less common sense seems to prevail. One might think that all the subsequent political teams' main aim is to develop the vicinity of the Palace on such a grand scale that the architecture of the new Poland overshadows the symbol of Soviet domination. Each new proposal has its respective supporters, but the majority admit that it is not beautiful enough, not sufficiently powerful architecturally, not satisfying enough, and that something else much better has to be found.

If it were only a question of developing a central city quarter that no longer bore this ideological burden, one of the political groups would have accepted a better or a worse design long ago, in order to quickly start enjoying the dividends of the precious land. But as far as the vicinity of the Palace is concerned the issue is evidently not merely to make a profit, but also to come up with a dignified Polish response to the Soviet intrusion in the cityscape. Meanwhile, none of the solutions submitted so far has been convincing enough to stand up to the task.

In early December 2008, Warsaw councilors submitted a proposal to rename Defilad Square "Fryderyka Chopina Square." This bizarre idea, coming almost straight from the realm of quasi-magical acts, proves how helpless the democratic authorities feel in the face of this legacy of totalitarianism, or as some prefer to call it, this post-colonial experience.

I am not willing to voice my clear position here on whether the period of Soviet domination in Poland should be analyzed from the post-totalitarian or post-colonial perspective, since in recent years the latter seems to have been an alternative proposal for understanding many phenomena of post-war Polish history.[36] It is difficult to declare one's position on the matter unambiguously, especially since the Poles have long been seeking to establish their self-identity through the "Orientalization" of the Russians, as Maria Janion has recently pointed out.[37] In her turn, Ewa Domańska claims that "post-colonial theory shall not provide us with methodological directives on how to study Poland's past, but it consolidates a context, a reference point for analysis. It allows us to formulate research issues and questions that do not appear in other options."[38] If we agree with Domańska, and simultaneously accept Janion's view, then the new facets of the problem will be revealed.

The Palace of Culture and Science and the vast Defilad Square at its front elevation, surrounded by the huge park complex—the entire architectural and urban planning setting—result from and therefore also symbolize both political domination and domination by an alien culture (architecture). If we thus admit that it incorporates both totalitarianism and colonialism, then a double research perspective, i.e., post-totalitarian and post-colonial, is justified.

It seems obvious that the Palace of Culture, just like other grandiose architectural projects from Stalinist times, is "socialist in content and national in form," thus deriving from the repertoire of forms considered typical or characteristic of the architecture of a given country or region. Dozens of similar examples of juggling with decorative elements from a national or regional vocabulary can be quoted, for example the complex in Berlin's Warschauerstrasse with a pair of circular belvederes recalling the structure of the twin Baroque church towers in the Gendarmenmarkt, or the elevation of the Press House in Gdansk with its rhythmicized tri-axial arrangement resembling old-Gdansk tenement houses.

The difference, however, is that these examples show how "our" architects sought "our" national forms, while the Palace is a Soviet gift in which an "alien" architect tried to penetrate "our" forms. He was trying to fake that he was one of us! And what is worse, after a two-week trip and followed by leafing through several albums, he thought he had grasped the essence of our culture! Thus the Palace of Culture is not merely the symbol of a totalitarian regime, but also of an alien culture trying to dominate, clumsily hiding its intentions. Adding Polish attics to the elevations and allowing Polish designers to decorate the interiors with their upholstery and hand-painted chandeliers from Włocławek charmed us and almost won us over. The Palace of Culture is an "alien in disguise."

The last twenty years spent seeking the right solution for the Palace and the square not only constitute a post-totalitarian experience, i.e., the new power's attitude towards the overwhelming power of a symbolic building entangled in ideology and embodying the old regime, which is seemingly an obvious attitude and the only one. The post-colonial perspective, in its turn, allows us to perceive another possible relation: that of the entity searching, so far in vain, for its "own" artistic expression (be it architectural or related to urban planning) in opposition to the Soviet, or more appropriately, the Russian "alien" element in the cultural cityscape. Even worse, this was an alien element benefiting from Polish national architecture, thus applying the strategy of impersonating something that it is not.

Regardless of whether we take the post-colonial perspective proposed by Domańska as our departure point, or agree with Janion's thesis on the "Orientalization" of Russia in Polish culture (or both), the Palace of Culture and Science is an obvious sign of an alien culture. Such an understanding of the building has been most clearly demonstrated in the strategy, adopted in recent years, of attempting to "tame" it, starting out from the moment we accepted that it cannot be annihilated.

In the academic analyses of art historians, the infamous Polish Renaissance attics attached to particular masses of the Palace have been perceived simply as an absurd combination of incongruent forms, resulting from a total misunderstanding of architectural rules.[39] Thus it is obvious that the Palace's architecture and its urban presence in the heart of our city constitute an alien element.

Other individuals however, primarily politicians, journalists and certain architects, adopt a post-colonial attitude and follow the strategy of enhancing this "Polish" element of the building, namely the national forms propagated by Stalinist doctrine, which seems to be a way of helping to "appropriate it," or more accurately, to culturally "tame" it.[40]

Thus the arguments used more or less successfully by the Stalinist propaganda in the publications of the nineteen-fifties within the framework of the aforementioned "strategy of pretending" to be Polish national culture by juggling with the Polish ornamentation details, repeated fifty years later by Polish feature writers, proved to be an effective "taming strategy."

Even more surprising, or indeed rather absurd, is a legend that has been increasingly popularized in Warsaw recently, claiming that Lev Rudniev designed the Palace's proportions after being enraptured by the Franciscan monastery in Niepokalanów.[41] The legend is most unlikely to be based on truth since, although Zygmunt Gawlik's design for the church was completed in 1939, the church itself was not built until 1948–54. What is more, it is hidden away and cannot be seen from any major road by chance, and it is certainly quite unimaginable that a Soviet architect would have been taken to see a church. An essential aspect of this legend is that the church is an element of the Franciscan monastery complex founded in 1927 by Maksymilian Kolbe. Kolbe was murdered in Auschwitz by the Nazis and canonized by Pope John Paul II in 1982. The Saint is said to have personally sketched the church's tower before World War Two. So the Palace of Culture and Science would not only have been an intentional conveyor of national contents, but also, unintentionally, of Catholic values. This shows that the cited legend also helps us to tame the Palace in ideological terms: Christianity versus atheist communism, demonstrating the Polish cultural superiority to which the Soviet architect unintentionally submitted.

The huge building, which is still the highest in Warsaw, along with the colossal undeveloped Defilad Square, remains an unsolved problem for the city. The complex connotations of the building itself together with its vicinity, its deep entanglement with the most recent episodes in Polish history, and most of all the enormous size of this symbol of the past and its omnipresence within the city tissue will not allow simple solutions, unambiguous judgments or easy decisions to be made in the future. Regardless of its totalitarian Soviet roots, it constitutes an element of the Polish cultural landscape, due to its consistent role in Polish history and the Warsaw cityscape for over fifty years.

Defilad Square and its surroundings are seen as a huge construction site awaiting development. As yet no one has attempted to save the already existing elements in the vicinity of the Palace, i.e., small squares, green spaces, and lesser architecture, which are regarded as integral parts of the building. None of the designs presented so far has tried to even partially respect these elements, in the belief that a complex of huge modern office buildings would redefine this part of the city and thus take away the spell cast on the giant. Fifty years after the construction of the Palace of Culture and Science and twenty years after the collapse of communism, architects, urban planners, and city authorities, along with a large section of the public are unable to free themselves from the ideological entanglement of this place and treat the Palace and its vicinity in an objective way, in keeping with a healthy attitude towards monument conservation, as the Palace and the square form part of the Polish cultural heritage.

Endnotes

1 Alfred Wiślicki, ed., *Budowa PKiN* [Constructing of the Palace of Culture and Science] (Warsaw: Państwowe Wydawnictwo Naukowe, 1957).

2 Aleksander Jackowski, "Marginalia," *Konteksty. Polska Sztuka Ludowa* 1 (1991): 33–34.

3 Tadeusz Barucki, *Maciej Nowicki* (Warsaw: Arkady, 1986), 10–12.

4 Jacek Friedrich, "… a Better, Happier World," in *Urban Planning and the Pursuit of Happiness*, ed. Arnold Bartetzky and Marc Schalenberg (Berlin: Jovis, 2009), 98–115.

5 *Konkurs nr 148 na usytuowanie zespołu gmachów centrali "Społem" i P.Z.U.W.* [Competition no. 148 for the Location of the Społem and P.Z.U.W. Buildings Complex], *Architektura* 2 (1948:6/7): 23–29.

6 Bronisław Baczko, ed., *Warszawa stolica Polski* [Warsaw, the Capital of Poland] (Warsaw: Społeczny Fundusz Odbudowy Stolicy, 1949), 147.

7 Jan Minorski, ed., *O polską architekturę socjalistyczną. Ministerstwo Budownictwa. Instytut Architektury i Urbanistyki. Materiały z Krajowej Partyjnej Narady Architektów, odbytej w dniu 20.–21.06.1949 roku w Warszawie* [Striving for Polish Socialist Architecture. Ministry of Housing, Institute of Architecture, and Urban Planning. Material from the National Congress of Architects Held in Warsaw on June 20–21, 1949] (Warsaw: Państwowe Wydawnictwa Techniczne, 1950).

8 Edmund Goldzamt, *Architektura zespołów śródmiejskich i problemy dziedzictwa* [The Architecture of City Center Complexes] (Warsaw: Państwowe Wydawnictwo Naukowe, 1956), 453–58.

9 Bolesław Bierut, *Sześcioletni plan odbudowy Warszawy* [Six-Year Plan for the Rebuilding of Warsaw] (Warsaw: Książka i Wiedza, 1950), 265; see also: Bolesław Bierut, *Der Sechsjahrplan des Wiederaufbaus von Warschau* (Warsaw: Książka i Wiedza, 1951).

10 Józef Sigalin, *Warszawa 1944–1980. Z archiwum architekta* [Warsaw 1944–1980. From the Archives of an Architect] vol. 2 (Warsaw: Państwowy Instytut Wydawniczy, 1986), 422–25.

11 Sigalin, (see note 10), 428–30; Jackowski, (see note 2), 33–34.

12 "Z dyskusji architektów na temat wyniku konkursu SARP na centrum Warszawy," [From the Debate of Architects on the SARP (Association of Polish Architects of the Republic of Poland) Competition for Warsaw's Center] *Architektura* 7 (1953:5): 118–26.

13 Sigalin, (see note 10), vol. 3, 29–47.

14 Goldzamt, (see note 8), 498.

15 Helena Syrkus and Szymon Syrkus, "Moskiewskie wysokościowce i amerykańskie 'drapacze nieba'," [Moscow's High Buildings and American 'Skyscrapers'] *Przyjaźń* 7 (1952:19): 8–9.

16 See: Waldemar Baraniewski, "Miezdu davleniem i ravnodusiem. Architektura v svete polsko-rosijskich otnosenij (XX viek)," [Between Pressure and Balance. Architecture in the Light of Polish-Russian Relations (20th Century)] in *Moskva-Varshava/Warszawa-Moskwa, 1900–2000*, ed. Maria Poprzęcka and Lidija Iovleva (Moscow: ArtKhronika, 2005), 139–47.

17 Jerzy Gieysztor, "Centralny Plac Warszawy," [Warsaw's Central Square] *Architektura* 7 (1953:7/8): 166–88; "Zasady realizacji wschodniej ściany placu J. Stalina zostały ustalone," [The Directions for the Development of the Eastern Wall of the Stalin Palace Have Been Settled] *Stolica* 74 (1954): 8–9.

18 Adolf Ciborowski, *Warszawa. O zniszczeniu i odbudowie miasta* [Warsaw. On the Destruction and Reconstruction of the City] (Warsaw: Polonia, 1964), 275–76.

19 Marta Zielińska, "Największy plac w Europie," [The Largest Square in Europe] *Kronika Warszawy* 4 (1989): 105–32.

20 Agata Passent, *Pałac wiecznie żywy = Long Live the Palace!* (Warsaw: Spis Treści, 2004), 76–81.

21 Edmund Goldzamt and Oleg Szwidkowski, *Kultura urbanistyczna krajów socjalistycznych: doświadczenie europejskie* [Urban-Planning Culture of Socialist Countries: European Experience] (Warsaw: Arkady, 1987), 368.

22 Grzegorz P. Bąbiak, "Pomniki władzy w krajobrazie Warszawy XIX i XX wieku. Od Soboru Newskiego do stalinowskiego Pałacu Kultury," [Monuments of the Authorities in the 19th and 20th Century Warsaw. From the Nevsky Cathedral to the Stalinist Palace of Culture] in *Pałac Kultury i Nauki. Między ideologią a masową wyobraźnią* [The Palace of Culture and Science. Between Ideology and Mass Imagination], ed. Zuzanna Grębecka and Jakub Sadowski (Cracow: Zakład Wydawniczy Nomos, 2007), 31–50; Agnieszka Haska, "Rozebrać czy zostawić?

Sobór pod wezwaniem św. Aleksandra Newskiego i Pałac Kultury," [To Demolish or to Leave It? The Aleksander Nevsky Cathedral and the Palace of Culture] in Grębecka/Sadowski, (see note 22), 51–58.

23 "Warszawski czakram. Dyskusja panelowa," [Warsaw's Chakhram. A Panel Discussion] in Grębecka/Sadowski, (see note 22), 9–22.

24 Marina Dmitrieva, "Der Traum vom Wolkenkratzer. Die Imagination des Urbanen in sozialistischen Metropolen," in *Imaginationen des Urbanen. Konzeption, Reflexion und Fiktion von Stadt in Mittel- und Osteuropa*, ed. Arnold Bartetzky, Marina Dmitrieva and Alfrun Kliems (Berlin: Lukas Verlag, 2009), 119–56, here 150.

25 Wojciech Włodarczyk, *Sztuka polska 1918–2000* [Polish Art 1918–2000] (Warsaw: Arkady, 2000), 163–64. See also German edition: Wojciech Włodarczyk, *Kunst in Polen in den Jahren 1918–2000* (Warsaw: Arkady, 2000).

26 Dariusz Bartoszewicz, "Planistyczna opera mydlana," [Planning Soap Opera] *Gazeta Wyborcza* (Gazeta Stołeczna), February 16 (2008): 2.

27 Michał Wojtczuk, "Warszawa ma plan zagospodarowania placu Defilad," [Warsaw Has the Development Plan for Defilad Square] *Gazeta Wyborcza* (Gazeta Stołeczna), March 10 (2006:59): 1.

28 Dorota Jarecka, "Konkurs odwołany, będzie nowy," [Competition Cancelled, Will There Be a New One?] *Gazeta Wyborcza* (Culture section), June 27 (2006): 12; Dorota Jarecka, "Kto nam zaprojektuje muzeum?," [Who Will Design the Museum Building for Us] *Gazeta Wyborcza* (Culture section), November 02 (2006): 14.

29 *Komunikat SARP* 2/3 (2007), 8–22.

30 Dariusz Bartoszewicz and Michał Wojtczuk, "Tunel przetnie muzeum?," [Will a Tunnel Cross the Museum?] *Gazeta Wyborcza* (Gazeta Stołeczna), November 26 (2007:276): 3.

31 Bartoszewicz, (see note 26), 2.

32 Michał Wojtczuk, "Pałac kultury ma być częścią miasta," [The Palace of Culture Must Be Part of the City] *Gazeta Wyborcza* (Gazeta Stołeczna), May 27 (2008:122): 4.

33 Dariusz Bartoszewicz, "Centralne jezioro stolicy," [The Central Lake of the Capital] *Gazeta Wyborcza* (Gazeta Stołeczna), June 12 (2008:136): 2.

34 Michał Wojtzuk, "Nowy plan placu Defilad," [The New Design for Defilad Square] *Gazeta Wyborcza* (Gazeta Stołeczna), November 24 (2008:274): 1.

35 The best analysis so far of the Palace of Culture and Science together with its cultural and social role viewed from the perspective of cultural anthropology has been carried out by Zbigniew Benedyktowicz, "Widmo środka świata. Przyczynek do antropologii współczesności," [The Phantom of the Center of the World. A Contribution to the Anthropology of the Modern Time] *Konteksty. Polska Sztuka Ludowa* 1 (1991): 16–32.

36 Ewa Thompson, *Trubadurzy imperium. Literatura rosyjska i kolonializm* [Bards of the Empire. Russian Literature and Colonialism] (Cracow: Universitas, 2000); Ewa Domańska, "Obrazy PRL w perspektywie postkolonialnej. Studium przypadku," [Images of the Communist Poland in the Post-Colonial Perspective. Case Study] in *Obrazy PRL. Konceptualizacja realnego socjalizmu w Polsce* [Image of the Communist Poland. Conceptualization of Realist Socialism in Poland], ed. Krzysztof Brzechczyn (Poznan: Instytut Pamięci Narodowej, 2008), 167–86, here 169.

37 Maria Janion, "Polska między Wschodem a Zachodem," [Poland between the East and the West] *Teksty drugie* 6 (2003): 140.

38 Domańska, (see note 36), 185.

39 Tomasz Torbus, "Die Rezeption der Renaissance im Nachkriegs-Polen: die Suche nach einem Nationalstil," in *Hansestadt, Residenz, Industriestandort: Beiträge der 7. Tagung des Arbeitskreises deutscher und polnischer Kunsthistoriker in Oldenburg, 27.–30. September 2000*, ed. Beate Störtkuhl (Munich: Oldenbourg, 2002), 313–25.

40 Maria Strelbicka, "Współczesne tendencje 'oswajania' Pałacu Kultury i Nauki," [Modern Tendencies in "Taming" the Palace of Culture and Science] in Grębecka/Sadowski, (see note 22), 177–88.

41 The legend was recently quoted by Marta Lesniakowska at the debate held at the conference: "Perspectives of Seeing Art and Cultural Traditions in Poland against the History of Central-Eastern Europe in the 19th and 20th Centuries—Consequences of Colonialism or/and the Experience of Totalitarianism," on December 8–9, 2008.

CULTURAL POLICY AS THE POLITICS OF HISTORY

Independence Square in Kiev

Wilfried Jilge

Independence Square (Ukrainian: Maidan Nezalezhnosti, popularly referred to simply as Maidan) in the center of the Ukrainian capital city of Kiev is today, without a doubt, the "main square" of the Ukrainian nation. It serves as the central public space in which all of the major political forces in the country assemble their followers when they want to highlight their political demands and programs. As is the case with other central squares in major European cities, Independence Square in Kiev fulfills a number of functions simultaneously. It serves, on the one hand, as a formation ground for the public, and thereby is the site for military parades, state celebrations, and is also a meeting place for opposition protests and demonstrations. On the other hand, the square is a central site of remembrance and a symbolic landscape, in which competing and intertwining imperial and national narratives leave their mark. The significance of this symbolic landscape has not only been modified by the changes in the composition of monuments, but also as a result of important national events and the manner in which they are remembered.[1]

The focus of this article is an investigation into the comprehensive reconstruction of Independence Square during the second term of office of the Ukrainian President Leonid Kuchma. As such, and in accordance with the previously mentioned functions of a central square, this article will start out from the proposition that an inquiry necessitates an examination not only of the meaning and function of the square's symbolism and its concordant view of history and identity, but that consideration must also be taken of the institutional framework (planning, political decision-making processes, and the execution of the reconstruction work) as well as how the initiators of the project dealt with the public. Only in this manner is it possible to assess the assertions made concerning the various dimensions of a historical culture, and, thereby, the political culture of the authorities and their allied groups, as well as the culture of remembrance in society.

From the Representational Site of Soviet Ukrainian Statehood to the "Main Square" of the Ukrainian Nation

The *Maidan* assumed the importance of a central political square and place of memory of an independent Ukrainian nation through the events of the late Perestroika period. Until then, and since 1977, the square bore the name October Revolution Square (Ukrainian: Ploshcha Zhovtnevoi Revoliutsii; 1935-77: Kalinin Square) and served together with Khreshchatyk Street, the city's main street, as a march and parade venue for Soviet state holidays. Between 1977 and 1991, the Monument to the October Revolution stood on the site of the present-day Independence Monument. It consisted of a central granite figure of Lenin with three bronze statues representing the revolutionary people, thereby cementing the ideological foundations of the Soviet state. The transformation of the square's significance into a national memory place of remembrance and a public democratic meeting place is primarily the result of the student hunger strike by the Kiev branch of the *Ukrainian Student's Union* that took place on October 2–16, 1990. In protest against the government of Soviet

Ukraine, Kiev students pitched tents in front of the Monument to the October Revolution and began a hunger strike. The prime minister of the government of the Ukrainian Soviet Republic was eventually forced to resign. Even though most of the students' demands were not met, their action symbolized by the tents in front of the monument is regarded as an important step in the national movement *Rukh* on the path towards independence.

After the proclamation of independence of Ukraine in August 1991, the change in meaning of the square was symbolically corroborated by the removal of the Lenin Monument. At first, no new monument was erected in the place of "Lenin." However, the official renaming of the square in 1991 as Independence Square, a name already common parlance since 1990, indicated a significant change in terms of identity politics. Even the use of the Ukrainian term *Maidan* for "square" instead of the word "ploshcha" cast a specifically national Ukrainian hue to the name of Independence Square, as it referred back to rural and perhaps even Cossack traditions.[2]

The present form of Independence Square only took place since a full-scale reconstruction project was instigated by President Kuchma in the late nineteen-nineties. The crisis-ridden post-Soviet regime, which also felt under threat by a growing democratic opposition movement, attempted to win back the prerogative of interpretation over the nation through a massive program of monument building, thereby masking its own post-Soviet authoritarian behavior in the process. During the Orange Revolution the square once again assumed the role of the central public space of the nation and society thanks to the actions of the democratic protest movement, which reacted against the falsification of the results of the autumn 2004 presidential elections and which, in part, deliberately positioned itself in the tradition of the 1990 student protests. Thus, the orange-colored demonstrators rebelled against the same authoritarian behavior that found itself expressed in the reconstruction process of the square and which has still not been completely overcome.

Cultural Policy as the Politics of History

This article is based on the position that cultural policies in Ukraine are, to a significant extent, subject to the politics of history (Geschichtspolitik) pursued by the state. The cultural policy in Ukraine can accordingly be regarded as conforming to the conceptual framework of the historical culture proposed by Jörn Rüsen, being subdivided into three dimensions—the political, cognitive, and aesthetic.[3]

The dominance of the politics of history in Ukrainian cultural policies is the result, among other things, of contemporary historical conditions. During the period of Perestroika, culture in Ukraine was a primarily political phenomenon. In the late nineteen-eighties and early nineteen-nineties, intellectuals belonging to the Ukrainian national movement *Rukh* highlighted the issues surrounding the importance of language, the culture of language, and the allegedly fully suppressed national history during the Soviet period with the aim of conceiving the nation in terms of a society of cultural integration and to legitimize the claims of Ukrainian statehood. In the process, they alluded to a threat posed to the ethnic and cultural foundations of the society in order to justify their claim to serving as the guarantors of these foundations. Yet, within the framework of this "societal identity policy"[4] and in the context of construed national views of history, innovative connotations were also derived, which were oriented towards democratization and the opening up of the authoritarian Soviet society. Due to the fact that nation-building and the consolidation of the state is still incomplete, culture in Ukraine remains to this day a particularly important factor in the legitimization of the new political order and the resultant political decisions.

As in the Soviet Union, an extremely political and functionalist notion of culture is often maintained by the representatives of Ukrainian cultural political institutions that aim to legitimize the existing power structure. Because the concept of the "nation" also serves as a central means of legitimizing power, art has been used to popularize national themes in society. Artistic works created on this basis tend to be characterized by a combination of nineteenth-century ethnographic style and a Socialist Realist artistic conception. In addition, they frequently serve the claims to legitimacy of their state patrons. Since President Kuchma's term of office, the main timeframe of these observations, the pluralization of the cultural scene has undoubtedly progressed. Nonetheless, the tendencies described here can be seen even today in the various branches of artistic activity in Ukraine, especially in the context of key monument and architectural projects.

The Significance and Function of Monuments

The main function of the monuments to be considered was supposed to be "from the start purposeful remembrance."[5] In this context, a monument is a means to create a group identity or, respectively, a national community. In addition, the erecting or the removal of monuments serves to legitimize or delegitimize political systems. Culture in modern society is understood here as a sort of societal memory.

Monuments are important elements of a society's historical culture. If one takes the three-dimensional conception of Rüsen's historical culture as a basis, then the central, *national* monument to independence on Independence Square in Kiev belongs to the political dimension of the historical culture. Monuments, however, are also works of monumental art, which demand artistic professionalism and expert competence. Moreover, the aesthetic dimension and the cultivated artistic realization of a monument play an important role in their acceptance by society. This is why the autonomy of a work in terms of its artistic-aesthetic and cognitive-scholarly dimensions is essential if the significance of a monument is to correspond—at least to some degree—to the interests and intentions of the citizenry, in particular when the purpose of the monument is to mobilize legitimacy.[6] The state also intends that central monuments present their "own" national culture to the outside world or positively distinguish them from "others," which is why great importance is often given to considerations on international developments in culture and art.[7] An examination into how the different dimensions of a historical culture relate to each other and the issues of the autonomy of these dimensions also permit conclusions to be drawn with respect to an understanding of power and the political culture in a society or social group.

The Monument as a Symbol of the National Idea

The initiative to erect an Independence Monument in Kiev was mobilized by the Ukrainian President, Leonid Kuchma. With the Ukaz (decree) of March 15, 1996, he appointed the *Cabinet of Ministers and the Kiev City Council* to initiate an open competition for a monument dedicated to Ukrainian independence. The Ukaz emphasized the political significance of the monument, therewith establishing the monument's legitimate function.[8] Following a directive by the *Cabinet of Ministers* to the *Ministry of Culture and the Arts of Ukraine*[9] on October 23, 1997, the cultural minister's council composed a ratification,[10] stating that all ideas involving a political monument would have to be state controlled.

According to the competition's brief, Ukraine became "an independent democratic state" in 1991 and declared its sovereignty and the "realization of a Ukrainian national idea." The competition was to promote the development of a project for a monument that would symbolize the "harmony among the citizens" and the "social constitutional state." Independence Square was chosen as the site for the monument. This first competition was acknowledged for its careful preparation of criteria and organization. The competition was broken down into two phases consisting of several months each, which gave artists throughout the country sufficient time to apply and develop their ideas. Additionally, the terms of the competition specified that maximum respect must be given to the urban environment. It was also clearly stated that the competition was for a monument dedicated solely to the theme of independence. The jury, however, did not find any of the seventy projects sufficiently acceptable—conceptually or aesthetically. Subsequent competitions were equally unsuccessful. By the year 2000, the competition was no longer of public or political interest.

De-Institutionalization and Patronage

Erecting the monument was taken up again after a decree by the Ukrainian president on April 14, 2000, instructing the *Cabinet of Ministers* to assume planning the tenth anniversary celebrations. One of the main events was the erection of a monument in honor of the declaration of independence, planned for August 24, 2001. The program was supplemented by additional symbolic and historical political measures that aimed to "establish political stability in society, and to consolidate the Ukrainian people around the idea of statehood." This also included the final establishment of the state symbols.[11] In further presidential decrees on June 8, 2000, Prime Minister Viktor Yushchenko and Mayor of Kiev, Oleksandr Omelchenko, were instructed to carry out plans for a competition for a *Pantheon of National Glory*, which would be "dedicated to the outstanding fighters for Ukrainian freedom and independence."

An order to find the best project for a memorial by the *Kiev Municipal State Administration*, signed by Omelchenko on August 7, 2000, led to the announcement of the "Express Competition," which was to be carried out by August 19, 2000 by the *Kiev Municipal Monument Protection Authority* in cooperation with the *Ministry of Culture of Ukraine* and the *Ukrainian State Committee for Architecture and Housing.* The manner in which the competition was organized violated key laws that regulate the execution of such competitions.[12] One very grave violation of the law was setting the deadline for August 19, 2000, meaning that architects and artists only had ten days to prepare a model. The short amount of time and the lack of public information made it almost impossible for them to conceive and design a necessarily complex model. This was especially true for artists from regions that particularly suffered from poor information politics. It was therefore not surprising that most of the competition entries came from Kiev.

The de-institutionalization was fostered by a nontransparent decision-making process that took place within a closed, post-Soviet clientelism of the official Ukrainian cultural administration. Even the manner in which the jury was chosen was typical of large-scale cultural projects in independent Ukraine. The majority were representatives of the state's executive branch and were not specialists in the field of monuments. Independent experts, such as artists, art historians, architects, were underrepresented.

The awards were to be presented at the end of September by a jury headed by Anatolii Tolstoukhov, deputy head of *Kiev Municipal State Administration.* The jury initially found they were incapable of making a selection. However, the sculptor Anatolii Kushch was ultimately awarded first prize for his project "Slava" (in collaboration with the architects Ruslan Kukharenko,[13] Ivan Mel'nykov, Yurii Tyzh). His design consisted of a thirty-eight-meter-tall Ionic column, on top of which stood a six-meter-tall figure of a "forever young Ukraine." At the base of the column, the legendary founders of Kiev were allegorized as Kyi, Schchek, Khoriv, and their sister Lybid,' who symbolized the beginning of the "over one-thousand-year-old history of 'Ukraine-Rus.'" Behind the column is a semi-circular formation of additional columns, between which are twelve sculptures (each three meters tall) that represent the nation's founders. The two other projects awarded for the square (second prize went to the project "2001" by the sculptor Valentyn Znoba/Architects: Oleksandr Komarovs'kii, Serhii Babushkin and third prize to the project "Vinec," by Anatolii Kushch/Architect: Stulakov) also included female figures, and an "altar of the fatherland," plus similar monumental, historically and politically symbolic, additional elements.[14]

Both the members of the jury and the winning artists had all previously been commissioned by the state to create important socialist monuments in Kiev and other regions in Ukraine during the nineteen-seventies and -eighties. For example, Valentyn Znoba and his son Mykola, in collaboration with other sculptors, to design the Great Socialist Revolution Monument on October Revolution Square in 1977. Znoba is also the author behind "Kosak Mamaj," which was erected on the southeast side of Independence Square

in autumn 2001. This monument was built at the personal wish and by decree of President Kuchma, soon after he visited Znoba's workshop. After the conclusion of the competition, it was decided that the first three prizewinners would form an "associated author collective" and develop a final model for the Independence Monument based on all three individual ideas. Plans were to be presented as early as autumn, but in August 2001, shortly before the monument's inauguration, there was still no final version of a politically and legally valid memorial project available to the public. One sign of the lack of public involvement is that, despite its significance, the project was neither discussed nor decided upon in the city parliament or in the *Verchovna Rada*.

In early autumn 2000, rumors began trickling through that the entire square on the northwest was to be rebuilt and would include multipurpose, underground centers, businesses, and restaurants. By order of the Municipality of Kiev of January 4, 2001, it was decided retroactively to reconstruct the entire square, a plan that, until then, had not been announced or made public in any document. Work began at the beginning of February 2001. An intervention of this size and scale in the cityscape should have required another competition procedure, but, instead, designing the northwest of the square was also delegated to the "associated authors' collective." The ideas for the new monuments on this side were developed by an associated collective headed by Komarovs'kii, parallel to those for the square. Bringing together various authors, who have completely different approaches and points of view, to design a square is difficult for aesthetic reasons, to say the least. It could be why the results of the reconstruction are eclectic and unsystematic. Yet, moreover, the project's financing was equally obscure. According to official communiqués, the reconstruction of the square, which cost 86 million Hryvnja (at that time 18.5 million euro) on the northwest side alone, did not come from tax monies, but rather exclusively

1   Independence Monument, figure "Maiden Ukraine" by Anatolii Kushch, Kiev, Ukraine, 2005.
2   Independence Square, baroque arch of the Independence Monument, Kiev, Ukraine, 2005.

from an investor group, called "Delight," consisting of investors from Ukraine, Russia, and Israel. To secure their use of the shopping malls, they paid a certain amount to the city council, which supposedly covered the costs of reconstructing the square and erecting the monuments. The origins of this money have never been disclosed, nor do the investors want to be named publicly.[15]

As far as the lack of transparency and the retroactive decision behind close doors to redesign the northwest of the square is concerned, independent journalists and human rights activists pointed out the fact that large-scale projects to reconstruct historical monuments in Ukraine have always served as a pseudo-legal way of attaining large sums of money and was often somehow connected with corruption.[16] This lack of trust was emphasized by the fact that corruption is a major issue in Ukrainian economics and politics, that the symbiosis between state bureaucracy and the oligarchs is considered typical of the Kuchma era, and that, according to surveys, much of the populace believes that true state power lies in the hands of "criminal structures" and "private capital."

The Reconstructed Independence Square

Independence Square, located at the main post office, straddles the Khreshchatyk, the main pedestrian zone. Following the Khreshchatyk toward the river Dnieper leads to the southeast side of the square—the location of the Great Socialist October Revolution Monument during Soviet times. It consisted of a statue of Lenin and four bronze figures that represented the honored heroes of the revolution. Shortly after the failed coup d'état in August 1991, the monument was destroyed.

In August 2001, the Independence Monument that honors the tenth anniversary was erected on the southeast side of the square. It is a 61.34-meter tall group of columns, crowned by a figure of a woman often referred to in documents as the "Maiden Ukraine" (the figure is 8.98 meters tall) (▶ 1). The column rests on an arch reminiscent of the "Ukrainian Baroque" or "Cossacks Baroque" styles of the seventeenth and eighteenth centuries (▶ 2). Behind this monument, there is a large, glazed, titled and, reminiscent of an amphitheater, ascending semi-circle in front of a glass dome. A cast bronze sculpture group entitled "Cossack Mamai" is situated to the left of the independence memorial (▶ 3). To the right is a sculpture group, approximately 8.5 meters tall and wide, which is dedicated to the legendary founders of the city of Kiev, Kyi, Shchek, Khoriv, and her sister Lybid' (▶ 4). This group is positioned in a circular fountain, surrounded by several other fountains. There are two more fountains situated between the memorials.

Since 2001, there has been a long, rectangular, flat, curved glass structure with a small dome on the Khreshchatyk end, located roughly in the middle of the northwest side of the square, with an equal number of fountains located on both sides. There is a smaller glass pyramid on each of the four ends of this ensemble. The main memorial on this side is a baroque gate built in 2001; it is approximately eleven meters high and majestically crowned by a 4.5- or

3   4

5-meter-tall sculpture of the Archangel Michael. This gate refers to the former Pechersk Gate of the seventeenth and eighteenth centuries that used to lead to the old city (▶ 5). The imposing, forceful archangel with broadly stretched, golden wings, and a flaming sword in his right hand and a round shield in his left, is the traditional symbol of the city, and replaced the symbolism of the Soviet city coat of arms. Behind the gate is a large round glass dome that leads to the "Globus" underground shopping mall. "Metrograd" shopping mall extends under the Khreshchatyk towards the Bessarabian Market. Visitors to the square can no longer enjoy the earlier strict, symmetric-systematic post-war construction that formed a successful contrast to the more complex construction of the Khreshchatyk. Nor does the ostentatious historicism of the monuments harmonize with the glass dome elements that, during the reconstruction work, replaced a part of the pyramid-shaped glass structures, fashionable in post-Soviet Ukrainian architecture. The glass dome elements make the reconstructed square very suggestive of Manege Square in Moscow.

A Monumental View of History: Soviet in Form, but National in Content?

The most striking element of the Independence Monument is its over sixty-meter-tall, white granite Corinthian column with a golden capital. Of the three types of columns (Doric, Ionic, and Corinthian), the Corinthian belongs to the Roman tradition, and is meant to embody the glory, power, and imperturbability of the state. According to Anatolii Kushch, the use of these antique formal elements is intended to symbolically immortalize

3   Independence Square, bronze sculpture "Cossack Mamai" by Valentyn Znoba, Kiev, Ukraine, 2002.
4   Independence Square, sculpture group by Anatolii Kushch, dedicated to the legendary founders of Kiev (Kyi, Shchek, Khoriv and their sister Lybid'), Kiev, Ukraine, 2002.

the independence of Ukraine. Kushch's antique column has been severely criticized in public discussion. It was referred to as "thirty-eight-meter conformism" and appropriately linked to the formal language of Soviet imperialism and the premises of Socialist Realism. According to critics, this position stands in contrast to the democratic claims of the state. Columns and stylistic elements of Socialist Realism were frequently employed in the other competition projects as well.

The crowning figure of the "Maiden Ukraine" (or "Lady Ukraine," "Ukraine") is intended by the artist to represent the core symbol of Ukrainian independence. She is meant to em- body the "Oranta-victress" or "Maria Oranta," in reference to what is probably the most significant mosaic image in the Kiev Sophia Cathedral. In the national tradition, she is regarded as the protector of the Ukrainian people. The nationalist appropriation of the praying Mother of God is a good example of the reformulation of an East Slavic, Orthodox religious symbol into a deliberate national figure. Concurrent with the stress on the link between the state and the Kievan Rus' is a reference to the Christian tradition in Ukraine. Nevertheless, the female figure also bears witness to the Soviet tradition. A woman with raised hands carrying a sheaf of wheat over her head was the symbol for Soviet Ukraine, as was the case, for example, in the monument erected in 1958 for the "Exhibition of Achievements of the Ukrainian Socialist Soviet Republic National Economy" in Kiev. The monument of a woman with outstretched hands holding palm leaves, as can be seen in the Park of Glory in the southern Ukrainian city of Kherson, is a typical Soviet symbol of vic- tory. Finally, one could also link the female figure with the massive sculpture rising from the banks of the Dnieper River, the Defense of the Motherland Monument. The use of the female figure illustrates the attempt by the artist to transform a Soviet monumental tradi- tion into a national tradition.

5

5   Independence Square, gate styled in "Ukrainian Baroque" with the Archangel Michael at the top, Kiev, Ukraine, 2005.

The reference to Soviet tradition was initially stressed by the artist through the figure holding palm leaves in her hand. It was only after the architectural competition that the project was revised and a decision was made to have her instead hold a branch of a snowball bush, which is a heraldic emblem of Ukraine, thereby serving to stress the national character of the monument.[17]

A main element in the discussion concerning the interpretation of the "Maiden Ukraine" is the image of the Berehynia (protectress), the original symbol of matriarchy. In the eclectic post-Soviet Ukrainian cult surrounding the Berehynia, there is an attempt to unite archaic pagan beliefs concerning the "Great Mother Earth" with matriarchal myths, the Christian cult of the Virgin Mary, folklore motifs, as well as character traits from literary and historical personalities from within the national tradition. The Berehynia stands on the one hand as a rendering of a woman's reproductive function in terms of absolutes, namely, as the "custodian of the tribe" and, on the other hand, she represents the preserver of all spiritual values of the nation and serves as the symbol of Ukraine par excellence.[18] The Berehynia cult links a patriarchal post-Soviet mother cult to a transnational, decidedly nationalist Virgin Mary cult that simultaneously incorporates Christian, universal Eastern Slavic, and Soviet elements. When the Independence Monument was erected, President Kuchma stressed its central significance: the monument evokes the "image of the Oranta as protectress [Berehynia] of our tribe," which constitutes the essence of the national idea.

The arch ensemble upon which the Corinthian pillar stands is meant to attest to the national character of the Independence Monument. The Komarovskii architectural office clearly looked to the Zaborovskii Gate, built from 1744–1746 on the grounds of the Kiev Sophia Cathedral, as a historical paradigm. The gate is one of the most significant monuments of the Ukrainian Baroque epoch. The approximately seventeen-meter-high, square arch ensemble consists of four arches with a three-tiered gable on each side. The Ukrainian Small Coat of Arms, the trident, is mounted on the second level of the gable on all four sides and is flanked by side ornaments.

The detailed citing of the baroque corresponds to the declared aim of the "association of authors' collective" to popularize the period of the Ukrainian Baroque from the seventeenth and eighteenth centuries as a time of national fruition. Likewise, the period of the Cossack Hetmans and Cossack statehood (sixteenth to eighteenth centuries) is also recalled, as it forms a central epoch in the historical viewpoint that stresses Ukrainian national statehood. Altogether, the Independence Monument—its copy and combination of various stylistic periods and use of national symbols—is meant to evoke the Kievan Rus' and the Cossack period. Evoking these founding epochs, it constructs a national Ukrainian view of history (Geschichtsbild), whereby the trident of the independent Ukraine is presented as the logical result of historical development. As such, the national theme contrasts with the Soviet style of architecture.

Kushch refers to the sculptural ensemble featuring the legendary founders of Kiev as representing the "courageous defenders of the fatherland." Kyi is the most important of the four figures and embodies "fire," which is held to be particularly meaningful in pre-Christian Ukrainian beliefs. A pagan symbol is visibly depicted on his shield, supposedly the origin of the trident, and, in turn, the state coat of arms. Through the trident, the artist manages to link the Ukrainian nation to the ethnic, national folk traditions all the way back to pre-Christian times. The ensemble, however, primarily recalls the monument erected on the banks of the River Dnieper in 1982 as part of the extensive 1,500-year celebrations of the city of Kiev organized by the state. The monument was meant to serve as the symbol of the unity of the ancient Russian Eastern Slavic peoples and embody the "unswerving friendship of the Russian, Ukrainian, and Byelorussian fraternal peoples." By citing this important monumental symbol exemplifying the Soviet Ukrainian view of history, the Soviet period is also incorporated into the national view of history.

To the left of the Independence Monument is a bronze sculpture of the "Cossack Mamai" or the "Cossack Bandurist" with a bronze horse, erected in September 2001. The Cossack Mamai is an extremely popular figure in Ukraine and dates back to Ukrainian portrait painting from the end of the seventeenth century to the nineteenth century. The literary model of the "Mamai" originates with the figure of the *Zaporozhian Cossack* (Zaporožec') in the Vertep Theatre, a popular puppet theater in the sixteenth and seventeenth century. The hero of these images is a young Zaporozhian Cossack, who sits cross-legged playing the *bandura*, just like the Cossack on Independence Square. His horse stands in the background. In most depictions, the Cossack Mamai is portrayed as a comical and burlesque figure. Even though he is regarded simultaneously as a symbol for the love of liberty and one who defends the people from its enemies (Poles, Jews, and Turks), texts and elements of the images in many portraits express a certain self-irony with respect to the central figure that can be perfectly interpreted as a form of hero deconstruction.

By contrast, the bronze sculpture created by Valentyn Znoba clearly evokes the stylistic language of Socialist Realism and bestows the Cossack with the characteristics of heroic Soviet monuments. By changing of the artistic form from painted portrait to a monumental sculpture, an authentic, laconic, and self-ironic folk art image has been transformed into a monumental Soviet-style memorial. The authoritarian connotations of the monument are further highlighted by the fact that it was commissioned by presidential fiat, accordingly to persons interviewed. All in all, one is left with the impression that a symbol *of the people* has become a gift from the authorities *for the people*. In addition, the monumental rendering of the "Mamai" is a good example of how aesthetic and art historical criteria can be subjugated to popular pedagogical thematism with a resultant loss of authenticity.

The authoritarian connotations are also revealed in terms of the use of the monument. Since the time of Perestroika, Independence Square has always been the place where Ukrainians assembled to demonstrate. In early 2001, against the background of domestic political crises, the symbolic tent cities once again became a sign of protest. At the same time, construction began and the square lost its function as a public political meeting place. It only regained its importance as a central public meeting place with the protests directed against the authoritarian Kuchma regime immediately preceding, and during the Orange Revolution.

Consecrated Heroism

The still unrealized plan for a *Pantheon of National Glory* featuring "outstanding fighters for the freedom and independence of Ukraine"—a project already prejudiced by President Kuchma's decree of June 2002 and part of the original plan as conceived by Kushch—illustrates the dominant personalist view of history represented by the monument ensemble. Kushch envisaged twelve sculptures for the pantheon, including the first "founders of the Ukrainian state," the early Rus' princes from the time of Oleh, the Princess Ol'ha, Sviatoslav the Conqueror, Volodymyr the Holy, Yaroslav the Wise, Bohdan Khmelnytsky, the "founder of the Cossack state," Ivan Mazepa, and Mykhailo Hrushevskii, the "first President of the *Ukrainian People's Republic* (UNR)." With the inclusion of the Hetman Mazepa and Hrushevskii, Kushch explicitly chose national heroes with which Ukrainian patriots can clearly distance themselves from the Soviet past and their Russian neighbors. The view of history developed in the pantheon, which traces the current state back in a continuous line to the *Ukrainian Rus'* through the *Cossack state* and the *Ukrainian People's Republic* of 1918, was presented in a similar form in the motifs designed for the Ukrainian Hryvnia currency notes in 1991.[19] Leading historians from the *Ukrainian Academy of Sciences* recommended a similar composition of heroes for the ensemble of figures and thereby provided a form of scholarly legitimization for the pantheon. In this way, the semi-official cultural policy and the state leadership have accepted the view of history promulgated by the national movement.

According to statements by the project's design collective, the aim was to arouse discussion among citizens on the history and culture of the state as portrayed in the monument as well as to solidify the independence of the state.[20] It remains to be seen, however, whether a sustainable interest in the history of the state and the nation is possible through the traditionalist presentation of a monumental, unconfined, and "from the top down" dictated view of history. Taking into account the continuing pluralization of Ukrainian society and its regionally diverse historical traditions, such a goal appeared questionable even during the planning stage of the pantheon.[21]

The Dominance of the Political Dimension of Historical Culture

The fixation on "national historical" symbols and themes in the construction of Independence Square resulted in the project's failure to achieve an appropriate artistic expression. As a result, the various stylistic epochs and formal design vocabularies employed in the Independence Monument are not even creatively assimilated, but are instead assembled in a schematically and aesthetically questionable manner in order to construct a useable popular pedagogical national view of history.[22]

A further example of an affected and occasionally kitsch historicism is the Pechersk Gate topped by the Archangel Michael, likewise constructed in a baroque style. The greatly oversized angel acts as an aesthetic burden on the gate. In addition, the gate serves no function on the square and stands completely out of context between modern glazed structures. This impression is only strengthened by the askew and asymmetrical position of the gate. According to the urban planner, the position of the gate was determined by the historical remains of the gate's foundations, upon which the current edifice supposedly stands. This is another example of a historical site being preserved as witness to a scientifically based fact, in order to make the national myth constructed on the square all the more believable.

Yet, it is precisely this neglect of the urban context and the dissection of the square with numerous monuments that has led to a lack of authenticity and aesthetic quality. As the original and impossible to reconstruct historical environment into which these colorful and ornate monuments once might have passed is absent, the construction of a "true" national history reveals itself as a superficial myth.

The ornate, pompous, and cost-intensive reconstruction of historical buildings and churches is a feature of Kiev's policy towards historical monuments in recent years. The leading post-Soviet cultural scene thereby attempts to present itself as the guarantor and preserver of national and religious traditions that were destroyed under communist rule. This patriotic claim, however, stands in contrast not only to the neglect of aesthetic considerations, but also to the lack of long-term professional preservation of historical monuments and outstanding cultural assets in the nation's capital.

Conclusion

Under President Kuchma, whose representatives were largely recruited from the late Soviet nomenclatura, or from the "second nomenclatura guard," the state administration adopted the national movement's view of history with the monument politics of Independence Square, so as to legitimatize their rule. This is particularly valid if one includes the not yet realized *Pantheon of National Glory*. The monumental view of history underscores the focus on the legitimization and representation of authority. Yet, if one includes the connotations of aesthetic form into a complete analysis of this view of history, then the monuments—if perhaps at times in an aesthetically degraded form—often refer to the tradition of Social Realism and a Soviet-imperial formal language. In a certain sense, the historical culture the square expresses could be interpreted as an unsystematic use of the guiding principle of "Soviet in form and national in content." The eclectic, at times kitschy, overall ensemble in the square represents a synthetic, and at times politically contradictory, view of history that attempts to cater to the country's varied cultures of remembrance reflected in the national preferences of the capital's populace.

Moderating and balancing different memory and political cultures under a deliberate, symbolical inclusion of the Soviet era is typical of the historical politics of the state leadership. Moreover, it could even boast a certain amount of success, as far as short-term legitimization of existing authority and power relations is concerned. Whether or not achieving such a level of authoritarian integration from above actually contributes to a sustainable national consensus was already questionable during the reconstruction of the square. Because, on the one hand, the secrecy of the process ruled out any chance of securing a sustainable agreement on a national consensus "from below." On the other hand, this historical political strategy in fact conserved the Soviet traditions and authoritarianism. The elements of this politics of history and political culture (patriarchal communication of a national view of history, lack of transparency) are indeed still perpetuated through the conception and realization of large monuments and cultural projects even in the post-Kuchma era—albeit depending on the chosen symbols—with an even stronger emphasis on national traditions.

Analyzing the monuments on Independence Square, as well as the conditions under which designing the square took place, illustrates a functional transformation of the national symbols of an independent Ukraine, popularized by the monument politics. The national symbols, popularized by the *Rukh* national movement at the end of the nineteen-eighties, and the destruction of monuments served to legitimize the political change of system. The connotations here were not only connected with risking ethnic exclusion, but also pointed perhaps more to a democratization and withdrawal from the authoritarian Soviet system. There was a direct link between the symbols and their connotations on the one hand and the ideological program and politics on the other.

After independence, yet especially since the end of the nineteen-nineties, the symbols served to legitimize existing, authoritarian structures and the veiling of the Soviet ways of thinking and behavior from which these structures and what they represent, emanate.

A society's or a certain social group's historical culture also allows an assumption of that particular group's political culture. The subordination of aesthetic criteria in the form of restricted autonomy and the exclusion of independent experts from art and science, which is still characteristic today of monument projects, reveals the one-sidedness of the presentation of authority and the will of state power. Scientists legitimize, afterwards, the mythic, post-Soviet, state-loyal, clientelism view of history that defines the official culture industry. Lack of clarity between politics, science, art, myth and, hence, between the individual dimensions of the historical culture (as well as the lack of autonomy of each dimension of historical culture) has always been typical of authoritarian societies. This is emphasized by the conformist aesthetic of monuments, which is dominated by imitation, a focus on state canonized themes, and the rehashing of existing monuments in the capital.

Their authors, who had all previously fulfilled state commissions in Soviet Ukraine and thus were awarded the authority cultural sanctification, justify their own existence in post-socialism by a thematic take over of the "national." This also overrides any possibility of creating an aesthetically innovative work of art that does not exclusively persist with preexisting historical thematic façade, which provokes discussion, includes present independent Ukraine in an authentic manner, and offers various forms of identification, beyond that of politicized views of history. The conformist culture of imitation may well be representative of a part of the semi-official cultural industry of Ukraine today, which has a limited interest in contemporary new forms of art.

This essay is a revised and condensed version of the following article: Wilfried Jilge, "Kulturpolitik als Geschichtspolitik. Der Platz der Unabhängigkeit in Kiev," *Osteuropa 53* (2003:1): 33–57.

Translated by Laura Bruce

Endnotes

1 Peter Stachel, "Stadtpläne als politische Zeichensysteme. Symbolische Einschreibungen in den öffentlichen Raum," in *Die Besetzung des öffentlichen Raumes. Politische Plätze, Denkmäler und Strassennamen im europäischen Vergleich*, ed. Rudolf Jaworski and Peter Stachel (Berlin: Frank und Timme, 2007), 13–60, here 34–36.

2 The Ukrainian word Maidan is Persian in origin and was incorporated into the language by the Slavs through contact with Turkic-speaking peoples. In general, Maidan indicates a large, vacant central square in a village or a small town with a church and a market place. This traditional Ukrainian designation for square was only employed during the Soviet era in a few remote villages with less than 100 residents. The term referred to the production site of saltpeter during Cossack times as well as the center of the Zaporizhian Sich, a fortified military camp of the Cossacks on the Dnieper River. These cultural references and, in particular, the historical references with respect to the Zaporizhian Sich, require more thorough research. One reason for this is the fact that, since the end of 2004, an element of the "orange" politics of history has been to establish a link between the Maidan as a symbol of freedom and the student revolution of 1990 with the "freedom-loving" Cossack tradition. The aim is to present the "Ukrainian nation" as particularly revolutionary and freedom-loving. *Maidan* in: *Ukrains'ke kozactvo. Mala Encyklopedija* [Ukrainian Cossack Nationality. Small Encyclopedia] (Kiev: Heneza, 2006), 357–58. In the year 2002, i.e., in the edition that was published before the "Orange Revolution" there is no mention of the meaning of Maidan in connection with the Zaporizhian Sich.

3 With respect to the concepts, cf. Jörn Rüsen, "Geschichtskultur," in *Handbuch der Geschichtsdidaktik*, ed. Klaus Bergmann et al. (Seelze-Velber: Kallmeyer, 5 1997), 38–41.

4 Wolfgang Kaschuba, "Geschichtspolitik und Identitätspolitik. Nationale und ethnische Diskurse im Kulturvergleich," in *Inszenierung des Nationalen. Geschichte, Kultur und die Politik der Identitäten am Ende des 20. Jahrhunderts*, ed. Beate Binder, Wolfgang Kaschuba and Peter Niedermüller (Cologne/Vienna/Weimar: Böhlau, 2001), 19–42, here 20.

5 Hans-Ernst Mittig, "Das Denkmal," in *Funkkolleg Kunst. Eine Geschichte der Kunst im Wandel ihrer Funktionen*, ed. Werner Busch (Munich/Zurich: Piper, 1997 [1987]), 539. The emphasis is in the original text.

6 Rüsen, (see note 3), 39.

7 This was also stressed by the chief architect of the reconstruction project for Independence Square, Serhii Babushkin, "Stadtarchitekt in Kiev seit 1996. Die erste Bilanz," *Stadtbauwelt 152*, *Bauwelt 92* (2001:48): 36.

8 Decree no. 191/96 from March 15, 1996 "Pro sporudženna Monumenta Nezaležnosti Ukraïny" [On Erecting the Independence Monument in Ukraine] *Urjadovyj kurjer* March 19, 1996.

9 Order of the Ukrainian Cabinet of Ministers no. 5508/1 from October 23, 1997, mentioned in the Cabinet of Ministers resolution.

10 Cultural minister council resolution no. 12/33–2 from December 22, 1997, "Pro Vseukraïns'kyj vidkrytyj konkurs na krašcyj eskiznyj proekt Monumenta Nezaležnosti Ukraïny" [On the All-Ukrainian Open Competition for the Best Design of an Independence Monument for Ukraine] (with 3 attachments), handed to the author by the Kiev Monument Protection on June 15, 2001.

11 Decree no. 597/2000 from April 14, 2000 "Pro pidhotovku do vidznačennja 10-ï ričnyci nezaležnosti Ukraïny" [On the Preparations of the Celebration of the 10th Anniversary of the Independence of Ukraine]; Wilfried Jilge, "Staatssymbolik und nationale Identität in der postkommunistischen Ukraine," *Ethnos-Nation* 6 (1998:1–2): 85–113.

12 Resolution of the Cabinet of Ministers no. 2137 from November 25, 1999 "Pro zatverdženna Porjadku provedennja architekturnych ta mistobudivnych konkursiv" [On Establishing Competition Guidelines for Architecture and Urban Planning] *Oficijnyj visnyk Ukraïny*, October 17, (1997:47): 68; Law of Ukraine no. 687–14 from May 20, 1999 "Pro architekturnu dial'nist'" [On Activities in the Field of Architecture] *Vidomosti Verchovnoï Rady* (1999:31): 246.

13 Kukharenko is a good example of closed, post-Soviet clientelism, because at the same time he headed the monument protection authority of the City of Kiev.

14 See jury protocol no. 3 from September 20, 2000 and the project description for the awarded designs provided by the Kiev Monument Protection Agency on June 15, 2001.

15 I am indebted to the journalist Susanne Reumschüssel for this information. She prepared a radio commentary for "Westdeutscher Rundfunk" (WDR) on the reconstruction of the square and its commercial implications.

16 K. Ščetkina, "Lazivka v istoriju," [History as an Excuse] *Dzerkalo Tyžnja*, March 16–22, 2002.

17 The president, together with the mayor of Kiev, most likely influenced the selection of a female figure that appeared in most of the projects submitted to the "Express Competition" starting in the summer of 2000.

18 See: Oksana Kis', "Modeli konstrujuvannja gendernoi identyčnosty žinky v sučasnij Ukraini," [Models of the Construction of Gender Identity in Today's Ukraine] *I. Nezaležnyj kulturolohičnyj časopys* 27 (2003): 37–58.

19 Jilge, (see note 11), 103–06.

20 See the author collective's internal circular: "Monument nezaležnosti Ukraïny," [Independence Monument of Ukraine] presented by the head of the Institute "Kyïvinžproekt" at the corporation "Kyïvprojekt," Mykola Marčenko in November 2002.

21 The pantheon has yet to be realized.

22 For literature available on the debates and documents mentioned, see: Wilfried Jilge, "Kulturpolitik als Geschichtspolitik. Der Platz der Unabhängigkeit in Kiev," *Osteuropa 53* (2003:1): 33–57, here 53–55.

THE PRESENCE OF THE OF THE RECENT PAST

Difficult Transformations of a
"Paradigmatic Socialist City":
Dunaújváros

Béla Kerékgyártó

Are our former socialist cities now post-socialist cities? Have they transformed and/or overcome their socialist heritage? In the following, I will try to investigate these general questions in a case study on the first and paradigmatic Hungarian socialist town, Dunaújváros (the former Sztálinváros). I will first reflect on the changes in the use of the term "socialist city" in past and present discourse. Then I will sketch some characteristics of the development of Dunaújváros as a socialist city, and conclude with a short assessment of the consequences of its socialist heritage and of post-1989 developments, plans, and perspectives.

First of all, let us take a short look at the changes in the discourse surrounding the term "socialist city" in Hungary. A significant difference can be observed between the time before the fall of state socialism and afterwards, not only in terms of ideology—this would be a truism—but even in the critical efforts to keep a distance from them.

The establishment of socialist cities had been a highly ideological issue, which was why, in the nineteen-sixties, social scientists and the public at large preferred not to address it. The researchers and planners who did try to investigate the subject in a more autonomous way sensed that it contained an ideological phantom. They replaced the term with "cities under socialism"[1] or stressed the parallels with new cities in the West and the centralistic interventionism of the welfare state after World War Two, in order to neglect the originality of the socialist model.[2] An ideological demystification, an attitude critical of the system, played an important role in both cases.

After 1990, however, researchers reevaluated the term and used it as a descriptive and analytical tool for the interpretation of the *historical* phenomenon. The general characteristics of state socialism justify the use of the term in its own right.

According to these researchers, ideological and political ideas and decisions played a decisive role in the historical development of this type of city. Why not call cities as they had called themselves, argued a comprehensive analysis of socialist-era urban development. The author summarized the difference between new Western cities and socialist cities as follows: "new cities in the West were developed with the aim of decentralization and regional integration, while new cities in the socialist countries aimed at centralization and had no concern for regional context/contextualization."[3]

We can therefore use the term socialist city in both a narrower and in a wider sense. The latter concerns "cities under socialism" generally. The narrower sense relates to new industrial cities, especially the few paradigmatic cities that were designed to demonstrate, even urbanistically and architectonically, the specific socialist, historically new character of society.

Industrialization and urbanization as a means of modernization—urgent tasks in the underdeveloped regions of Eastern Europe—had to follow the Soviet model of the nineteen-thirties and -forties in the short Stalinist era. While the development of heavy industry (mining industry and steelworks) and the foundation of new industrial cities had represented an important share in the urbanization of the Soviet Union (1,000 new industrial cities with forty

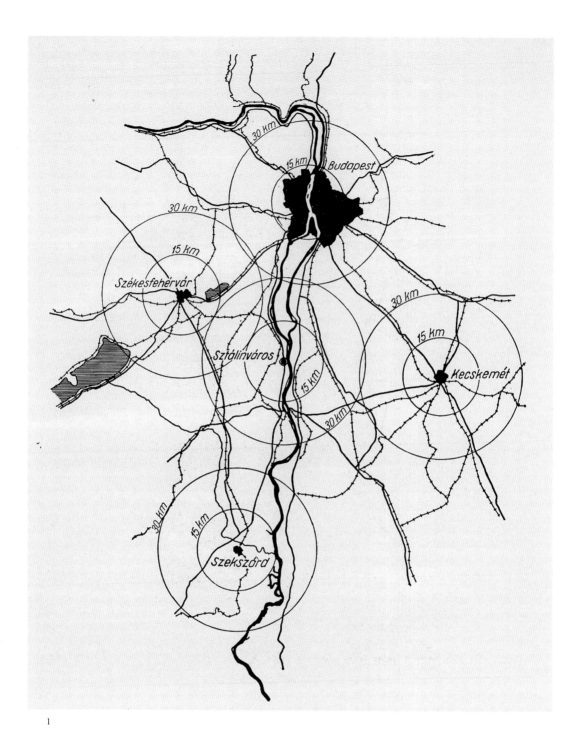

1   Stalin City in its regional context, today Dunaújváros, Hungary, 1959.

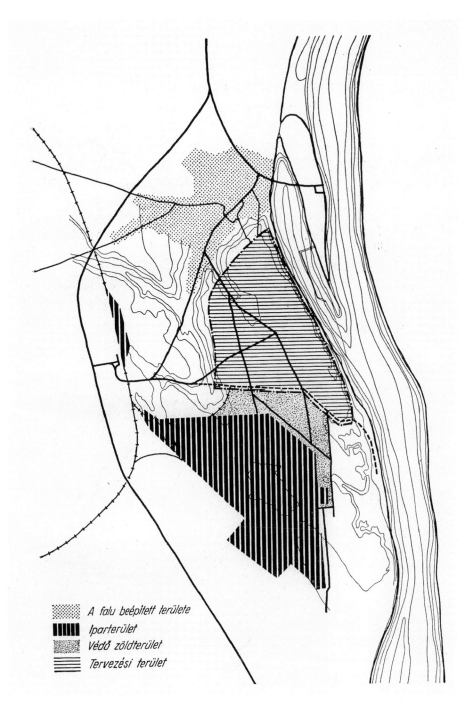

A falu beépített területe
Iparterület
Védő zöldterület
Tervezési terület

2

2   The area of the village, the new city and the ironworks (from top to bottom), Stalin City, today Dunaújváros, Hungary, 1959.

million inhabitants), this proportion remained quite low in the so-called socialist countries (approximately 120 new towns in Eastern Europe altogether; in Hungary itself twelve, the proportion of which within the population remained only around 6 to 7 percent).[4]

The dogma surrounding the priority of heavy industry was a highly ideological and, in some sense, utopian claim that could only be brought close to "reality" through a dictatorial or even despotic wielding of power. The regime tried to create a "brave new world," but it was able to do so only in a few exceptional cases, the show cases (as it were, the positive counterparts of the show trials). Closed as they were, most of these highly orthodox, newly founded socialist cities of the Stalinist period could not be maintained later, and remained the expressions of their outdated period. But some of their fundamental characteristics— i.e., a centralized and paternalistic power with territorial and architectonic consequences— remained decisive factors throughout the existence of state socialism.

The former *Stalin City* (known as Dunaújváros, or *Newtown-on-the-Danube* since 1961) is the paradigmatic Hungarian example of the new industrial cities built on "virgin soil" in the orthodox Stalinist period. Some well-known examples from other bloc countries include Nowa Huta in Poland and Eisenhüttenstadt in the former GDR. They were typically connected with the foundation of huge ironworks (with the aim of becoming "the land of iron and steel"). They not only had to function as housing estates for the ironworkers but also to demonstrate, by means of urban development and architecture, the superiority of life under socialism. "Architecture as art is both a mirror and a monumental means of the propaganda of the social system, a certificate of the value of the society which produced it."[5]

The Hungarian Stalin City remained unfinished, partly because of Stalin's death a short time afterwards, partly because of the exaggerated ideological ambitions that treated the city center as a site for mobilized masses.

In the case of Stalin City (Dunaújváros), even the choice of site for the industrial plant had been determined by external political factors. The more appropriate site located in the southern part of Hungary, near the border, was dropped because of the worsening political relationship with Tito's Yugoslavia. Instead of Mohács, the village of Dunapentele on the Danube was chosen. Although its loess was excellent for agriculture, it was not so favorable for building a city. As builders failed to pay enough attention to this fact, an extremely dangerous landslide occurred in the loess river bank at the beginning of the nineteen-sixties. The construction of the embankment to protect the steelworks and the city cost billions (▶ 1, 2).[6]

Planning in Stalin City primarily meant voluntaristic, dogmatic decisions, which were always at odds with real conditions and spontaneous development. The declared unity of the industrial site and the city, the place of work and the living quarters, in fact, hid a deterministic relationship, because the building of the ironworks always had priority over the urban development. The ironworks management even had a say in matters concerning the city.

At the beginning, even the number of newcomers to the town had been underestimated.

While 7,000 people had worked on the construction of the ironworks in 1950, this number had reached 25,000 by 1952. The authorities had thought that primarily singles and nuclear families with one or two children would come to the town, but they soon had to correct these expectations. According to the 1950 plan, the city would have a total of 25,000 inhabitants; however by 1952, when the first urban development for the city was adopted, this number had already reached 40,000. Services necessary for everyday life had not been planned for, and had to be developed in an improvisatory and spontaneous way. This alone demanded a more systematic answer to the question: how to create a living city organism? The fast changes of concepts and solutions illustrate the differences and tensions between voluntaristic planning attempts and spontaneous, evolutive development. The realized ensemble clearly bears the ideological stamp of the time; nevertheless, from within, it looks more like a collage of different urban patterns and architectural solutions.

An interesting aspect of this development can be seen in the story of the chief architect and urban planner of the project, Tibor Weiner (1906–1965).[7] He had studied at the Bauhaus in Weimar at the end of nineteen-twenties, then went to the Soviet Union with Hannes Meyer at the beginning of the thirties, and later emigrated to South America (Chile). After World War Two he returned from exile to Hungary, and at the end of the nineteen-forties was placed in charge of planning the city, remaining its chief architect until his death in 1965. His contemporaries dubbed Stalin City "Weiner Neustadt" (alluding to the actual Austrian town, Wiener Neustadt) (▶ 3).

The first streets and houses were planned and built in a modernist style. But soon an ideological turn took place, replacing modernism with Socialist Realism and Stalinist dogma. This second, monumental phase was connected to the elaboration of the urban development mentioned above, the focus of which was a monumental city composition. In accordance with the plan, the city was organized around two axes. The main road, "Stalin Avenue," was 120 meters wide, and connected the city center with the main entrance of the ironworks. This connection between working and living space, factory and city, proved to be more virtual than real because of the distance and a forest belt in between. The plan for a monumental center at the intersection of the two axes, with important political, administrative and cultural institutions, and a gigantic Stalin memorial had been drawn in no less than twenty versions, but was not realized in this period. Politicians regarded the designs either less monumental than required, or far too monumental. However, although they themselves had envisioned a monumental Stalin statue like the Soviet War Memorial in Berlin-Treptow (!), this plan was dropped from the agenda after Stalin's death (▶ 4, 5).[8]

The monumental avenue differed radically from the original concept of the chief architect, who had imagined a concave skyline for the city with relatively small public buildings at the midst of a wide green area, surrounded by high-rise apartment houses.

The official concept of Socialist Realism was just the opposite, with masses piled up towards the center, ending in monumental public buildings. However, the city center has remained

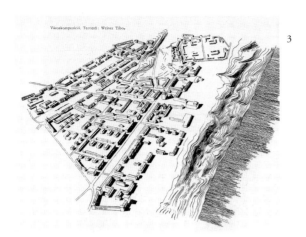

3

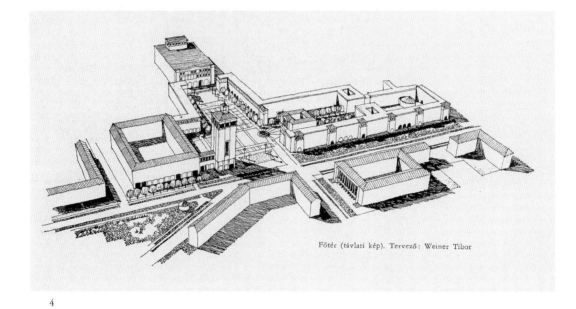

Főtér (távlati kép). Tervező: Weiner Tibor

4

unresolved to this day. The disproportionate width of the main avenue and the lack of a commercial and cultural center have been repeatedly criticized.[9]

The core idea determining the layout of the city was an adapted version of the neighborhood principle, an authoritarian version of a community-based ideology. It structured the city in self-contained quarters with their own public utilities and communal institutions. The basic idea was that individual flats would be enhanced by the provision of daily services, educational and cultural institutions such as laundries, canteens, nurseries and schools, cinemas, a theater, and a cultural center.

Architecture and art being a means of "monumental propaganda and revolutionary romanticism" (Weiner), 5 to 10 percent of investments were to be spent on works of art related to

3　Tibor Weiner's plan for the new city (1952–53), Stalin City, today Dunaújváros, Hungary.
4　One of the plans for the center of Stalin City, today Dunaújváros, Hungary, 1953.

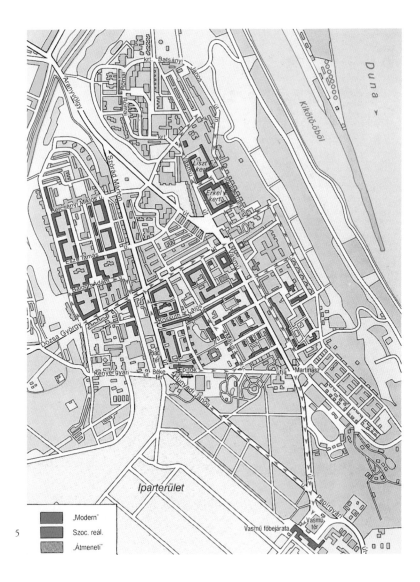

5   „Modern"
    Szoc. reál.
    „Átmeneti"

the construction of the city. These were to mirror the people/community and their happy future, so that everyday people would face their own images in public places. According to a monumental plan, twenty statues of Stakhanovite workers were to line Stalin Avenue. Buildings, squares, and roads were to be decorated with representations of the workers and their heroic labor, like the mural above the entrance of the ironworks or the mosaics on the wall of the department store (▶ 6, 7).[10]

The elimination of social and spatial differences was also an ideological and urbanistic dogma. The flats including amenities, all of them approximately of the same sizes, were built in great numbers. They were better than the average in the country at the time, but the rigid repetition and homogenization turned out to be disadvantageous in the long run.

5   The realized ensemble. Dark: building blocks in the Socialist Realist manner; gray: modern from the 1960s and 1970s, Stalin City, today Dunaújváros, Hungary.

6

After the death of Stalin, another abrupt change took place in the ideological and political order. Though Stalinist orthodoxy was no longer accepted, the city continued to be built according to the original Stalinist principles, the original projects having been carried through to their completion at the end of the nineteen-fifties and early -sixties—although, due to economic and ideological reasons, they were finished in a somewhat simplified form. The Dunaújváros of the nineteen-sixties saw the return of international modernism in—as it turned out to be—a faceless, bureaucratic-industrialized mass version. Prefabricated housing estates dominated city development in the nineteen-sixties and -seventies. This in turn triggered a second large wave of immigration and led to the demographic peak at the end of the nineteen-seventies (1965: 43,500; 1970: 45,874; 1975: 54,738; 1980: 60,736—but by 1990, as a clear sign of the economic crisis and stagnation, the number of inhabitants decreased to 59,000). Even the long-planned city center, the City Hall, was built in a combination of the typical high-rise with an extended low wing (a "flan") in the sixties.

When we look at this heritage today, we are faced with certain far-reaching structural consequences. The city has retained its industrial character and the ironworks—although sold to foreign investors and divided into different parts—continues to dominate employment in the city. Layoffs were not as dramatic as in other industrial areas of the country, employment remaining at a high level. Despite efforts to bring in other firms and enterprises and the foundation of an industrial park to counterbalance the ironworks, it still provides work for nearly 50 percent of the city's employees.

6   Stalin Avenue in the 1950s, Stalin City, today Dunaújváros, Hungary.

One of the most important factors influencing the quality of life is the housing situation. The composition of Dunaújváro's housing stock significantly deviates from the average found in other cities, especially the older cities. This is clearly the consequence of the ideology-driven homogenization in the center of the town and in the industrialized mass housing estates erected in the nineteen-sixties and -seventies. The housing stock is dominated by two-room apartments (66.5 percent—in contrast to the countrywide average of 40.8 percent!), while the share of apartments with three or more rooms amounts only to 20.8 percent (the countrywide rate being 45.3 percent). The average size of apartments is 54.7 square meters (compared to a countrywide average of 60.5 square meters).

Due to the one-sided qualitative development and a lack of space for expansion, the population density of the city is extremely high at 1,003 people/square kilometer (higher than any other city in Hungary, except for Budapest). The proportion of the housing stock built by the state is also very high (approximately 90 percent as opposed to 60 percent in other cities and 40 percent in the country). After 1989, privatization resulted in a similarly homogenous structure (approximately 95 percent of the flats are now privately owned). Communal politics has thus lost one of its most important means of intervening and main-

7   The gate of the ironworks, Stalin City, today Dunaújváros, Hungary, 2008.

taining a sense of land value and land use, especially in the center of the city. Under these circumstances, the chances of population mobility are far too limited.

A typical symptom of retort cities is the underdevelopment of commerce and services. This is demonstrated by e.g., the number of shops and restaurants in a given area (Dunaújváros has an average of 14.9 shops per 1,000 inhabitants, while the countrywide rate is 19/1,000). The constant decrease in the population, in spite of a relatively high employment rate, is certainly related to general tendencies such as the processes of segregation and suburbanization, but also to the mono-structured employment and the homogeneity of the housing stock and living conditions of the city. The population has become older, with an extremely low proportion of young people (0–24).

In the last ten years, a growing awareness of the need for reinvention and reconstruction has evolved in the city. Once planned and centrally directed, the city now has to relearn the importance of planning and active strategic building. As a result of different initiatives, important documents have been prepared, such as a settlement construction plan, a strategic concept for urban development, and a marketing plan. Various professional and civic groups have taken part in this work, including the city council, the college, and the association of artists. The city council has submitted an application for EU funding, entailing a project-based renewal process.

A new comprehensive city plan study states that, because of the physical and moral deprivation of the city center and the housing stock, the city needs a complex program that would make it more livable for its inhabitants and more attractive for visitors and tourists. Even from the point of view of new regional possibilities (a new bridge on the Danube, the building of new international roads close by), the main question is the redevelopment and rebuilding of the city center. On the one hand, this reconstruction would include the Socialist Realist ensemble as a whole, but the center at the crossing of the main axes was never really completed; a problem that has not yet been solved, despite many plans and interventions at different periods. The administrative center mentioned above has caused more problems than it has solved. Its buildings have no architectural and environmental value. The buildings need to be renovated, modernized, and even completed with some new parts with additional functions. With the demolition of the low wing, the "flan" of the City Hall, the city center would be opened up towards the Danube. The relationship of the city to the Danube, incorporating the river bank, the island, and the water is crucial from the point of view of any possible development plan.

The axis that leads from the territory of the administrative center to the railway station has great potential for further development. From the nineteen-sixties it has developed into a commercial and financial center, providing functions typically lacking in the centers of the socialist cities: shops and a college. A spontaneous process has been under way since the nineteen-eighties. First smaller shops (boutiques) were opened on the ground floors of the blocks. In the nineteen-nineties, even new buildings—banks and a service center—sprang up. This development could now be continued at the corner of the axis, opposite the city hall. On this strategic site a significant building (wing tower) with complex functions (hotel, trade, banks, restaurants, et cetera) could be erected.

Recently, important developments related to the college have been made in the area connected to this axis. Besides industry-related disciplines, the college provides training in economics, communication, and management. Furthermore, not only does it contribute to the transformation and differentiation of the employment structure, but plays a very important role from a demographic point of view, given the proportion of children and young people in the city, which is generally extremely low. The development of the institution has been very dynamic. Recently, it has won significant support from the state for further projects. The construction work at the campus is also exemplary from an architectural point of view. The quality of the new buildings and the reconstruction of former industrial ones could serve to stimulate the development in the city center.

In its more or less consistent composition and temporal unity, the socialist realist ensemble now represents a value in its own right—particularly in contrast to the later mass housing estates (▶ 8, 9).

8

8   The department store with the mural, Stalin City, today Dunaújváros, Hungary, 2008.

9

But this value should be discovered by and advertised to both the local community and visitors. The first important step in this direction was made when a systematic historical investigation of the building stock was carried out, followed by the publication of an architectural guide based on it.[11] There is an ambiguity between the modernist and the Socialist Realist parts of the ensemble, between the more low-rise buildings—even in the case of institutions located in the wider green area—and the monumental closed or semi-closed blocks decorated with historicist elements. But, as an urban analyst stated: "behind the representative, ostentatious neo-classicist avenues, we often find provincially warm, closed units with inner courtyards or houses with only three or four stories."[12] The scale of the ensemble, the size of the houses, and the spaciousness of the green areas make it a pleasant environment. Nevertheless, the criticism formulated in the nineteen-sixties holds true to this day: the loose dissemination of public buildings resulted in a loss of functionality and importance. The representative hotel building ceased to function as a hotel (it was privatized and is now used for other purposes, although demand for a new, quality hotel has in the meantime arisen). The cinema nearby, one of the most characteristic buildings of the ensemble, is in a terrible state; it urgently needs to be renovated and provided with new functions.

9   The theater (former community center), Stalin City, today Dunaújváros, Hungary, 2008.

The former department store is now rented by various small shops, and has actually lost its communal functions and significance in spite of the fact that, together with the surrounding neighborhood consisting of the theater, the square, and the surrounding modernist houses, it is one of the most attractive parts of the ensemble. Changing its commercial function to a cultural and a communal one would be justified. It could be imagined to house a restaurant, a café, a multifunctional center, not to mention a museum of social and urban history, presenting everyday life in the founding period.

The spaciousness and rich vegetation of the ensemble are two of its main attractive features, but these public areas have more in common with parks. What is lacking is differentiated, multifunctional use. For example, the ground-floor level of the buildings along the main street and the inner squares would be suitable for quality shops and public services, and together with the various transitional spaces, could be developed to form a living urban microstructure.

Whether and how these plans can become more specific and actually be realized, whether the interested parties can effectively cooperate, and whether the city dwellers actively participate, are questions that will be answered in the near future. The transformation of Dunaújváros into a post-socialist city is under way, and hopefully this process will be continued at a faster rate than has been the case thus far.

Special thanks to Péter Pásztor

Endnotes

1 Iván Szelényi, ed., *Szocialista városok* [Socialist Cities] (Budapest: Kossuth, 1971).

2 Viktória Szirmai,*"Csinált" városok* ["Created" Cities] (Budapest: Magvető, 1988).

3 Pál Germuska, *Indusztria bűvöletében* [Under the Spell of Industrialization] (Budapest: GONDOLA NOVA BT, 2004), 49.

4 Zoltán Kovács, "A szocialista korszak városfejlődésének jellemzői Magyarországon és Kelet-Közép-Európában," [The Characteristics of Urban Development in the Socialist Era in Hungary and East-Central-Europe] in *Rendszerváltás és Kádár-korszak* [System Change and Kádár Period], ed. György Majtényi and Csaba Szabó (Budapest: Kossuth, 2008), 314–16.

5 Quote from a critical article about experiences in and with Dunaújváros: Rezső Szíj, "Építészeti problémák," [Architectural Problems] in *Új építészet, új társadalom 1945–1978* [New Architecture, New Society 1945–1978], ed. Máté Major and Judit Osskó (Budapest: Corvina, 1981 [1967]), 277–92, here 292.

6 The area has been inhabited for a long time. Intercisa was the name of the Roman settlement. The settlement Dunapentele was founded in the Middle Ages. In the nineteen-forties it was an agricultural village with 4,000 inhabitants. The ironworks and the city were planned independently from the village. Cf. Ferenc Erdős and Zsuzsánna Pongrácz, *Dunaújváros története* [The History of Dunaújváros] (Dunaújváros: Dunaújváros Város Önkormányzata, 2000).

7 See: Tibor Weiner, Károly Valentiny and Miklós Visontai, *Sztálinváros, Miskolc, Tatabánya. Városépítésünk fejlődése* [Sztálinváros, Miskolc, Tatabánya. The Development of City Building in Hungary since 1945] (Budapest: Műszaki, 1959)

8 Cf. the description of the monumental plan for the city center in: *Építészet és tervezés Magyarországon, 1945–1959* [Architecture and Planning in *Hungary, 1945*–1959], ed. Endre Prakfalvi and Virág Hajdú (Budapest: Országos Műemlékvédelmi Hivatal Magyar Építészeti Múzeum, 1996), 139–41 (only in Hungarian).

9 For example in: *Magyar építészet 1945–1970* [Hungarian Architecture 1945–1970], ed. Jenő Szendrői et al. (Budapest: Corvina, 1972).

10 On the role of artists and works of art in Dunaújváros see: *Acélecset. Művészet az ország közepén* [Steelbrush. Art in the Center of the Country], ed. Tamás Fehérvári (Dunaújváros: Dunaújváros MJV Önkormányzata, 2006). See especially the study by Edit Sasvári, 10–29 (with a short English summary).

11 Unfortunately, the guide is only in Hungarian.

12 Tamás Meggyesi, *A városépítés útjai és tévútjai* [Urban Concepts and Misconcepts in the 20th Century] (Budapest: Műszaki Könyvkiadó, 2005 [1985]), 72.

PROJECTED HAPPINESS

Old Myths and New Ambitions
in a Bucharest Neighborhood

Carmen Popescu

This text explores a seemingly insignificant or marginal aspect of the post-socialist city as far as substance is concerned, analyzing the development of the *Floreasca* district in the north-eastern part of Bucharest from the beginning of the twentieth century onwards. After 1989, few transformations were made to the district and these were introduced slowly, without dramatically altering its image, at least not in an apparent way. The time of radical changes had already taken place with the development of the neighborhood in the socialist years, throughout the nineteen-fifties and at the beginning of the nineteen-sixties, as well as in a later phase in the late nineteen-seventies. The image of the district was formed during those years and—as I will argue below—it was precisely its "labelization" that mattered as far as its later perception was concerned.

However "mild" or barely discernible the changes in the last few years have been, they still represent unmistakable signs of the mutation of post-socialist Romanian society. Due to the "settled" character of the district, these transformations are revealed in a subtle manner; they can be interpreted as a reaction to the socialist system, directed against its centralized urban thinking, but they also result from other factors. Thus, this text deals with architecture and urban form as a material culture, analyzing the ways in which their appropriation expresses specific features of the community that uses them.

For methodological reasons, the article is divided into sections determined by space and time coordinates. This not only allows us to consider the district as a distinctive unity within the body of the city, but also to vary the instruments of analysis as necessary. Thus, while the central role of socialist thinking in the forming of the district (along with its image) becomes clear, the structure of the frame serves to justify the different (methodological) perspectives adopted: a succinct presentation of the "pre-history," an analytical radiography of the different layers of "history," as well as a curious (ethnographic) look at the present. Here again, considering the present as "post-history" is a tongue-in-cheek way of looking at the post-socialist city, reminding us of the connections between modernity and socialist thinking. It also implies that "the end of ideology" is equivalent to "the end of history."[1]

The versatility of the methodological approaches was dictated by the transitional character of post-socialist trends. This specific situation, translated as the reuse of preexisting structures (transformed, adapted, valorized, or depreciated) and the contraction of time horizons (short term strategies able to respond to the needs of transformation/adaptation),[2] is opaque to the "traditional" tools of art history, which I thus converted into an approach related to the new ethnography/anthropology.

Geography

Situated in the northeastern part of Bucharest, Floreasca's boundaries evolved during its various chronological phases (▶ 1). The south part of the district was developed after 1914 as a low-income housing area which, in the nineteen-twenties, was still situated at the periphery of the expanding capital, hence the location of the hippodrome (1922; Paul Smărăndescu)

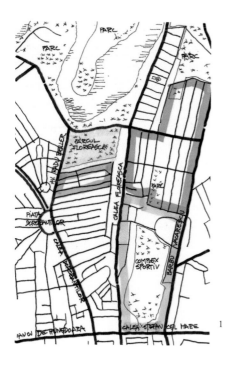

built here by the *National Society for the Improvement of Horse-Breeding*. A decade later, when the society decided to replace the hippodrome with a residential project, the district's boundaries progressed northwards; on the Bucharest map, this project corresponded with the intentions of the newly promulgated Master Plan (1934)[3] to develop the city towards the series of lakes to the north. The socialist neighborhood was built within the street-grid designed at the end of the nineteen-thirties: it is this particular part of the district, mainly shaped in the nineteen-fifties, that came to embody the "label" image of Floreasca.

From the inter-war period onwards, the western limit of the district had a certain versatile character, reflecting the intentions of the urban planners to connect, in one way or another, the elegant residential area of Dorobanți (whose development began in the early part of the twentieth century according the principles of the "garden-city") with the recently created neighborhood of Floreasca. The first concretization of this intention was realized in the early nineteen-sixties when the Floreasca park was designed, and the western limit of the district thus duplicated, since Aviator Radu Beller Street, rather insignificant by then, became an alternative to Calea Floreasca. The role of this street as a border was reinforced in the late nineteen-seventies, in an operation that extended the socialist neighborhood to the "bourgeois" (read capitalist) residential area. As I will argue below, after 1989 this expansion towards the west was to be "canonized" by symbolic means. Since 2000, the district has developed further to the north along Calea Floreasca (with profuse expansion at its eastern side).

1   Map of Floreasca district and surroundings, Bucharest, Romania.

These two extensions that took place after 1989—one virtual, to the west, and the other effective, to the north—were crucial in (slightly) shifting the image of Floreasca into an icon of post-socialism.

Very early on, the peripheral positioning of Floreasca on the city map was perceived as a blessing: at the margins of the crowded capital, but not far from its center, the neighborhood had always benefited from an extremely pleasant natural landscape: lush vegetation (enhancing its "garden-district" character) and beautiful lakes, which were used in various ways. This blessed context propelled Floreasca, in its diverse phases, to the status of the potential starting-point of a new urbanity. Its distinct character, which had set the neighborhood apart since its beginnings, shifted to an image of uniqueness, which was accentuated in the post-socialist years.

Pre-History

The Floreasca of today was formerly part of a large village, Florești upon Colentina, founded in the sixteenth century and composed of three large residential units: Low-, Middle-, and High-Florești. The latter of these was developed into the Floreasca neighborhood.[4] It is probable that the reputation of the future district was forged at the beginning of the eighteenth century, when this piece of land was given (as a wedding gift) to the son of the prince's doctor, Antonache Caliarh-Florescu, who built a residence on the border of the lake for himself and his wife Ancuța (also known as Floreasca), with a garden pavilion for meditation and intimate celebrations.

Today, the only reminders of this era are a small chapel near the residence (restored in 1926 by the architect commissioned with the hippodrome's design) and two streets named after the aristocratic owners.

At the end of the nineteenth century, the village of Floreasca belonged to the larger rural community of Băneasa-Herăstrău, an area with woods and lakes highly valued by the Bucharesters. With a surface of 153 hectares and 174 inhabitants, the village had seven pubs. The chapel was abandoned, and the entire area became overgrown with vegetation.[5] At the turn of the century, the limits of the capital were extended as part of the envisioned measures of modernization. Floreasca started to be developed as a district after the *Communal Society for the Construction of Economic Housing* was founded in 1911. In 1914, the society built its first housing development, with semi-detached two-story houses and a small school (later turned into a kindergarten), whose structure followed the principles of the garden-city, with architecture inspired by local tradition (▶ 2).[6]

After World War One, the built-up area was developed towards the east in a similar project. To the north, the *National Society for the Improvement of Horse-Breeding* commissioned a hippodrome, taking advantage of the geographical position (the meadows of the former village) and the reputation of this northern area as a place for outdoor leisure activities. However the hippodrome was soon to be demolished; in 1937, the society decided to replace it with

a residential project. This decision was certainly motivated by the new urban development of the capital envisioned by the 1934 Master Plan, but probably also by the construction of the Ford plants (1932–34, Emil Miclescu) on the east side of Calea Floreasca, not far from the low-income housing district. A grid of perpendicular streets was traced, the land was parceled and sold to private owners, and the first sparse villas were raised before the beginning of World War Two.

History 1. The Story

The socialist regime inherited this empty grid, purveyed with installations for public lighting and canalization, with a few villas (of no particular architectural merit) scattered here and there. There were cornfields between the streets, and the inhabitants had improvised vegetable gardens around their houses.[7] As a consequence of the frozen economy during the war, but probably also due to the unsolved proximity of the slum known as Groapa Floreasca (Floreasca Dump), which was situated more or less along the perimeter of the future Floreasca Park, the projected residential area did not develop at a normal pace.

Given the context, the municipality did not consider the district to be among the propitious places for embodying the new face of socialist architecture. While Vatra Luminoasă (Alexandru Iotzu and Victor Aslan) and Bucureştii Noi (Nicolae Sburcu and Zoltan Grundl), also situated at the periphery of the capital, were designed in the early nineteen-fifties as vast and articulated compositions of *kvartaly*,[8] Floreasca had a slower and definitely a more modest start.

---

2 Houses built 1914 by the *Communal Society for the Construction of Economic Housing*, Calea Floreasca, Bucharest, Romania, 1994.

The first activities began around 1953, with the realization of a few two- and three-story buildings commissioned by the *Ministry of Agriculture* for its employees, who made a financial contribution to the construction costs. Erected between the existent villas, the small blocks had the same tile roofs, but their composition was otherwise most basic, with long façades deprived of any adornment. In no way did they compare to the elaborate rhetoric of Socialist Realism adopted for the emblematic building projects of the new regime.

Two years later, however, Floreasca became the site of a large-scale construction project of this kind: a new district was envisioned, on thirty-seven hectares, consisting of 2,479 residential units (entirely financed by State funding) and numerous facilities. The general scheme followed the Soviet model: the buildings were grouped in three *kvartaly* formed out of closed urban units of apartment blocks, with Socialist Realist façades.[9] The symbolism of the architecture was but a lure: the neighborhood was not planned to reflect the glorious image of socialism, as did other districts and new towns, but rather to embody the normality of everyday life. Designed at the beginning of the period of ideological relaxation in Romania—which had immediate effects on architecture[10]—the message of Floreasca was no longer heroic but comforting on both a political (public) level and an individual (private) one. Politically, it promoted the new goals relating to the architectural policy, economy and efficiency of the building process and of urban thinking: low-rise blocks of flats (which did not necessitate the use of elevators), composed of repeatable units; for the inhabitants-to-be, the district provided affordable (but modest) homes in a green environment (advertised as such by the chief architect of the project);[11] and—thanks to the numerous facilities—an almost autonomous neighborhood. Hence, Floreasca aspired less to the glorification of the socialist ideal than to the fulfillment of a social idea.

A series of circumstances and factors contributed to the transformation of this ordinary neighborhood into an exemplary one. The most influential of these were the changing political context and the evolution of architecture in the Communist Bloc after the famous speech made by Khrushchev at the 1954 *Constructors' Congress*.

As the project was scheduled on the basis of three successive phases, the architects had the opportunity to reduce the constraints related to the conception and to take advantage of the opportunities presented by the recently adopted norms (▶ 3). The urban units were opened up by suppressing the corner buildings at the close perimeter, thus creating the relaxed appearance of an incipient freedom of disposal, while preserving the advantages of the common courtyard. The buildings lost their Socialist Realist adornments, embracing the minimalist aesthetics of a functional (and economic) architecture: terrace-roofs, simple façades enhanced, only in some cases, by balconies and small porches. The number and character of the facilities slightly evolved towards a lower level of collectivization; the public baths and collective laundry, reminiscent of Stalinist planning, disappeared. Gradually, planning began to conform to a more modern everyday life-style—the working-men's club, initially projected to be built in the middle of the southern *kvartal*, was eventually replaced

3

4

by a trendy cinemascope; on the first floor of the pastry shop a bar was installed, a rarity in socialist Romania (▶ 4).

Moreover, the third *kvartal*, which was added later (1958–60) in the north part of the neighborhood, benefited from special conditions. The appearance of the blocks of flats was amended: the typologies were diversified, (small) balconies became systematic, and the façades interpreted in a simple but suggestive manner vernacular architecture (pitched roofs, red brick decoration, porches with pergolas, et cetera). These transformations were the result both of the relaxation process (which was progressing) and of a shift in social targeting; this third kvartal being destined mostly for the use of the *Central Committee of the Communist Party* employees (such as doctors, nurses, but also drivers, et cetera).

3 Aerial view of the neighborhood, period postcard, Bucharest, Romania.
4 Cinemascope, Bucharest, Romania, 1950s.

Finally, the architect behind the planning of the project constituted another essential factor. If the official coordinator was Corneliu Rădulescu, the main designer seems to have been Virgil Nițulescu, who worked on Rădulescu's team at the *Urban Planning Institute in Bucharest*.[12] Considered one of the most promising of the young generation, Nițulescu had been marginalized for political reasons related to his inflexible deontological position and his explicit adherence to the principles of modernism (proscribed by the Stalinist ideology for its "bourgeois" character). If his career was not entirely broken, it was certainly held back by a permanent subordinate position. The general conception of the Floreasca district benefited from his ideas, inspired both by modernist housing experiments (mostly German *Neue Sachlichkeit*) and recent theories in the field.

Some of the articles published on the construction of the district suggest that the proposed solutions were more daring than the accepted final version. For instance, the realization of the third kvartal was envisioned originally, in 1955, as a "park" parceling with detached villas.[13] Eventually, the accepted formula was a compromise, the villas being replaced by small blocks of flats mimicking a cozier appearance.

History 2. The Mechanics of an Urban Project

The original "banality" of the district turned out to be deceptive. During its realization the project evolved into an exemplary case, for several reasons. The most important of these was the shift in architectural norms: the new direction severely criticized the excesses of Socialist Realism, promoting an economic and competitive way of construction based on the industrialization of the building process. Floreasca was declared an experimental site,[14] applying the demands of the new socialist architecture on a large scale, which led to the construction of some 2,600 apartments in less than a decade, a real achievement for the Romanian architecture of the time. Neither the aesthetic appearance nor the urban disposal were truly groundbreaking, but nevertheless they represented an important step forwards, opening the way towards the more modern solutions to be adopted in the districts built a few years later.

The experimental character of Floreasca's architectural planning was also designed to show that a decent, enjoyable life could be offered to its inhabitants using "modest" solutions. In response to the remarks made by the population,[15] the architects improved the design of the flats after the first construction phase. The next phases featured increased surface areas (within the limits of the economic norms), elements of built-in furniture for the kitchens and the corridors (to ease the problems arising from the lack of space), replacement of the showers with bathtubs, et cetera.[16]

Floreasca was conceived as a model of *micro-raion*, which replaced the Stalinist *kvartal* in Soviet urban planning. A critical response to the rigidity of the latter, the *micro-raion* officially represented the materialization of a new way of socialist urban thinking: "create the best conditions of work, rest and recreation for the entire population."[17] Officially,

5

it perpetuated (and elaborated on) CIAM urbanism:[18] an autonomous unit, but clearly integrated within the body of the city, placing considerable importance on nature. Adopted as the common theme of the "Vth UIA Congress," held in Moscow in 1958, this concept connected the capitalist and socialist blocs in their efforts towards rethinking the shape of post-war urbanity.

The district's autonomy constituted another reason for its exemplarity. The numerous facilities integrated in the three urban units were thought to respond to the primary needs of the population: two schools (one from the first to the eighth grades, the other including a high school), two kindergartens and a day-nursery; a dispensary with various medical cabinets for children and adults; a post office and a savings bank; a modern cinemascope and a pastry shop with a "day-bar"; a small market (with fruit and vegetables from the countryside) and a number of different stores—three general food-stores, three bakeries, three butchers, three groceries, a bookstore, a small general store (selling clothing and furniture items, textiles, cosmetics, and perfume), a tailor, a shoe store, a pharmacy, three tobacconist/newsstand (▶ 5).

A third factor ensuring the success of the district was the vegetation, which was carefully studied and seen as an essential element of the planning. The first aim of the architects was to provide both a healthy and enjoyable environment. Taking advantage of the particular micro-climate of the neighborhood, praised as a major advantage, they planned the district as a "vast park, without closed courtyards."[19] The oppressive feeling engendered by the former *kvartaly*, where private life seemed to be under constant control, was to be amended by the new fluid urban structure, which conciliated private and public spheres. Vegetation played an important role in this process, studied by a team of landscape architects who designed the parks and the green spaces between the blocks of flats.[20]

Two parks were planned: the first in the center of the southern urban unit and the second on the northern boundary of the neighborhood, where the vestiges of the hippodrome had

5   Pastry shop, Bucharest, Romania, 1960s.

been turned into a garbage dump.[21] In designing the parks, particular attention was paid to the playgrounds and installations for children (▶ 6).[22]

The spaces between the blocks of flats were treated as green squares, with alleys and benches, swings for the children, and practical devices for the households, thus combining necessity with leisure. Stripes of lawn bordered the main façades of the blocks, while trees were planted all along the streets. Initially, each street was to be differentiated with a variety of trees: chestnuts, elms, linden-trees, et cetera; on the same principle, each entrance was individualized by diverse decorative shrubs: jasmine, lilac, roses, et cetera.[23] Hence, the uniform aspect of the architectural composition was enlivened by adding the picturesque touch of various types of vegetation. This approach was in keeping with the preoccupation of Romanian architects with finding remedies against the monotony of repetitive modernist aesthetics.[24]

The diversified unity of the ensemble, the balance between symmetrical and free structures, was designed to create a harmonious composition. The image also responded to the demands of socialist urbanism: in their writings, the Soviet architects of the time compared the urban composition, with its interdependence between the various parts and the whole, to symphonic music.[25] Symptomatically, the streets of the new district were named, with few

6 Playground equipment for children, Bucharest, Romania, 1950s.

exceptions, after famous composers, including: Bach, Beethoven, Mozart, Chopin, Strauss, Tchaikovsky, Rachmaninov, Glinka, Verdi, Puccini, Donizetti, Rossini, Bizet, and Bartok.

History 3. Living in Eu-topia

Such a striving towards harmony was barely dissimulating the utopic mechanics that activated the ideology of the time. At the beginning of this "pragmatic" phase of socialism, it resonated with the echo of the heroic ideals of building a new world. It was probably these mechanics that provided inspiration for the writer George Călinescu, who took the building of Floreasca as the subject of his novel, *Scrinul Negru* (The Black Chest, 1965). Set in the large area of the neighborhood (on the grounds of the former village), the novel explores the inevitable tensions engendered by the creation of a new society: the capitalist reminiscences are embodied by decrepit aristocrats forced to live in the miserable huts around the old chapel, while the construction of the socialist district epitomizes the birth of the new world, with its vigor (the dynamics of the building site) and beauty (its harmonic structure). The book describes the transfiguration of the new district, which appears as having almost miraculously "burst out of the soil," its harmonic structure forming an "architectural landscape created for the pleasure of the eyes," a place of "joy and calm."[26]

This glorious image—Émile Zola's *Cité heureuse*, revisited by the aesthetic principles of Socialist Realism—represented a literary license coupled with a political hint. Călinescu, who lived in a small house across the road from the new district, attempted to capture the spirit of the urban project: a place for good living, reinterpreting in what could have seemed a banal setting the great myths of the communist utopia—the new world, the golden age, eternal youth.

In spite of its ordinary appearance, Floreasca embodied such a model of eu-topic life. If not (always) for the same reasons, the new district thus became an iconic image, praised by the political officials, very well received by the architectural milieu and, above all, highly appreciated by the population. Its iconicity was fabricated by the intensive use of its image, disseminated by all the media of the time. The urban project of Floreasca was presented in numerous architectural shows abroad,[27] published abundantly in the pages of the specialized journal *Arhitectura RPR* (The Architecture of the Romanian People's Republic), and used to illustrate several entries of the new Bucharest city guide (▶ 5).[28]

Symptomatically paralleled with the prestigious (but much larger) operation on the Black Sea coast,[29] in the perspective of the politicians the district capitalized on a number of advantages. Less glamorous than the resorts at the seaside, it corresponded instead with everyday reality, thus making life in a socialist society appear more valuable. The fact that it was constructed partially on the site of a slum made the *topos* of a new world rising up from the debris of the capitalist regime convincing: the contrasting images of the district, before and after, were abundantly circulated in newspapers, newsreels, and TV documentaries.

In the eyes of architects, Floreasca's exemplarity was reflected by its experimental character, but also by its "normality," proving that ideas could be put into practice and function outside of the rhetoric of ideological discourse. If innovations were limited both by the economic norms and censoring ideology, the project was appreciated for other reasons, such as its capacity for integration, i.e., the harmonious relationship created between built and natural landscapes, a topic that was being widely discussed all over the world at the time. The integration of older architectural structures represented a delicate subject[30] in the political context of the period. In Floreasca, this matter was fortunately resolved by the economic principles that ruled the entire planning process:[31] had the architects not been placed under the constraint of preserving the preexisting pattern of streets, the disposal of the buildings would probably have been closer to the free urbanism of post-war modernism.

The sense of continuity resulting from this integration had an essential impact on the inhabitants of the new district. The vicinity of the pre-1945 housing developments, the continuing presence of the "bourgeois" villas, the preservation of the traditional street-gridding and the active part played by nature all converged to provide an enjoyable environment, where the new socialist space was no longer built on the denial of the values of the past. The structure of properties, a mix of rented apartments (approximately nine-tenths of the buildings) and privately-owned ones, also provided a certain sense of continuity.

Inhabited by over 10,000 people, the new district seemed to be the home of a large family. Most of those who moved here were working in the same institutions, and had thus already formed friendships at their workplace. Moreover, most of them were young, which contributed ideally with the eu-topical nature of Floreasca. If the neighborhood was not a source of eternal youth, it was certainly an ideal place for the happy young people of the present to live (▶ 7).

History 4. Addenda

Like many other districts built at the time, in the east and west alike, Floreasca appeared to signify the personification of everyday happiness.[32] Moreover, like Novye Cheremushki (1956–57, Nathan Osterman et alii), the muscovite district that certainly influenced Romanian architects, it was an urban icon.[33] Built more or less during the same period, both were experimental projects that subsequently became "household names,"[34] and both were the inspiration for works of art.

The iconicity of Floreasca was increased by a further related project, realized at the beginning of the nineteen-sixties (Victor Agent et alii).[35] The former Floreasca Dump was removed and replaced by a vast park, whose contemporary design was enhanced by a display of statues by some of the avant-garde sculptors of the time. This park was bordered to the east by a skating-rink and to the south by six tower-like residential buildings, thirteen stories high (▶ 8). The affirmed modernity of the ensemble was also enhanced by the Floreasca Hall of Sports (1949, Titu Evolceanu et alii), a key edifice of Romanian architecture before its Stalinization, which stood opposite the park to the west.

7

8

9

10

7   Young family in the park, Bucharest, Romania, 1961.
8   Skating rink, Bucharest, Romania, 1960s.
9   Herd of goats across Barbu Văcărescu Street, Bucharest, Romania, 1963.
10 The sports hall of the high school, Bucharest, Romania, 1960s.

In spite of its popularity—in the late nineteen-sixties and -seventies, the district featured in movies and TV dramas, long after its architectural fame started to diminish—Floreasca was a place of contrasts.

To the north, the district was juxtaposed with the vestiges of the old village, which was progressively transformed into a garbage dump in the twentieth century; a large terrain vague (whose construction was not begun until the nineteen-nineties) bordered it to the east. This unfinished character, the mixture of built landscape and untamed nature, was a permanent feature of the neighborhood. After the war and during the nineteen-fifties, the inhabitants of the villas continued to buy fresh milk from a woman who had a cow and lived in a cottage near the stables of the former hippodrome.[36] Later on, when the area was redesigned as Verdi Park, shepherds continued coming here until the nineteen-eighties. In the nineteen-sixties, on the arid land of the terrain vague across Barbu Văcărescu Street, children played with goats and sheep (▶ 9). The duration of the building site and the disruption it entailed created a certain lack of homogeneity in the neighborhood. One inhabitant, living in a villa in the northern part of the district, which was developed in the last construction phase, relates that in the early nineteen-sixties her children referred to going to the recently built cinema as "going into the city."[37]

The other contrasting aspect of the neighborhood was related to the ambiguity of its social composition. On the one hand, there were subtle stratifications in the community. Its inhabitants neither belonged to the working class—the prototype of the "new man"—nor to the numbers of the "happy few"—the population was mixed, with a slight predominance of white-collar workers. In the beginning, the leveling factor was an affiliation to the same institution, which compensated for this stratification. After years of living together, a certain sense of community developed, enhanced by the common use of public spaces, particularly the parks and the squares between the blocks of flats. On the other hand, the inhabitants of the third urban unit were not "ordinary" people like their neighbors: the fact that they worked for the *Central Committee* made them a privileged class. In spite of their belonging to the low hierarchy of the privileged, their presence created a certain aura in the district.

Symptomatically, the school located in this northern part of Floreasca was declared an experimental school for the intensive teaching of English, which implied not only phonetic laboratories but also teachers invited from the United States and Great Britain. The founding year of the new program is also symptomatic; the first English classes started in the autumn of 1968. Reputed for its high standard of teaching, but also for its "cool" attitude, the school attracted pupils from all over the capital and, of course, some of the *nomenklatura's* offspring.

In addition to vast grounds, the school—published as an exemplary building in *Arhitectura RPR*[38]—had a multipurpose annex, used as a community center (the first cinema of the neighborhood was located here) and as an indoor sports hall during bad weather (▶ 10).

In 1973, an open-air swimming pool was added, which fell into disrepair in the nineteen-eighties.

Around 1980, the number of the "privileged" suddenly increased when blocks of flats were built on a small perimeter situated between the Floreasca district and the elegant Dorobanți (where most of the prominent figures of the regime resided). A little further to the south an "alimentary complex" was erected: given the shortages imposed by the harshening politics of the regime in those years, these buildings were known as "temples" or "circuses" (depending on their architectural scheme) "of hunger."

Post-History. Big Changes or Small Transformations?

Thus was the heritage of the district in 1990.

Its reputation had somehow faded, although it had not completely disappeared. Its inhabitants still enjoyed living here, and on the rare occasions that someone moved away, this was most often due to the limited size of the flats. This led to a stable population, which actually grew old at the same time as its environment.

The dynamics of the changes observed after 1989 were rather unspectacular, and the general impression given by the neighborhood in the first half of the nineteen-nineties was that of

11   The former pastry shop transformed into a grocery store, Bucharest, Romania, 2009.

slow decay. The well-balanced system of stores disappeared, and new structures were not only scarce but of poor quality. The infrastructure was almost deserted, while the population was mainly made up of elderly people, often disoriented by the new system for which they had been waiting for so long.

Any "small transformations" that were introduced in the "micro world of day-to-day life," i.e., in the neighborhood, were symptomatic of the mechanics of society in general, of the macro-structure.[39]

Naturally, the first changes concerned the former socialist commercial system. The privatization process began almost at the same time, but with a far slower and much more complicated evolution. Partly as a consequence of these two processes, but also as a result of the general transformation undergone by the Romanian capital in the nineteen-nineties, a third type of change affected the neighborhood: a process of gentrification. The three processes had separate dynamics and sometimes followed parallel tracks; however, their evolution was often intermingled, even though their effects differed.

Post-Socialist Consumerism

The socialist stores were not only privatized, but in many cases there was a change in the range of goods they stocked. This progressive process led to a drastic reduction in the number of actual stores. The most affected were the food stores, which disappeared with the exception of one bakery. Meanwhile, the elegant nineteen-sixties pastry shop regressed into a sort of grocery store, selling an improbable mixture of goods ranging from bottled beer, sunflower oil, vegetables, and sweets to underwear and pajamas (▶ 11). The former "temple of hunger" was transformed into a mini "mall" housing a (short-lived) supermarket.

The former small shops were turned into offices or services, until the neighborhood was gradually deprived of its (partial) autonomy. Moreover, the cultural (and consequently the communal) life of the district suffered when the cinema was closed at the end of the nineteen-nineties. This decision was probably due to the lack of state subventions, but also to some hidden economic private interests reflected in the various attempts at reconversion, for example as a bingo hall, a destination that was symptomatic for the troubled economic situation during that period. Finally, its transformation into a discotheque proved successful—if the new destination did not really benefit the life of the district, it certainly boosted its glamorous image.

At the end of the nineteen-nineties, and particularly after 2000, Floreasca entered a new era of glamour, partly related to its gentrification. This repositioning on the social map of Bucharest had an immediate effect on the nature of the commercial and service spaces, targeting a wealthier population. Successive attempts were made at establishing (expensive) stores, while three of the former food stores were replaced with banks. In their stead, new gastronomic outlets appeared—ranging from fast-food to "chic" restaurants, their aim was clearly to provide "hype," if not always of an exclusive kind.

This gradual (but constant) "glamorization" of the neighborhood projected a cone of shadow on the less prosperous part of the population. Very few of the new structures took this large mass into consideration. Apart from the grocery store mentioned above, and a few kiosks, the most prominent example of these was a second-hand shop (recently closed), which mainly proved successful with the many pensioners living in the district.

But the big change in terms of commercial structure was brought about by the opening of two large supermarkets. This huge undertaking should be seen in relation to the late revitalization of Floreasca's potential. The urban criteria,[40] which should apply to this type of store, were deliberately ignored for economic reasons that seemed to be justified by the particular situation of the district.[41] Indeed, the two stores were opened on the wasteland that had for years bordered Barbu Văcărescu Street, a rather wide urban road leading to the city center and linking the district with the expanding north section of the capital. Apart from the favorable circumstances, the labelization of the district—as a latent consumerist area—certainly played a role in the choice.

The opening of the supermarkets marked a significant change, both on the urban level (a rupture in the traditional fabric of the urban space on a huge scale, accompanied by equally vast parking spaces) and at the societal level (new consumer behavior). Even the less privileged inhabitants of the neighborhood became regular clients of these commercial paradises. If the concurrence between the two supermarkets benefited the population, the image of the district certainly profited at least as much. This was an image that, as in the old socialist days, was not so much glamorous (as projected by the new elite who moved there), but reflected the "good life," with consumerism as its key. Happy people strolling along the alleys of the supermarkets with their (more or less) full shopping trolleys, against the acoustic background of happy music inviting them to buy more—an image as beautiful as the happy new man promoted by the former socialist regime. As beautiful as a TV commercial.

Privatizing Public Spaces

The process of privatization developed at various levels and followed several directions. The most significant of these was the privatization of the state-owned apartments, which were sold to their tenants. However—as elsewhere in the country—the reprivatization of the formerly nationalized dwellings proved to be a much longer and more complicated process. Albeit for different reasons, the privatization of sections of public space—mainly referring to the common open yards between the blocks of flats—also posed a problem. Where real estate interests requested it, the land was partially split up and sold to private owners.[42] On the sections sold, with one exception, only residential buildings were raised—multistory blocks of flats and individual villas. The new dwellings were clearly meant to represent a life of ease. The blocks of flats promised high modern standards (even if their windows were frequently far less than the quoted distance away from the modest, uniform socialist façades

12

neighboring them), while the villas, hidden behind high fences, profusely displayed all the characteristics of the new "capitalist realist" architecture.[43]

The harmonic structure conceived by the team of architects who designed the district in the nineteen-fifties was dismantled, little by little, by interventions which neglected any attempt at integration. Paradoxically, Floreasca was the victim of its success during the socialist years. The residential focus of the densification reflected its high position on the new list of real estate values. The municipal services closed their eyes at the new commissioners' irregularities; the mayor of the local urban jurisdiction pretended to take a closer control of the situation, taking advantage of the fluctuant and ambiguous regulation of the green spaces.[44] However, in spite of the public billboard installed in 2006, ostensibly showing the zonal plan of Floreasca, there was neither halt in the diminishing of communal property, nor in the dismantling of the urban structure of the district. The high school lost part of its sports ground, which was split up into sections: the new dwellings built here represented a strategic investment, due to the close proximity of Verdi Park (▶ 12). The park itself was under risk of becoming privatized and built up as a residential area, an undertaking that was eventually frozen.

The most famous case of the privatization of Floreasca's green space was linked with Elena Udrea, a disputed figure of the Democrat Liberal Party.[45] Udrea bought a parcel of land

12 The new villas built around it, Bucharest, Romania, 2009.

situated at the perimeter of an open yard and obtained permission to build a block of flats. The neighbors, organized in associations, protested immediately against the planned construction and the engendered damages, such as the cutting down of twenty trees in the yard and the ensuing loss of visibility and light for the surrounding buildings. In the meantime, the owner of an adjacent parcel of land was not allowed to take back his property, since the municipality considered it a green space. Questioned on Udrea's case, the chief architect of the local urban jurisdiction replied that "not all pieces of land where trees and grass are growing can be automatically considered as green space." As a result, a full-page article was published in one of the most influential national newspapers; one week later, a short note, accompanied by a photo, informed the readers of the same newspaper that the politician had already started to cut down the trees on her parcel.[46]

Another process of privatization developed parallel to the main stream, implying the recuperation or transfer of property. More subtle, and thus insidious, it evolved around two poles: affirming the individuality of the owner and appropriating public space. Both of these manifestations were meant to domesticate what was perceived (and experienced) as standardized life. Hence, their original motivation was not that of recovering privacy after the reign of (controlled) publicity, but of differentiating the individual from the mass.

The yearning for individualization, combined with a progressive social demarcation, transformed the uniform façades of the blocks of flats into patchworks of diverse patterns: window frames, iron lattices and balustrades, closed balconies, et cetera (▶ 13). Through their diversity of material, shapes, and color, they sometimes became clear indices of the owner's fortune, for example in the case of Termopan window frames, the chimneys of individual heating systems, or the ventilation for air conditioning.

Hence, a new symbolism of representation invaded the post-socialist city, architecture being reduced to the role of a support mechanism.

But the former tenants, who had meanwhile become private owners, also expanded their activities to incorporate the collective space allotted to their dwellings. The stripes of greenery in front of the blocks were systematically closed in with trellises and grilles of various shapes and sizes, to delineate what was seen as a personal garden (belonging to the community living in the block) from the public space of the sidewalk. The same type of fences proliferated in the open backyards, where they partitioned off certain areas such as the place for garbage bins, but also small parcels of land appropriated by the most "individualistic" members of the community (▶ 14).

Apart from being an explicit sign of property (due to their very function), fences also became a symbol of orderly attention to detail.[47] Soon, besides private owners competing in the size and decorative elaboration of their enclosure, public instances also began to increase their displays of border definition. An impressive but useless fence was raised in front of the main façade of the school in the southern section. The park in the center of the district had its lawns surrounded by metal grilles, carefully painted; and as in many other parks in

Bucharest, the fathers of the local urban jurisdiction put up a board drawing attention to the care they had taken, just in case the inhabitants had missed the meaning of their fencing project (▶ 15).

And in Floreasca Park, the minimalist nature of what was conceived as a piece of modernist landscaping was turned into an exuberant festival of vegetal species, crowned with a giant flower clock (▶ 16).

Regardless of their particular manifestation, all the cases discussed above deny the concept of public space as defined by modernist thinking. The correction of the decried "anonymous" socialization maintained and controlled by the socialist state is undertaken by imposing the rules of the individual/community—an attitude that implies a sort of return to rurality, a societal governance concept, blurring the limits between privacy and publicity. Meanwhile, the new buildings, whether they be villas embodying the notion of property as a "place to hide"[48] or the spacious flat in a "high-standing" block, introduce a new form of (anti-) urbanity, which is obviously postmodern, since it obeys the logic of the fragment,

13   14

13   Patterns on window frames, Garibaldi Street, Bucharest, Romania, 2009.
14   Fencing in public spaces: common yard, Aghires/Garibaldi Street, Bucharest, Romania, 2009.

15

16

15 Beautification: grilles and marble fountain in the cinema park, Bucharest, Romania, 2009.
16 Floral clock in Floreasca Park, Bucharest, Romania, 2009

its scope being to create a viable microcosm (the extreme expression of which would be the "gated community"). Disregarding integration in almost all cases, these microcosms deliberately ignore the unity of the macro urban structures.

Hence, the revenge of "privatization" reflects the failure of what was believed to be the material transposition of communist society. This failure of modernism seems to amount to the collapse of modernity itself, another symptom of the "end of history."

It is not that the "new man" disappeared; but that the modern man ceased to exist.

A New Varnish for an Old Icon: Gentrification of the Neighborhood

The illusion of a classless society[49] was quickly relinquished after 1989. The urban structures of the socialist regime, whose composition with regards to population was carefully controlled by the Party,[50] started to reveal their breaches, which grew progressively wider.

Behind the pretension of social uniformity, socialist Floreasca had already experienced these breaches, arising between owners and tenants; between those living in the tiny one-bedroom apartments designed in the first building phase and those enjoying the benefits of a more spacious, two-bedroom apartment built in the later periods; between the inhabitants of socialist blocks of flats and those living in "bourgeois" villas. And, above all, between "normal" employees and the "elite" serving in the *Central Committee*. If 1989 erased this last discrepancy, along with the property regime, it caused new social demarcations to arise.

The process of gentrification was fueled by two different motives. On the one hand, Floreasca benefited from the successful image gained in the socialist years, which now became even more attractive due to the increased dynamics of the real estate market. This attractiveness was reinforced, on the other hand, by a change in the mapping of this market, whose focus shifted to the north of the capital. Copying the model of developed metropolises, the new moneyed elites started to migrate out of the city, favoring the suburbs in this area, which was already reputed for its climatic and leisure qualities. Thus they forced the emergence of a new urbanity, which was neither adapted to nor necessary for the Romanian realities of the time, but which, paradoxically, constituted in a certain manner a continuation of the tendency announced by the 1934 Master Plan. Floreasca, situated close to the urbanized limit of the socialist city, was caught up in the maelstrom of these changes. If the neighborhood itself did not allow significant construction activities to be carried out, building fever inflamed two of its vicinities instead, both of which possessed a hybrid structure reminiscent of the inter-war slum-like peripheries. In the narrow streets linking Calea Floreasca with the chic area of Dorobanți, many of the tiny houses were demolished and replaced with "luxury" apartments; meanwhile, more lavish dwellings along with small terraced villas emerged in the former core of Floreasca village. Both building operations had an impact on Floreasca, increasing its gentrification.

It is not clear if the newcomers praised the neighborhood for its acknowledged quality of life or for its newly boosted real estate value. The fanciness of the Dorobanți/Beller neighborhoods contaminated Floreasca as well, with new places opening to cater for an "elite" clientele. The former bookshop was turned into a fashionable minimalist café, attracting large groups of wealthy young people at all the times of the day, whatever the season (▶ 17). The magnate who enriched himself by selling parcels of land in the northern suburbs bought a part of the former "Temple of Hunger" and opened a luxury restaurant there, with potted topiary, statues and bodyguards at its entrance. Ceaușescu, who was said to be the originator of the "hunger temples/circuses," would have been astounded by the shift in his concept. The earliest of these cafés/restaurants is also the most popular: installed on the foundations of the former public toilets in Floreasca Park—and hence nicknamed "At the two closets"— it has become the meeting place for the *nouveaux riches*, who gather there to show off their exclusive accessories. Their considerable presence in the area inspired the media to pin down the nouveau-riche populace as a distinct species, scornfully labeled as the "Dorobanți gross/Dorobantio ostentativus."[51]

This self-proclaimed "elite" now has its own magazine, entitled *Băneasa, free neighborhood guide*. The first issue published a map of "the zone where the Bucharest high-class chose to live"; surprisingly, this area also includes Floreasca.[52] The district is thus acknowledged as an icon of post-socialist glamour.

Conclusion: A Set of Questions

The inclusion of Floreasca in this new mapping of a trendy, upmarket Bucharest is rather paradoxical.

Offering mainly modest-looking blocks of flats, built according to socialist principles, Floreasca does not really personify the lavish image promised by the new architectural standards, as advertised by glossy magazines and catchy billboards. Moreover, its gentrification remains superficial—the main part of its population is, as much as its architecture, a "vestige" of socialist times, while the new moneyed inhabitants who have installed themselves here are neither very numerous nor extremely wealthy. Finally, its leisure/commercial potential is limited—the new stores and services have decreased in number and, in spite of being a good showcase of contemporary aspirations, they are not among the top luxury establishments of the moment.

So what is it that makes Floreasca so desirable? The most probable answer resides in the affordability of the myth: under the socialist regime, it already embodied a rather pragmatic reconversion of unattainable utopia into a concrete, enjoyable eu-topia. But is this approach still viable in contemporary times? What is the value of eu-topia today? The project of "public happiness," the aim of communism, seems to have been replaced by the happiness of the "happy few"—presented as an ideal for the "ordinary" citizen to strive towards. This also explains the "beautification" operations carried out by the municipality: although the fathers of the sector deliberately left the cinema to perish, they built an out-of-scale fountain in front of it, covered with marble. Sitting on the benches surrounding it, the "traditional" inhabitants of the district can now sympathize with the young moneyed people sipping their drinks, two hundred meters away.

However, what Floreasca has to offer seems to be more than mere consumerism, pointing to the desirable state of "luxe, calme et volupté." There is an ambiguous note to all of this, blurring the line between reality and projection. The hyped new generation appears to have restored, on an imaginary level, what could be called the "aura" of the district. An image cleansed from political conjectures.

But is there such a thing as a space that bears no mark of politics?

17

17   The terrace of the café situated in the former bookshop, Bucharest, Romania, 2009.

Endnotes

1 Michael Burawoy and Katherine Verdery, "Introduction," in *Uncertain Transition. Ethnographies of Change in the Postsocialist World*, ed. Burawoy and Verdery (Lanham et al.: Rowman and Littlefield Publishers, 1999), 1–17, here 1.

2 Burawoy/Verdery, (see note 1), 2–3.

3 See: Luminiţa Machedon and Ernie Scoffham, *Romanian Modernism. The Architecture of Bucharest 1920–1940* (Cambridge, Mass.: MIT Press, 1999), 82–87.

4 Nicolae Stoicescu, "Un valoros monument de artă din Bucureşti. Biserica Floreasca," [A Valuable Bucharest Art Monument. The Floreasca Church] *Glasul Bisericii* 18 (1989:6): 141–55.

5 Stoicescu, (see note 4), 151.

6 See: Nicolae Lascu, "Legislaţie şi dezvoltare urbană," [Legislation and Urban Development] (PhD dissertation, University of Architecture, Bucharest, 1997).

7 Interview with Florica Vasilescu, inhabitant of the district, summer 2004.

8 The *kvartal* was the basic unit of Soviet urban planning; see: Jean-Louis Cohen, "La forme urbaine du réalisme socialiste," in *URSS 1917–1978: La ville, l'architecture*, ed. Jean-Louis Cohen, Marco de Michelis and Manfredo Tafuri (Paris/Rome: L'Equerre Editeur/Officina edizioni, 1979), 140–97.

9 Corneliu Rădulescu, "Cartierul de locuinţe Floreasca," [Floreasca Residential Neighborhood] *Arhitectura RPR* (1955:8): 3–5.

10 See: Carmen Popescu, "Looking West: Emulation and Imitation in Romanian Architectural Discourse," *Journal of Architecture* 14 (2009:1): 109–28.

11 Rădulescu, (see note 9).

12 Interview with Alexandru Beldiman, September 2008. See also: Ion Mircea Enescu, "Anatomia unor vremuri abominabile," [The Anatomy of an Abominable Period] in *Arhitecţi în timpul dictaturii* [The Architects in the Time of Dictatorship], ed. Viorica Iuga Curea (Bucureşti: Simetria, 2005), 29–91, here 42, 68.

13 Rădulescu, (see note 9).

14 Corneliu Rădulescu, "Cartierul de locuinţe Floreasca-Bucureşti," [Floreasca-Bucharest Residential Neighborhood] *Arhitectura RPR* (1957:7): 28–29.

15 Rădulescu, (see note 14), 28.

16 Corneliu Rădulescu, "Cartierul de locuinţe Floreasca," [Floreasca Residential Neighborhood] *Arhitectura RPR* (1958:12): 8–11.

17 Alexandru Budişteanu and Romeo Rău, "Microraionul—element esenţial în sistematizarea oraşelor noastre," [The Micro-Raion—an Essential Element in the Systematization of Our Cities] *Arhitectura RPR* (1960:6): 22–25, here 22.

18 See: Juliana Maxim, "Mass Housing and Collective Experience: On the Notion of *Microraion* in Romania in the 1950s and 1960s," *Journal of Architecture* 14 (2009:1): 7–26.

19 Rădulescu, (see note 14).

20 "Plantaţii in cartierul Floreasca Bucureşti," [Plantations in the Floreasca Neighborhood Bucharest] *Arhitectura RPR* (1957:7): 4–5.

21 Rădulescu, (see note 9).

22 See note 20.

23 See note 20.

24 On combating architectural monotony through the use of plantations, see: Rică Marcus, "Parcuri şi amenajări sportive," [Parks and Sport Installations] *Arhitectura RPR* (1957:7): 2–3. The article was the editorial of a special issue dedicated to parks and plantations, where Floreasca figured as an exemplary case.

25 See: Georgii Minervin and M. Fedorov, "Despre calităţile estetice ale construcţiei de masă," [On the Aesthetic Qualities of Mass Construction] *Arhitectura RPR* (1958:5): 23–25.

26 *Scrinul Negru* [Black Chest] (Bucharest: Editura de Stat pentru Literatură şi Artă, 1960), 605–07.

27 Among which the large exhibition organized for the Vth UIA in Moscow, in 1958; See: "Al V-lea Congres al Uniunii Internaţionale a Arhiteţilor," [The Vth Congress of the International Union of Architects] *Arhitectura RPR* (1958:7): 16–20

28 *Bucureşti. Ghid* [Bucharest. Guide] (Bucharest: Ed. Meridiane, 1962).

29 The modernization of the Black Sea coast was undoubtedly the most iconic operation, which gave Romanian architecture of the time a name abroad (see note 10). For the parallel with Floreasca, see "Sarcinile ce revin arhitecţilor in vederea aplicarii hotaririlor plenarei Comitetului

Central al PMR din 26-28 noiembrie 1958. Referatul biroului UA la Plenara a V-a," [The Report of the Union of Architects Board at the Vth Plenary] *Arhitectura RPR* 7 (1959:1): 5–11, here 7.

30 For the difficulties of integrating the Socialist Realist architecture in a preexistent inter-war housing development see: Nicolae Sburcu, "Locuințe noi în cartierul Vatra Luminoasă-București," [New Dwellings in the Vatra Luminoasă Neighborhood] *Arhitectura RPR* (1954:9): 19–25, here 20.

31 See note 20.

32 Cor Wagenaar, "Cities and the Pursuit of Public Happiness. An Introduction," in *Happy: Cities and Public Happiness in Post-War Europe*, ed. Cor Wagenaar (Rotterdam: NAI Publishers, 2004), 14–23.

33 Pictures of Novye Cheremushki were published in connection with the Vth Congress UIA in Moscow, "Congresul al V-lea UIA Moscova iulie 1958," [The Vth Congress UIA Moscow July 1958] *Arhitectura RPR* (1958:10-11): 61–66, here 63.

34 Iurii Gerchuk, "The Aesthetics of Everyday Life in the Khrushchev Thaw in the USSR (1954–1964)," in *Style and Socialism. Modernity and Material Culture in Post-War Eastern Europe*, ed. Susan E. Reid and David Crowley (Oxford/New York: Berg, 2000), 81–100, here 88.

35 Victor Agent, "Blocuri-punct cu 12 niveluri in parcul Floreasca," [12 Stories Tower-Blocks of Flats in the Floreasca Park] *Arhitectura RPR* (1963:12): 18–21.

36 Interview with Florica Vasilescu.

37 Interview with Florica Vasilescu.

38 Dan Bacalu and Gabriel Cristea, "Noile școli cu 24 de clase, construite în București," [The New Bucharest Schools with 24 Class-Rooms] *Arhitectura RPR* (1960:1): 30–34.

39 Burawoy/Verdery, (see note 1), 1.

40 For the locational practices of supermarkets, see: Konstantin Axenov, Isolde Brade and Evgenij Bondarchuk, *The Transformation of Urban Space in Post-Soviet Russia* (London/New York: Routledge, 2006), 159–63.

41 On the lack of regulation, see: Asociația Salvați Bucureștiul, "Bucureștiul, un dezastru urbanistic," [Bucharest—an Urban Disaster]

no. 22 (supplement), March 18, 2008, 3–8.

42 Asociația Salvați Bucureștiul, (see note 41), 4.

43 See: Carmen Popescu, "Realismul capitalist. Rapidă incursiune prin parcurile bucureștene," [The Capitalist Realism. Quick Walk Through the Parks in Bucharest] *Dilema*, September 28, 2008. By capitalist realism I designate the architectural vocabulary forged after 1989, under the pressure of the commissioners, meant to display their social status by an eclectic mixture of prestigious references (columns, balustrades, gables, et cetera).

44 The Emergency Ordinance 195/2005 forbade the construction on green spaces; however, a year later, the law 265/2006 modified the article related to the property regime, opening the door to possible interpretations. As stated by the law 24/2007 (article 23) the situation remained ambiguous.

45 Tiberiu Lovin, "Elena Udrea plantează un bloc în loc de copaci," [Elena Udrea Plants a Block of Flats Instead of Trees] *România Liberă*, April 17, 2008.

46 The caption reads: "The Photo of the Day: One Cut Tree, One Planted Block," *România Liberă*, April 24, 2008.

47 Popescu, (see note 43).

48 Hannah Arendt, *The Human Condition* (Chicago/London: The University of Chicago Press, 2 1998), 71.

49 Hannah Arendt, *The Origins of Totalitarianism* (New York: Harcourt, Brace and Co., 1951).

50 Ștefan Ghenciulescu, "Everyone's Space, Someone's Space, No One's Space," in *Lost in Space*, ed. Augustin Ioan (Bucharest: NEC, 2003), 398–429.

51 This was the result of a recent campaign launched by Radio Guerilla in favor of urbane comportment. For a presentation of the various "species" see: http://byrev.blog-u.net/idei-bune/atlas-de-mitocanie-urbana-video-specii-rare-din-fauna-urbana.html (last accessed January 3, 2010). The campaign led to the publication of the book *Atlas de mitocănie urbană* [A Guide to Parvenus' Places] (Bucharest: Editura ART, 2009).

52 *Băneasa, Free Neighborhood Guide*, February 2009, 17.

BUCHAREST AS A BATTLE-GROUND, 1989–2009

Augustin Ioan

You are sure to have heard of Bucharest, the curious capital city of Romania. It is there that the last communist president, Nicolae Ceauşescu, decided to

    a) demolish 485 hectares of downtown neighborhoods;

    b) build the "House of the Republic," not only the second-largest building in the world but also the most architecturally retarded official building of the nineteen-eighties;

    c) lay a most impressive boulevard commemorating the Victory of Socialism which, quite appropriately, leads from nowhere to nowhere, stretching more than five kilometers through the demolished area.

In the process, not only did entire neighborhoods disappear, but churches and monasteries were demolished or moved to other locations. An impressive feat, it must be said. And, even more extraordinarily, the story doesn't end in 1989. Most of the blocks of flats along the boulevard have been completed, privatized, and now cost a fortune (of course, the word "socialism" has disappeared from the boulevard's name); the House is still under construction (and is already in need of renovation), while the demolished areas to the left and right of the boulevard are in precisely the same state of dereliction as they were in 1990, if not worse. In the meantime, we have experienced our own version of real estate boom, but the bubble has finally burst, propelling Bucharest from a communist borough with monumental aims to a post-socialist battleground with gated communities at its outskirts. Money has come and gone.

And here we are in 2009. This is not an academic text, but a synopsis of a 2008 public intervention regarding the city's future. It is my city and I am involved with its fate not only as an architect, but also as an (adopted) citizen of its rather peculiar structure.

Recently, one of the main topics of discussion among Bucharest's intelligentsia has become the urban disaster that is the downtown area.[1] *The Pact for Bucharest* has been published by several NGOs, only one of which counts a few professional urban planners and a very few architects among its members, while the overwhelming majority are just concerned citizens. Although this in itself is not a problem, it does explain why some of the demands issued in this manifesto, though motivated by good intentions, are impaired by a considerable lack of expertise in the field.[2] Needless to say, the professional architectural associations themselves, having produced no urban policies of their own, now complain about being ignored by the "fathers" of the city.

One would expect such a manifesto concerning the future of Bucharest to be taken into account by candidates for various positions in the local administration in 2008, and also by the new mayor (a *politician-cum-surgeon* with absolutely no previous expertise in city management) and the Local Council after the respective elections. Needless to say, at the time of this writing, this has not happened.

Obviously, this is a matter of faith, not politics: post-1989 Romanian civil society cannot help but crumble when faced with administration and/or politicians. The issues raised in this manifesto (with a bigger splash in various blogs than in public spaces) are considerably more serious than the ones discussed in this essay. The urban disaster of Bucharest did not happen in a day. Had the cultural domain been in any way open to architects and city planners, towards publicizing and debating their proposals to "fix" this city—few though the good ones were—these proposals could have had some positive effect by now.

The Pact for Bucharest is a text written by amateurs for politicians. It is a pretentious text (despite the presence among its signatories of a small number of extremely good and active architects and educators in the field), a collection of good intentions, passionately expressed and applied to empirical data without any mention of causes. The solutions offered range from the viable to the hilarious, many verging on sheer impractical naiveté. The willfulness of the text stands in lieu of expertise, or even replaces and represses professional know-how. Meanwhile, architects, urban planners, and other professionals who should be concerned with the making and organization of urban life stand idly by. Perhaps they are already absorbed in lucrative private contracts or simply caught up in their own nocuous mediocrity. Have we, as architects and urban planners, proposed sector designs, urban policies, and solutions for each field of expertise to politicians? Evidently not. So, if we have failed to do so and continue to fail to do so, even now in 2008, let us not criticize them for their administrative pretense or their lack of perspective in their plans for the capital. Painting investors black does not solve anything. Both of these approaches will only serve to create further problems. What is needed is for experts to supply solutions designed to promote public interests, taking into account the inalienable right to property. At the same time, the decision makers (local or national politicians) should adopt the best solutions in all negotiations between private entitlements (guaranteed) and the public good (which they represent, define and maintain).

What is missing is a vision of the city's development, a vision that logically lays out means of achieving its ends. We are still parochial; we believe development or the banning of development (and/or demolition) to be the cures for all ills. In the absence of an overall city design or a definition of the public interest within the city, all discussions are bound to appear patchy and all solutions, patriarchal, obsolete, and consequently of little or no use for the city as a collective entity, with regards to both its inhabitants and its buildings.

Private Property—The New Enemy? The Real Estate Developer as the Bad Guy

Of late, it has become trendy to give property a bad name. Born-again (or newly born) leftists joined hands with those who only got the leftovers when the public property of the former communist government of Romania—land, houses, resources, industrial sites—was doled out. Private owners and private property are allegedly bent on making a profit, generally without limitations or scruples. They speculate and do not show themselves in public, to avoid being dressed down by the upper crust of civil society, with its mighty pen or voice. The fact that the cultural press—unlike economic periodicals and newspapers—still approaches the matter of the city's development in an unprofessional way is a matter of grave concern. It corroborates once more that the Romanian public intelligentsia lags behind the very society it attempts to preach to from "above." The time is ripe to introduce a few principles into the debate that, once accepted by all parties, could finally lead to a discussion that would be of benefit to everyone.

Naturally each group, if entreated to voice its opinion, will try to promote its own interests. The people working in the Monuments Department will claim that preserving old buildings should be everybody's sole concern. The truth of the matter is that there is insufficient money and expertise to realize even the projects already on the list, which are already far too numerous. The members of Bucharest's urban planning commission will insist that their expertise is vital to the future of the city. Yet they will not look you in the eye if you ask them how it is possible to be a referee (i.e., a member of the commission) and a player (i.e., a designer presenting a project for approval before the said commission) at the same time, without the entire affair reeking of corruption. These are just a few of the most visible examples of the dozens of approvals a designer needs to gain from all sorts of institutions (civil defense, environment, water, gas, sewage). However, since not all of them have anything to do with the public character of the public space, the axioms appear invisible, or perhaps they are just uttered too infrequently:

1. Private property is guaranteed and, consequently, so should be its undisturbed exercise. Private space, be it one's own house or one's plot of land, is an expression of property—which is the concern of this essay.

2. Public space is the area on which arguments, negotiations, exchanges, and decisions are centered.

Focusing on this public space ensures that, in principle, each partial and partisan opinion is entitled to its own voice and visibility, no matter how few or weak its representatives. If the public good entails servitude applied to private property, this should be negotiated as a compromise in which the privileged party loses or delegates some of the uninfringed exercise/right of possession, and in compensation gains something equivalent. Fragmentary truths (pertaining to the various groups inhabiting the city) are presented in the public space by representatives of the citizens (local councilors, each according to their political affiliation; MPs; other elected figures) and/or delegates of the interests (experts and lobbyists from NGOs, themselves representing shreds of public interest, or specialized firms that openly promote private group interests). Decisions are made according to the principle of the voting majority (in a democracy) or by the imposition of assumed or delegated power (in autocratic, totalitarian regimes or dictatorships).

From this, it is evident that the exercise of private property must be allowed, protected, and what is more, *guaranteed* by the community in which one chooses to deploy it. It is a contract of coexistence by which one agrees to observe the same principle when it applies to others. How can it be that when a thief invades my property he is (or ought to be) punished by the law, but when a commission of experts from the city hall or the state decides (without asking my opinion) that on my property I am allowed to build only a percentage, or not at all, or in a certain manner, or only for others … the people who impose such restrictions are not treated in the same way as someone who fraudulently breaks into my dwelling? An initial answer could be that the city hall experts are delegates of the public good. I, as a citizen who owns private property, also contributed to the establishment of that particular instance when I voted for the Constitution or for Parliament (therefore for a government that enjoys the support of the majority of the elected) or the local council of the city. A second answer is expertise: a sum of experts is more qualified than us, the grassroots, to deal with the concerns of the city. For instance, urban planners are familiar with urban city planning, the science of a city undergoing a constant crisis (proof of this is found in the amazing studies of cities such as Lagos, the sprawl phenomenon, New Urbanism). Road makers are able to take the sketches made by urban planners and give them a transversal profile, endow them with a sewage system and lateral resilience. Renovators will tell you that you don't have to change a thing in your grandfather's house, that you ought to live just as he did (after dealing with mould and reinforcing the house after its decades of erosion) because the good and beautiful thing about an old city is perhaps that it stays old at all costs. At the same time, the new city should move to the outskirts. Not to parks, though, since regulations oblige us to plant four trees for each one felled, and we'd rather clog up the city than "waste time" making sure that the planting gets done.

The GUP for All and the ZUP for Everyone

In short, the state, the city hall, experts working for the public utilities, and even experts for hire by individuals will enumerate loudly and clearly the various limitations on your exercise of the right to property. Most of them behave as though they held the city's supreme truth. All of these people believe that the public good arises from them, exists thanks only to them, because their criteria for judgment are, if you please, absolute. Thus we have the general urban plan (GUP), a law for the development of the city—reminiscent of the early twentieth century, drafted by "experts" from whose ranks the actual movers and shakers (for instance, businesspersons) have been excluded. These experts have decided, for nebulous and uninformed reasons of "urban aesthetics," where tall buildings will and will not be erected. Yet the people of Bucharest—from the humblest citizens to the most important entrepreneurs—do not benefit at all from the laws governing the development of their city. Private property accepts what is imposed on it, although these restrictions are nowhere to be seen among the founding principles. A battle for exterior public space is being waged in Bucharest, and the fact that the city being built does not belong to its inhabitants at all—not even in the city center—is ignored. The demand to be made, as I have been saying since 1997, is that the ground floor (if not also the mezzanine) of all buildings erected in the center be declared urban space. New York shows us how this could be achieved: private property begins above ground level or next to the public atrium. Naturally, the builder should be granted one more floor upwards, to make up for the areas given over to public space. The percentage of public space in a private investment should be stipulated by a representative of the public interest (council and/or mayor), and stringently applied according to each zonal urbanism plan approved. If (large) public and private investments had been made in the center of Bucharest other than by architecture and city planning competitions, this problem would not have emerged in the first place.

It is widely believed, especially by those uninvolved in urban planning, that ZUPs (zonal urbanism plans) are a tool of real estate banditry, since they are generally financed by the developer and modify the master plan of the city, turning a more sympathetic eye towards his profit needs. However the master plan of the capital—adopted in 2000 and never updated—ignores the interests of businesses and private property, which essentially had no voice in 1999–2000, when it was drawn up. Therefore, the ZUP has remained the only instrument capable of setting the repression of urban voices to rights. Rather than condemning the plan in itself, we should beware its potential for abuse and try to compensate for its various shortcomings. The development of a city is the outcome of the joint presence of the often diverging interests of the various urban actors. The right to property is guaranteed by the constitution. Its exercise cannot be restrained other than by public interest, as legally defined in the constitution. If various laws restricting this constitutional right begin to clash with it, they obviously need to be brought into line with the constitution, otherwise they will encroach upon it. If this restraint is exclusively defined in terms of interdiction, then we should not be surprised that ways of eluding it are devised, both legal and illegal. Righteous indignation may make a good impression, but it is not sufficient. Public interest needs to establish a dialogue with private property, prohibiting one thing while giving another in exchange. In other words, negotiating.

This explains why the press demonizes the host of zonal urbanism plans by which this private interest is publicly expressed. What does private property want from the city? The unhampered exercise of its right, the way in which it has been exercised, by an "honorable" group of experts does not appear satisfactory. The voices represented are, at the same time, repressed voices: someone else knows what is best for you, acting in your stead and on your behalf. Why is this legitimate request to exercise the right to private property—within the legal parameters of public welfare—to be condemned? Why is it *a priori* bad to build tall things? It is also misguided to take up public space instead of extending it within the ground floor of new constructions: but otherwise, why do tall buildings give intellectuals such indigestion? Why must the maximum height of a certain ultra-central "protected area" be kept low, while businesses are banished to the outskirts, to unsuitable areas? Why should the city center be condemned to ruin and insignificance, to outlived memories, when there is simply not enough money for all this backbiting? Why is conservatism more important than urban development? These are all legitimate questions, yet no one is even trying to offer an answer. And the good people in the city-oriented NGOs mentioned above behave as if it goes without saying that small is beautiful, that less is more, and other such slogans recited by rote. Only the absence of critical thinking explains why dubious statements are taken at face value when, as a matter of fact, they have been called into question or even rejected by the respective contemporary professions for many years.

The first thing we all need to do is to accept the principles laid out in the beginning. The second is to sit down at the bargaining table. On one side, the public good—represented by the authorities, civil society and experts, in a humble frame of mind, since they have been elected and appointed by the citizens and are paid out of public funds to provide their most honest and qualified expert opinion. On the other side, private property—also humble, since it is surrounded by and beholden to public space, striving to develop while respecting the contribution it is obliged to make to the public good.

The third thing that all parties at the negotiating table should assume is that if the public good imposes something on private space, it should necessarily and concomitantly also grant a privilege in return. "You are expropriated, so be it." There are extreme cases motivated by a public cause, beyond a shadow of a doubt. But then the expropriation should be carried out at the best market value, following Berlin's reconstruction policies. "This or that building cannot be pulled down because it reminds us of our ancestors? So be it." Then we must take care of the maintenance of the old house and/or exact mild taxes on the property affected by our decision. "You cannot build anything on your property because the communists erected plants, apartment buildings, streets, and parks on it? Very well." In exchange we must provide compensation for you in the form of land of the same value somewhere else.

So far, interdictions related to public space mentioned above, without any of the compensation that ought to have ensued as a result of honest negotiations, have resulted only in increased prices and corruption. The restraints arbitrarily imposed on the right to property are the sole reasons for the corruption that arises in order to avoid the consequences of those very restrictions. At the moment, there is no form of negotiation process between the public good and private space. Instead, having no other recourse, the courts become the only forum available for such "negotiations." Tomorrow, the solution will certainly be negotiation between all the public figures involved in this city's space. If certain parties deliberately throw a wrench in the works of these negotiations by favoring their own field of competence, it is ridiculous that they should complain when the impeded right to property makes its just claim on the city.

Is Small Really so Beautiful?

Ever since the mid-nineteen-nineties when the topic of the Orthodox Patriarchal Cathedral in Bucharest became public for the first time, the subject of nanism came to the fore with a vengeance. Churches should be small, it was said, since they had always been tiny. Later on, the nanist aesthetic (readily psychoanalyzable, I might add) was applied to the city. From the perspective of someone afflicted by this height angst, Manhattan must be seen as the most terrible borough in the world. And yet it is not. It is not architectural height that defines the quality of the urban space, but the presence or absence of its public component. Consequently, limiting the land utilization coefficient, as is done in civic documents, appears arbitrary. "Large" and "small" do not exist as absolute values. Whether something is "large" or "small" is entirely dependent on the relationship between something that already exists and something that is proposed.

In the name of an enlightened, purely illuminist approach to urban space (the street as a trajectory between two ends of a monumental perspective), the altimetry study coordinated by Alexandru Sandu in 2002 (unpublished and, therefore, not available for public inspection) prohibits building within a given zone structures that fail to conform to that zone's regulations. The city would then no longer be a series of streets, preferably straight, with monuments or grandiose edifices as focal points at either end.

Before moving on to maximum height regulations, we have to answer other, more pressing questions: cornice alignment or isolated/individual buildings? Inner courtyards or dead ends or free space surrounding the built-up area? Urban island or four-façade edifices? Back-to-back housing or perimeter fenestration where we know that neighbors will be prohibited from expanding vertically?

The Crusade against the New

Preserving absolutely everything that was built "in former times," at all costs, is probably the holiest of today's causes. Of course, there are many more facets to this reality. We hear practically nothing about medieval Bucharest, although it was the real victim of nineteenth-century demolition. On the other hand, the just cause of protecting historic monuments has been extended to cover anything that is old, which is deemed valuable simply because it is old. There are not even sufficient resources to maintain the items on the list of structures classified as historical monuments. Virtually no protection is granted to pre- and post-war modern architecture, except for the efforts of the local International Council of Monuments and Sites. In short, let us concentrate on the real aspects of conservation—historic monuments—order to ensure that at least they will survive. Sadly, not everything that was built before our time will outlive us. If means of balancing public interest against private property (compensated interdiction) are not found, it will be quite unfair to blame investors, who perceive old edifices as a treadmill, for their decay.

Green Up

While protesters chained themselves to the Communist Heroes' Monument in Carol Park in the name of preserving the gardens, on another green area next to *Casa Scanteii*-turned-*Casa Presei Libere* (The Free Press House) a humongous office building was being erected; at the same time the Bordei green zone was traded in. Trees were felled in Izvor Park so that a motorcar race could be held, with no trace of the ostensibly mandatory five-fold replanting in sight. Actually, the diminution of green space rhetorically doubled [following] Parliament's attempt to restrict property by prohibiting construction on green areas that were returned to their former, pre-communism owners. This cannot be efficiently counteracted in the absence of civil projects that promote the expansion of green areas, public and private alike. For more than thirty years now, architecture and landscape art have been coming up with countless methods of integrating vegetation with the city and its edifices. Façades can be clad in green (speaking of traditions, Bucharest was once a settlement practically covered in ivy), and terraces can house just as many plants growing up towards the sky as their green counterparts on the ground. However, merely establishing these spaces will not be sufficient. The greenery gained in this way must be planted and tended. Bonn carried out a similar project throughout the city, and now enjoys a ribbon of vegetation based on biodiversity.

A Christian City?

Over 95 percent of Romania's population have declared themselves to be Christian. What could then be a consistent Christian outlook for the cities in which this population lives? A Christian outlook is not the same as a "Democratic-Christian" one. In the Catholic and Eastern Orthodox worlds, being a Christian does not imply political regimentation in terms of what can only be a reductive ideology. By its very definition, a Christian outlook is a holistic one: Christians aspire to be, to become and remain complete men, and thus they cannot be divided into fractions to the left, right or center. Consequently, their outlook cannot be other than complete.

A Christian view stresses the importance of the process of *becoming*, where others see objects and stagnation. It sees the same dignity of creation everywhere: in the nature within the settlement just as in the countryside surrounding the settlement. The same dignity can be perceived in the design and construction of the city, in the public parks and the private gardens, in every column and porch pillar.

It is not Christian to treat the city center as superior to the outskirts; the deluxe district as superior, from an urban point of view, to the slum (therefore more entitled to be blessed with communal services, investments and visibility); or the palace as superior to the humblest dwelling in the community. And finally, it is not Christian to grant more privileges to private spaces than to public space, or vice-versa.

A Christian outlook on urban development is participative. Its basic elements are the family (in the private space, incorporating the young and the old) and also the parish community (the neighborhood unit arranged in a close network, with the same charitable care available as in the family, extended to the scale of the social group). Special note should be made of migrant communities (those who have moved to or from the city), a topic to be addressed separately.

A Christian outlook on urban policies regards this notion as tautological. Christianity, an urban religion—born of hotbeds such as Jerusalem, Constantinople, and Rome—understands and affirms the idea that the prime concern of politics, as we know from Aristotle's *Politics*, is the solid construction, arrangement, preservation, and propagation of the city. This refers to the communities populating them, as well as to the space organized to take into account the construction, arrangement, preservation and propagation of those communities.

Having said this, it cannot be too difficult to understand what a Christian must do once he has reached by election or appointment a position of power, thus representing the community in the sense of administering its permanent settlement; just as this dignitary, be he councilor, mayor, or chief architect, must do if he is elected as a representative of any other ideology. He is obliged to assume the consequences of the principles underlying his public faith. Furthermore, since I have said that the Christian perspective is a holistic one, he has a duty to bear all of the consequences of his faith, which is equally important.

The city is a whole entity, and must be treated as such. In order to accomplish the task of governing a city, especially one as complex as Bucharest, a Christian mayor must have control over all levels of its infrastructure, from the public transport system to the police force. The city cannot be segregated into slices and responsibility diluted thereby. On the contrary, it must be comprised of neighboring units and districts with natural boundaries. For instance, the city is defined by the districts within the central ring, interior peri-urban villages (districts built inside the belt) and exterior areas (modern towns housing those who commute to Bucharest on a daily basis)—all autonomous and united to form a single metropolis. In all that he does, the Romanian leader should set out from elementary units of social, communal aggregation, and urban articulation. He must allow and by all means encourage the formation of micro-communities. At the same time, he needs to focus on the quality of individuals dwelling in their respective micro-communities as mirrors of the city. In short, no matter how small the district, it must be a city within a city. Like a fractal, the dwelling type and the neighborhood unit should have the same components as the city itself: center and outskirts, greenery and walls, public places, edifices and private spaces, all on equal footing. The dwelling itself should include all these spaces, as well as garden and yard, on the façades and/or terraces, as the case may be. Streets must connect rather than separate districts, while the city center should be the nexus of the neural-urban network, i.e., the public core of the various districts. If the city is an organism, then these districts will become more complex and evolved the more autonomous nervous centers they have, all coordinated by the primary center, the brain.

Thus the elected or appointed administrator should ensure that the urban subsidiary has both sense and substance. Problems that may arise should be resolved at the correct level. The mayor of a district (sector) will provide citizens with options and facilities for the joint creation and administration of parking space and garages, in public/private partnership. The city mayor will offer urban, fiscal, and administrative policies appropriate to each and every area, according to their specific needs: a certain set of policies may be suitable for the historic center, and others for communist boroughs built on the outskirts of Bucharest, for instance. A Christian mayor should not work hand in hand with large investors as a business partner. He must arbitrate in a proactive manner according to the Christian vision of the city's future, as defined in the program voted for by the residents, so that the city's business environment offers equal opportunities for everyone, more or less powerful, foreign or domestic.

A mayor should not construct houses for anyone, nor give away other people's homes, but should rather create the conditions necessary for interested communities to build accommodations, whether this be social housing owned by the communities or expensive private housing. No matter what their category, they should be thought out from the start as urban micro-communities, not as alienated buildings. Neither should a Christian mayor be a slave to the masses who represent a broader, more "poorly" articulated, less visionary interest group. A Christian mayor will not humble his fellow beings with any kind of alms, but will create the conditions and opportunities for everyone to preserve his/her human dignity: the right to shelter and worship; the right to a public space in which to develop freely, both physically and politically, as a citizen; the right to unspoiled nature; to private initiative; and above all, the right to shared beauty and collective memory.

Instead of a Conclusion

I was not born in Bucharest and therefore I do not nurture sentimental bonds with this agro-megalithic borough. I have never missed it, and as an architect I have always seen it as an object of theoretical and practical professional observations. The city is an *unfinished project*, a succession of layers of a *palimpsest* where each stratum replaces the next with catastrophic and/or political violence (fires, earthquakes, demolitions). Bucharest is a patchwork, a motley territory, lacking in professional and public urban policies. The local authorities here fail to represent the interests of the inhabitants of the capital, bowing down only to the interests of real estate capitalists.

The formation patterns of the city are amazingly utopian, like Sforzinda, or picturesquely debauched (slums, a city that has developed "organically"). The "mahala" (slum) threatens to engulf the center everywhere in Romania, and in Bucharest its "hideous specter" looms behind each new building, as George Matei Cantacuzino warned us as early as 1947.[3] From the Republic House, it has consumed public space, turning it into a mall. This ultimate edifice of Romania is subject to all sorts of symbolic (the Great Pyramid of Little Paris) or urban restructuring projects such as Bucharest 2000, a futile competition that started off on the wrong foot aesthetically. It is an excellent case study for the concept of the *Singular Object*,[4] resisting all attempts to exhaust its meanings. And the rigmarole goes on with the House of Republic, also known as Palace of Parliament. The building is still unfinished, yet it is already in need of repair, and apparently no form of maintenance program has been planned. It has actually not been fully mapped, areas of it still being uncharted. I think we still have to work hard to grasp the meaning of this peasant house, with a fence and garden at the front, and weeds at the back—which is a representative of the concept of Bigness,[5] of magnitude, in Bucharest. Then the location of the patriarchal cathedral is shifted from one place to another, seemingly in search of an ever more uncertain site, pointing towards the conclusion—not apotheotic but apocalyptic—of the hilarious destiny of the wretched city of Bucharest.

This essay briefly resumes the position I took on behalf of Bucharest in some cultural journals and on the internet. I very much hope that they make sense to the outside reader. On the whole, they say that being a Romanian is a full-time job. Being a Romanian architect in the capital city of Romania does not exactly make things easier.

Endnotes

1   See: http://www.salvatibucurestiul.ro (last accessed January 3, 2010).
2   See: http://www.petitieonline.ro/petitie/pactul_pentru_bucuresti_ca_ hotarare_de_consiliu_general-p15770050.html, with the text as proposed to become a decision of the City Council (last accessed January 3, 2010).
3   George Matei Cantacuzino, *Despre o estetică a reconstrucției* [Towards the Aesthetics of Reconstruction] (Bucharest: Cartea Romaneasca, 1947).
4   See: Jean Baudrillard, *The Singular Objects of Architecture* (Minneapolis, Minn.: University of Minnesota Press, 2002).
5   See: Rem Koolhaas, *Delirious New York—A Retroactive Manifesto for Manhattan* (London: Thames and Hudson, 1978).

4

ECONOMIC CONDITIONS

TURBO URBANISM IN PRISHTINA

Kai Vöckler

Since the end of the socialist system and the war that led to the break up of Yugoslavia, a substantial amount of informal construction activity has taken root across the region, resulting in a completely new type of urbanization.[1] This is a typical development in transformation and post-conflict situations, where the lack or weak presence of institutional structures makes regulating building activity problematic, as has happened in Prishtina and Belgrade, in Skopje and Novi Sad. The erratic sprawl of makeshift buildings is a product of the urban crisis that has shaped the region since its post-socialist transformations and wars. At the same time, these urban changes highlight a new topology, completely independent of regional particularities and differing significantly from informal settlements known until now from outside Europe. They are in fact an expression of the developments taking place across wide sections of society, developments that to a large extent bind investments. Their specific and as yet unexplored forms are the result of an interdependence of spaces linked by a media-based image world, migratory movements, and cash flows. Accordingly, the following question can be asked: to what degree has this uncontrolled and informal urbanism developed forms of city life that may eventually appear in other European states under the conditions of the continued neoliberal denationalization?

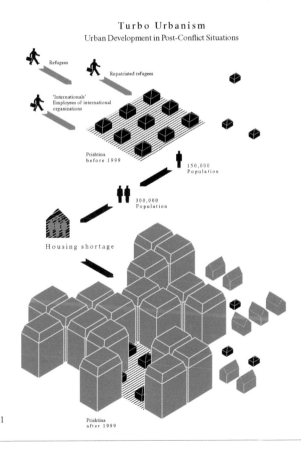

1

---

1   Prishtina, Kosovo, is a prototypical example of the transformation of a city following a conflict: Within a short period of time, rural migrants and returning refugees doubled the number of inhabitants and the lack of housing triggered a building boom, leading to the deconstruction of almost 70 percent of the city structure, serious safety problems, and social conflicts.

Prishtina after 1999

In 1999, the NATO-led *Kosovo Force* troops (KFOR) intervened in the war between the Serbian military forces and the *Kosovo-Albanian Liberation Army* (UCK). This ended the war, but owing to repressive measures that had been instituted in 1990 and sustained ever since by the regime of Slobodan Milosevic, the majority population of Kosovo-Albanians found themselves essentially isolated from the rest of society in the autonomous republic located in what had once been Yugoslavia. When the KFOR troops marched into Kosovo, Kosovo-Albanians regarded it as an act of liberation. Their newly found sense of freedom was basically expressed through an almost immediate frenzy of construction. The minority population—consisting of Kosovo-Serbs, Romas, Ashkali, and Kosovo-Egyptians—made up about 10 percent of the total population, but they were largely excluded from this development, or else saw no future for themselves in real estate investments. These minorities had been intimidated by the many attacks perpetrated by the Kosovo-Albanians when the KFOR troops arrived, and large numbers of Kosovo-Serbs and Romas (as well as other small ethnic groups suspected of collaborating with the Serbs) were persecuted and fled the country. The remaining Kosovo-Serbs believed the NATO intervention was an act of hostility. They had no trust in either the experimental, entirely new sort of peace mandated by the United Nations, or in the assurances of safety they had been given. Riots in March 2004 were triggered by Albanian hooligans, and spread all across Kosovo, leaving many dead and injured Serbs. Heavy damages were inflicted on Serbian cultural institutions. When the UN police and KFOR troops generally failed to put a stop to the rioting, the Kosovo-Serbs seemed to be justified in their fears. Considering all of this, it was not surprising that this part of the Kosovar population was not interested in building.

Rapid population growth in cities is characteristic of post-conflict situations (▶ 1). It is partially caused by migrants moving from rural to urban areas, looking for new and better prospects for the future; repatriation of refugees is another reason for growth. Germany, for instance, promptly revoked the asylum and provisional residency status it had granted to Kosovo-Albanian refugees, and sent them back to their own country. This meant that there was a vast increase in the numbers of inhabitants of Prishtina who first had to find some way that would allow them to settle in the city, and this increase subsequently led to conflicts. Due to the skyrocketing number of new residents, a huge demand for housing arose. This triggered a great deal of construction, which occurred under fuzzy legal circumstances, while the government structures meant to regulate development were either weak or dysfunctional. We can use Prishtina's problems and its potential as an example to better understand this development, but first it is necessary to analyze the sort of political and social conditions under which this development occurs. In this way, it should become clear who can successfully participate in such development. However, we should also be able to see how the development itself is structured, in order to better understand how to plan during this fragile period of the city's development, when very different interests are contesting.

This is the point where informal, local networks encounter governmental structures that are either undergoing transformation, or are in the process of being founded. Here, too, there is an international administration that is tied up in a murky construct of quasi-governmental, local, and international organizations. It is an unstable construct, whose labile power relations foster a kind of urban development that is problematic and conflicted, and this has resulted in an urban crisis.

"Unmikistan"—The UN Administration and the Local Population

In March 1999, the crisis in Kosovo and the military intervention moved the international community to decide to place Kosovo under the control of a provisional international administration. It was hoped that this would, at least, help to build a Kosovar administration that would eventually be able to govern the region. Another hope was that a functioning administration would be able to solve the problem of Kosovo's status.[2] Immediately after the KFOR troops marched into the territory, a temporary administration was set up. It was called the *United Nations Interim Administration Mission in Kosovo*, or UNMIK for short. Its task was to govern a territory that had no police, no judicial system, and no state institutions capable of functioning in a practical manner. The *United Nations* took on the task of rebuilding the police, the judicial system, and the administration, while the *Organization for Security and Co-operation in Europe* (OSCE), was responsible for democratization and the establishment of constitutional institutions. The EU, or *European Union*, was supposed to take care of rebuilding and economic development. Besides all of that, work was begun on structuring a provisional self-government *Provisional Institutions of Self-Government* (PISG). After the 2002 elections, most of the authority was transferred to this government, with the exception of the police and the judicial system. However, the UNMIK continued to control the actions of the provisional self-government, while the leader of the mission, the *Special Representative of the Secretary General* (SRSG) was essentially entitled to full authority. His authority enabled him to issue his own orders (UNMIK Regulations), as well as veto decisions made by the PISG. The UNMIK influenced practically every part of life in Kosovo until 2008.[3]

The UN administration was also guided by the belief that it was a positive role model, even though the local population regarded it in a completely different light. Although the KFOR troops were considered liberators, it was felt—especially by the Kosovo Albanians—that the UN administration was nothing but an obstacle blocking the way to independence. In addition, it was observed that a considerable amount of money set aside for aid went to equip the international organizations and to pay the salaries of the international employees— salaries that were high even by Western standards. However, it was the UNMIK resolution 2000/47 that turned out to be particularly problematic, since it essentially gave immunity to the KFOR forces and the employees of the UN administration. These people could only be prosecuted in a court of law, with the express permission of the *General Secretary of the*

United Nations.[4] This provided opportunities for the criminal energies of a few UNMIK employees, and the ensuing public scandal surrounding the failure to prosecute those involved in corruption and the misappropriation of funds discredited the UN administration in the eyes of Kosovars for a long time.[5] It is hard to imagine why an international organization with complete sovereignty in a territory would give itself so much more immunity than a democratic state would.[6] Some of the actions of the UN administration also seemed to be founded on the notion that simply setting up institutional structures would automatically lead to a strong, self-governing, functional democracy. This notion found itself in conflict with local, informal networks and authorities led by clan chiefs—former military commanders and party leaders—which had already proved their effectiveness in the previous decades. Local political forces were in so much conflict that they sometimes resorted to violence, but they all agreed on one thing: the introduction of democracy would make it possible to take over political responsibilities and hence to quickly achieve independence.[7] On the positive side, a substantial amount of stability was achieved. No one disagreed on the necessity for institutional structures. However, it is clear that the mere existence of institutions is not the only thing required for good government, and excellent evidence of the truth of this statement can be seen in the process of urban development. The technocratic approach assumed that establishing formally functioning, lawful institutions—such as an urban planning department—would "automatically" resolve all of the outstanding issues that affected not only the development of the city, but all of its residents as well. However, this approach ignores the fact that an administration has to achieve a specific balance of powers and deal with conflicts of interest. And it overlooks the fact that even administrative planning cannot be carried out independently of the norms and values of those affected by the plans themselves. UN agencies such as *United Nations Human Settlements Program* (UN-HABITAT) use a "stakeholder" approach in order to influence procedures and methods. This permits the process of moderation to include those who are affected by urban development measures or are pursuing some sort of interest, ultimately in order to achieve a consensus on the measures to be undertaken. However, this process, which requires a great deal of time, has never been pursued in Prishtina. In addition, the question arises as to whether this very formal approach should be adjusted to fit the specific cultural context. Meanwhile, the city redevelopment agency practiced the classic sort of "top-down" planning—to very little effect, as it turned out.

The Construction Boom

The massive "international" presence, headquartered in Prishtina, had a problematic effect on the city's development (▶ 2a–c). Rents skyrocketed, since the financially secure aid organizations and their employees were able to pay any price. Often housed in new buildings, which had been constructed without permits, a service industry sprung up around the international organizations. Cafés and restaurants mushroomed. During the first two years after the war, a rapidly expanding economy favored this growth. However, the economy depended upon international donors and the Kosovo-Albanian diaspora, and it soon began shrinking at a considerable rate. Kosovo today has one of the lowest per capita incomes in Southeast Europe, and is regarded as one of the least economically developed areas in the region. The unemployment rate is over 40 percent. Large portions of the population survive as day laborers or find themselves forced to participate in the illegal operations of well-organized criminal networks—such as smuggling, for example. The survival of entire clans of families depends on money sent by family members living either legally or illegally abroad.[8] For instance, about 400,000 Kosovo-Albanians currently live in Germany, Switzerland, and Austria—more then one-fifth of the entire population of Kosovo.[9] According to estimates from the *Kosovar Ministry of Finance and Economy*, monies transferred from relatives abroad

2

2a–c   Views of Prishtina, Kosovo, 2005.

comprised about 50 percent of the household incomes in Kosovo in 2002.[10] Although it is
difficult to ascertain the precise sum of money involved in these transactions, it probably
amounts to the entire budget of the provisional government in Kosovo. This means that the
diaspora exercises an extraordinary amount of influence over the development of Kosovo.
Even though this influence has decreased somewhat over time, it is still a significant factor.
Money is primarily invested in the construction sector. The reason for this is the increasing
demand for housing, caused by the migration of people from the country to the city and by
the return of refugees from abroad. In addition, the international organizations need office
and living space for themselves and their employees. This allowed everyone who had some
sort of a hand in construction to quickly turn a high profit. Investors, who had the necessary
financial means; owners of buildings or land; builders who had materials, skilled laborers,
and expertise at their disposal: all wanted to participate in the booming construction and real
estate sectors. However, there were also family-funded investments. During the Milosevic
era, Kosovo-Albanian families put a great deal of money into savings accounts in foreign
countries, which they began using to invest in housing for their families. This often consisted of large two-to-three-story single-family homes, which were built on farmland on the
periphery of the city (▶ 3). Anyone who did not have savings or was unable to raise enough
money through the family network was excluded from the construction boom. Housing
developments were not only built by migrants, but also by old, established families. All layers
of society were involved, with the exception of the socially disadvantaged. Apart from a few
pilot projects, there is no government-subsidized housing. Accordingly, there is very strong
pressure on the socially disadvantaged to solve their problems on their own.[11]

3 A family-based development is found primarily at the outskirts of the city. Permission is generally not
applied, but neighbors know one another. Buildings are constructed on the basis of estimates and experience, and are mostly erected by construction companies without the aid of architects. They are solid,
often oversized and have nothing in common with what we know as the "shanty towns" of non-European
countries. Prishtina, Kosovo, 2005.

The Failure of Administrative Plans

In Prishtina, unregulated construction went on. Even though there were regulatory plans that had been formulated during the Yugoslavian era (between 1967 and 1990), they existed only on paper. Nobody paid any attention to them—a result of the disputes over authority carried on by the international and local administrations. Up until 2005, it was not even possible to obtain a building permit, either because the city administration had no legally binding planning documents, or because the old plans from Kosovo's days as a Yugoslavian territory were deemed insufficient. Since no one could apply for a building permit, an important reason for working with an architect disappeared. Moreover, there were numerous disputes over property ownership. The legal status of many properties was unclear, since there was often no access to land registries. Many had been destroyed or had disappeared during the years of armed conflict. Many pieces of property were claimed by a variety of parties. A considerable number of abandoned flats and houses had simply been taken over, or pieces of land, including city property, were occupied. With regard to property ownership, the 2005 EU Progress Report stated that the dominant atmosphere was one of lawlessness and impunity.[12] In order to negotiate the continuing disputes between Kosovo-Serbs and Kosovo-Albanians over property rights, the UN administration set up two international, court-like authorities with exclusive jurisdiction over these cases. By 2005, they had settled half of the cases that had been brought to them. However, this still did not eliminate the fundamental legal uncertainties caused by incomplete or missing information. In 2008, a land registry for Prishtina was still in the process of being assembled.

Since the UN administration first had to build local and institutional structures, a great deal of legally binding data was still missing, and development plans had either been overtaken by actual construction projects, or else they were incomplete. The city's development continued without state regulation, governed only by economic factors and private interests. The result: about 75 percent of the city is overbuilt—with too many new buildings and numerous informal developments on the edges of the city. Remarkably enough, even though not much of Prishtina was destroyed during the war, the post-war construction has led to the destruction of the city. Public needs are of no significance to developers. In 2005, according to the city redevelopment agency, ten new buildings a day were being built in Prishtina. Public squares and parks are decaying, and the streets are in a terrible condition. The power supply regularly fails; this is not only caused by insufficient maintenance, but also by the illegal tapping of electricity lines. Water supplies are also strained, due to the many new, illegal connections. The historic inner city, with its typical, one-story, square houses, has been overbuilt, mostly with high-rise office buildings, hotels, and stores, which feature the typical blue glass façades (▶ 4, 5). Even buildings that were protected by historic preservation laws disappeared overnight.

In September 2000, the director of the city planning agency, Rexhep Luci, tried to put a halt to the destruction of the city by having students document illegal buildings—where-

4

upon he was shot to death. The murder has never been solved. In reaction to Luci's murder, the UN administration issued an order to regulate construction (UNMIK Regulation 2000/53), which required local authorities to enforce building regulations. However, it was not possible to block illegal construction or enforce building codes. First, Prishtina had only three building inspectors, so there were not enough inspectors to determine exactly which projects were not up to code. Second, no one was capable of enforcing the regulations. The Kosovo police force was in the organizational stage, and, with a few exceptions, the UN police and KFOR troops refrained from interfering, since they did not want to draw the wrath of the local population down on themselves—because, ultimately, almost every level of society was involved in the construction activities. The *Kosovo Protection Corps* (KPC) was a "catastrophe protection organization" chiefly made up of former UCK soldiers. They offered to intervene in the illegal activities, but no one took them up on their offer: nobody wanted to take the responsibility for this task away from the police. Besides the problem of enforcement, however, there remained the question of what exactly should be enforced. Here, the excuse was that plans first had to be drawn up, so that there would be a legal basis for enforcement. Considering the demand for readily available housing and the profit-motivated economic pressure coming from the building sector, it was clear to everyone that development could be neither slowed nor stopped.[13] Yet those in charge of the local and international governments deflected each and every flexible and pragmatic solution.

4   The blue glass façade, signifying business and "internationality," is a typical example of Turbo Style. Prishtina, Kosovo, 2005.

5

Planning the Utopian

Instead, in 2004, the city administration proposed its "Urban Strategic Plan 2020." It had been developed within a period of four months, in consultation with German planning agencies, and was henceforth supposed to be the basis for all future development. It was an astonishingly urbane vision based on fairly untrustworthy information. As a study by the *European Stability Initiative* (ESI) proved, the plan was based on an estimate of a half a million inhabitants—a figure that is not at all valid.[14] In fact, if one calculates the number of households connected to the water supply and the average size of each household, one can see that there is a population of between 200,000 and 250,000. This is still double the number of residents counted in the last census, conducted in 1981. In addition, the plan assumes that people will continue to leave Kosovo, but it nonetheless suggests that the city be expanded enormously, by building large apartment buildings and wide streets. Where the money is supposed to come from for all of this is not explained. Apparently—true to the old socialist tradition—the agency expects money from the European Union, from donor nations around the world, and—in Albanian tradition—from the diaspora.[15] In principle, this vision of the future is unobjectionable, but the question remains as to whether it is a viable model. To be practicable, it has to be plausible and based on realistic assumptions. It is aggravating that that the "strategic plan" did not deal with any of the problems it had created: the fact that large parts of the old Prishtina had been destroyed, that essential safety

5   This is a characteristic example of a "hybrid building." It is often unclear what a building is to be used for, the decision being left until later. Blue glass façades indicate office space, normal windows signify residential space. Prishtina, Kosovo, 2005.

standards had been ignored, that the infrastructure—especially water supplies and waste-water removal—either did not exist or was overburdened, and that social problems resulted from unregulated construction (violent disputes already having occurred). The "strategic plan" offered no strategies to cope with these things. Clearly, it did not occur to those who worked on the proposal that it might be preferable to analyze the actual situation and concepts for improvement, rather than to develop megalomaniac visions.

6

6   Entire houses are built on the roofs of privatized communal buildings. Roof extensions are often semi-legal, with basic permits whose restrictions are not fully adhered to. Raising the roof by up to three floors is a common practice in the development of housing and often raises serious safety problems, as it is carried out without the involvement of architects or engineers. Prishtina, Kosovo, 2005.

7

Planning without a Plan

The apparently spontaneous, uncontrolled urban development described here had to first figure out how to regulate itself. Self-regulation is essentially determined by each of the individual parties dealing with one another in construction projects (▶ 6, 7). However, the sum of all of these different interests and the ensuing activities does not necessarily serve the interests of society as a whole—as can be seen in the total neglect of public affairs. As far as the new structures are concerned, however, there are no really dangerous problems, aside from specific elementary deficiencies in safety. The examples named here—blocking emergency lanes, the removal of load-bearing walls on ground floors in order to create shop space, or the addition of extra floors on top of buildings, executed without engineering help—should be taken seriously, but they are the exception rather than the rule. Instead, the negative results are more obvious in the areas where the state should have been responsible from the start: supplying a functioning technical and social infrastructure, and allocating or maintaining public space.

This specific form of urban development is largely determined by traditional social networks founded on family, heritage, and clan structures. Only a portion of this development involves neighborhood initiatives. Individual interests dominate, and they tend to lead to conflicts with the neighbors. These networks are essentially para-state structures, which have historically been suppressed by the state, and they maintain distance from state authorities. The law of custom tends to play an influential role, but, as can be seen from the example of Prishtina, it is not enough to regulate development. The rapid rise in population and the

7   An oversized house in the middle of Prishtina. The investor tries to maximize profit by making the building as large as possible—up to seven stories high without an elevator. Because he knows that he will not gain legal permission for a building of this size, he uses a common "camouflage" strategy, claiming that the upper three stories consist of the "roof." Prishtina, Kosovo, 2005.

accelerated rate of construction obviously hindered the overall ability to differentiate among the various self-regulating procedures; this has led to numerous conflicts. In addition, those involved were confronted with a new, unfamiliar type of situation, so they could not resort to traditional patterns of behavior and negotiation. However, despite the enormous flow of refugees into the city, the high rate of unemployment and the terrible economic situation, no slums appeared (like the ones that are seen in countries outside of Europe). It is also worth noting that this development embraced almost all income brackets, and as a phenomenon, it affected society in general. Basically, two main groups can be identified: one is comprised of investors, who have the financial means to buy and develop property and buildings. The other group consists of property owners and owners of small houses, who do not have the money to increase the value of their property and who are therefore dependent upon others to act with them. Therefore, the second group—by far the largest involved in the construction process—usually acts as part of a team consisting of a small, local contractor and the buyers interested in purchasing the apartments. This form of organization, typical of Southeast Europe in general, is based on balanced interests: the property owner permits the local contracting firm —which has the labor, the material, and a relatively large amount of expertise—to construct a building of several stories. Afterward, the building is divided between the property owner and the contractor, and the units they do not use themselves are rented or sold.[16] If the building is a large one, the units are sold beforehand, in order to finance the construction. Another variation: construction is carried out while yet-to-be built units are sold at auction. Existing buildings—many of them smaller—are torn down, so that the largest possible profit can be turned. Architects are not involved; at best, a building engineer might be consulted. However, all of the parties do follow a common plan, and hence, the process is neither "spontaneous" nor "frenzied."

The group with money to invest can be divided into three. First, there are the non-local, foreign investors. However, because of the uncertain legal situation, there are only a few of these, and they have little to do with development. The second group is made up of local investors equipped with sufficient wealth, who also have enough of the right political connections to feel safe about making large investments in the building sector. Most of the money for new commercial buildings comes from this group. Architects are hired for these projects, in order to ensure the quality the investors want—meaning the signal effect of the buildings. Also, because it is more complicated, this type of building requires a great deal of expertise. The third group of investors is made up of family clans and private organizations. They buy empty lots (mostly farmland) on the city periphery and build houses there (▶ 8).

To sum up, it could be said that uncontrolled urban development has permitted landowners to maximize the value of their land in inner-city areas. However, individual interests clearly conflict with one another—as can be seen in the blocked windows and balconies of neighboring buildings in the shadow of illegal additions. The fact is that in the long term property values will decrease, since each and every addition changes the entire situation for the worse: there is a drastic reduction in unoccupied space. Moreover, room for traffic is severely reduced and the technical infrastructure—from water and power supplies to wastewater removal—is overburdened. The social infrastructure—such as kindergartens and schools—is also deficient.[17] Although it is true that this type of self-regulation permits a highly flexible use of space, this tends to happen by accident. Because its use is so random, the space becomes problematic, precisely because no planning or thought has been put into the framework in which it exists. It should be pointed out that these circumstances make it easier for small economic units, consisting of property owners and contractors, to be successful in the real estate sector. These smaller groups, however, are obviously dominated by the networks of wealthier investors with more political clout. Whereas the former group needs to prepare for the "emergency" that will be legalization, as well as a confrontation with the state administration, the latter already has the right "connections" to government agencies and will not have anything to fear from restrictions. Accordingly, if legalization occurs in the future, private groups will be in a far worse position to negotiate. Ultimately, these examples demonstrate that self-regulation in a society reaches its limits if it does not

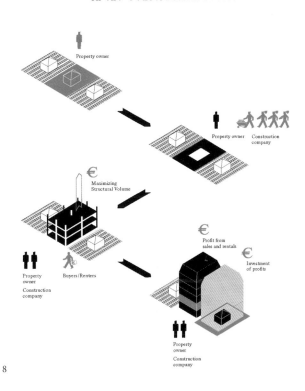

Maximizing Profits
in the Construction Sector

8

8   Architecture without architects—the way in which local individual investors, together with construction companies, try to maximize building profits. Only the poor, who do not own a plot or are not in a position to mobilize money for investments through family networks, are excluded from this business.

take into consideration all aspects of society as a whole. It does not take the entire city into consideration, and thus results in problems such as inadequate or insufficient connections to infrastructure and utilities.

Turbo Architecture

Besides all of this, there is another aspect that is crucial to our understanding of this phenomenon: the specific style of these buildings signals the belonging to an international urban culture. This culture is marked by media, especially television, where the "good life" and its accoutrements are prefigured. One of the neighborhoods in old Prishtina, "Pejton," with its typical, single-story houses, is centrally located; therefore it has, of course, been overbuilt with enormous high-rise office and commercial buildings, cafés, and restaurants (▶ 9). Locals call this area "Pejton Place," after the American television series *Peyton Place*. Imitating the styles of buildings seen in various media is a symbolic way of demonstrating modernity, at the same time it rejects modern architecture, since modern architecture also stands for socialist Yugoslavia and an epoch in history that is now past. The new "Turbo Architecture," as Srdjan Jovanovic Weiss calls it, can be found everywhere in the western Balkan regions. Its mish-mash of styles is a reference to "tradition," only this tradition now comes from elsewhere.[18] The rejection of one's own tradition is a sign of internationalism and sophistication. There are no references to traditional regional architecture. The usual

9 The "Swiss Casino" can be seen as "concrete poetry" of a deregulated city development. Prishtina, Kosovo, 2005.

10

11

10   Housing in Turbo Style expresses prosperity and modernity—it has nothing in common with traditional architecture. Prishtina, Kosovo, 2005.

11   This model of "Turbo Architecture" was erected by the international community in the middle of Prishtina—a "California-Victorian-Free Style" design, known from the United States, which inspires locals to copy it. Prishtina, Kosovo, 2005.

props, with their historic-looking elements of décor, can be found in local home improvement stores, having arrived there via the distribution networks of international chain stores. They are then blended with specific kinds of local architecture, which frequently imitate forms articulated in neighboring buildings. Characteristic of this is the preference for blue or green mirrored windows and curved façades. This creates a kind of Victorian, classical, oriental, American, free-style architecture, which, of course, also uses elements of modernism, such as the load-bearing steel and concrete structure (▶ 10, 11). "Turbo Architecture" has a pendant in the popular "Turbo Folk" music, which mixes traditional folk and pop

Turbo Architecture

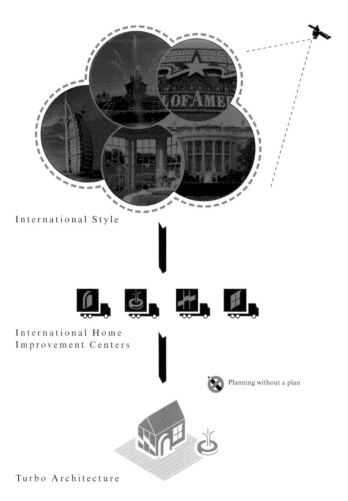

International Style

International Home
Improvement Centers

Planning without a plan

Turbo Architecture

music with international rock, pop, and techno. Just as abstruse as the character of this music, which is widespread in southeastern Europe, is the region's architectural language. It symbolically expresses a longing to be part of Europe. The mass distribution of almost identical stylistic elements does not lead to diversity, but to a uniform image of the city. It expresses dissociation from traditional rural architecture and testifies to the increasing social status of those who have left the country for the city. Here, the city is already an effective idea, even before it materializes.[19] It incorporates the hope of being allowed to participate in modern, European culture—the city might be capable of linking the local to the international. This idea is not only conveyed through the world of universal images and signs, but is also shaped by it.

Turbo Urbanism

Originally, the term "turbo" indicated extreme acceleration and escalation, and in "Turbo Culture," with its exaggerations and excesses, the word finds its correlation in the essentially random way in which regional and international props are used and mixed.[20] It is precisely the symbolic significance of randomness that is related to the actual informal character of this kind of cultural expression. The city and its architecture takes this informal, apparent randomness (the rules are not canonized) and symbolically relates it to the global. Implicitly, the architectural language refers to a phenomenon that can be seen happening around the world: the informalization of the urban space caused by a kind of unfettered, neoliberal capitalism.[21] This development, which Edward Luttwak sums up as "Turbo Capitalism," is characterized by a type of capitalist economics aiming for pure efficiency and maximum profit on a global scale, which goes hand in hand with the destruction of government regulation, all the way to the total abolition of government taxation.[22] This deregulation corresponds to the emergence of "informality," especially in the labor sector, which is attempting to adapt to the new conditions (▶ 12).

The new world order also gathered in Prishtina. As the old planned socialist economy was transformed into a market economy, after 1999 international administration encouraged neoliberal economic principles, which encountered weak formal structures—namely, the new state institutions that were just in the process of being organized. To this day, the economy is dominated by essentially informal networks of local investors (due to uncertain legal circumstances, there are only a few foreign investors). A concomitant feature of this basically deregulated situation is the informalization of urban space. In this sense post-1999 Turbo Urbanism, with its deficient self-regulation, is not just a phenomenon resulting from a kind of accelerated, excessive city planning based on a lack of state regulation. Turbo Urbanism is also a result of the specific economic situation—only the construction sector has offered a majority of Kosovars the chance to achieve some financial gain. Anybody trying to introduce regulations after the fact—attempting to establish a building code, for instance—would be forced to negotiate with private developers. However, these negotiations would also require Kosovar society to confront itself with the future of the city. Ultimately, the extraordinarily large number of construction projects and the involvement of almost all social groups will make it practically impossible to redress the illegality of the situation. Instead, guidelines for legalization will have to be developed, which will end in the balancing of interests. In turn, this balance will have to be negotiated and converted into generally applicable, legally binding regulations.

However, in order to properly judge the situation, one has to see it from the standpoint from which the relationship between "formal" and "informal" structures and procedures is evaluated. Undeniably, there are many problems that make it necessary to have state regulation, for the sake of general welfare. Accordingly, Prishtina might simply be a warning example of the consequences of strict deregulation, as well as of a kind of development that might possibly blossom in northern European cities, for instance, if they continue to retract communal taxation and focus on so-called public-private partnerships, whose only orientation is economic profit. The position held by a planning agency can be all too hastily taken over in the process. Looking at Prishtina, it can be seen that untaxed and unregulated city planning is the result of a political and social crisis that is typical of post-conflict situations. The negative aspects cannot only be blamed on the failure of international and local agencies and the politicians who lead them. Urban development is also a social process. It is the result of the different intentions of every group and individual participating in the process; it also incorporates the accoutrements of power, which form the basis for influence and economic success. The situation in Prishtina cannot be compared to the developments in western European cities. There, urban development is largely structured by economic interests and communal planning within a highly formalized framework. In Prishtina, family clans are mostly responsible for development, and it is marked by a system of economic patronage, or cronyism. In this sense, it is a unique kind of urbanization, where all relationships—whether market relations or legal relations—have to conform to the family system.[23] Economic interests are also pursued, but the primary goal is to secure the family household by owning real estate. This framework has its own values, norms, and regulations that cannot be applied universally. So it is necessary to conceive of a new combination of state and social regulation, which can form the basis for a subsequent successful regulation of the process. A way to negotiate the situation has to be discovered. The appropriate strategies will not strive for autocratic or bureaucratic solutions; instead, they will turn directly to Kosovo-Albanian society—which will have to consult with itself regarding its future welfare.

Excerpt from the publication: Kai Vöckler, *Prishtina is Everywhere. Turbo Urbanism: the Aftermath of a Crisis* (Amsterdam: Archis Publishers, 2008). A German edition is available under the title: *Prishtina is Everywhere. Turbo-Urbanismus als Resultat einer Krise* (Berlin: Parthas Verlag, 2008).

Endnotes

1 The term "informal" sector first appeared in the nineteen-seventies to describe the underground economy in the southern countries. It describes an economic area where generally accepted laws are not effective.

2 UN Security Council Resolution 1244 (1999).

3 See: Beate Kellermann, *Das Kosovo zwischen Standard und Status—vom bewaffneten Konflikt in die unsichere Demokratie* (Stuttgart: Ibidem, 2006); *Kosovo Wegweiser zur Geschichte*, ed. Bernhard Chiari and Agilof Kesselring (Paderborn: Schöningh, 2006).

4 UNMIK Regulation 2000/47 on the Status, Privileges and Immunities of KFOR and UNMIK and their Personnel in Kosovo (August 18, 2000).

5 A detailed description can be found in: Maciej Zaremba, "Wir kamen, sahen und versagten," *Süddeutsche Zeitung Magazin*, August 24 (2007:34).

6 According to the conclusion reached in Julia Tielsch's analysis. See: Julia Tielsch, *UN-Verwaltung und Menschenrechte. Die internationale Zivilverwaltung im Kosovo* (Frankfurt a. M.: Peter Lang, 2006).

7 See: Helmut Kramer and Vedran Dzihic, *Die Kosovo-Bilanz. Scheitert die internationale Gemeinschaft?* (Vienna: LIT, 2006).

8 Kramer/Dzihic, (see note 7), 123–25.

9 Other estimates go as high as 700,000 Kosovo Albanians. It is difficult to guess precisely, since estimates also include the many people who have no residence permits and are therefore not registered with the authorities.

10 Economic Strategy and Project Identification Group (ESPIG), "Toward a Kosovo Development Plan. The State of the Kosovo Economy and Possible Ways Forward," August 2004.

11 See: The Institute for Spatial Planning, *Kosovo Profile*, Prishtina, June 2004.

12 European Commission, Kosovo (according to Resolution 1244 of the United Nations Security Council), "2005 Progress Report," Brussels, November 9, 2005; see: Tielsch, (see note 6).

13 "Not Doing Anything is Definitely Not an Option." Quoted by the Institute for Spatial Planning in: *Kosovo Profile*, Prishtina, June 2004.

14 See: European Stability Initiative (ESI), "Utopian Visions. Governance Failures in Kosovo's Capital," June 8, 2006 http://www.esiweb.org/index.php?document_ID=78&id=156&lang=en (last accessed January 3, 2010).

15 See Michael Martens's comments in: "Prishtina, ein balkanischer Vorort von Utopia," *Frankfurter Allgemeine Zeitung*, June 14, 2006.

16 As shown, for example, by the metropolis of Athens, with its population of millions. See: Sotiris Choutiris, Elisabeth Heidenreich and Detlev Ipsen, *Von der Wildnis zum urbanen Raum. Zur Logik der peripheren Verstädterung am Beispiel Athen* (Frankfurt a. M.: Campus-Verlag, 1993).

17 For more on the positive and negative aspects of deregulated urban development as discussed here, see: Sotiris Choutiris, Elisabeth Heidenreich and Detlev Ipsen, "Eine Stadt baut sich selber. Formen der Selbstregulation in der Stadtentwicklung. Das Beispiel Athen," in *Metropole, Weltstadt, Global City: Neue Formen der Urbanisierung. Dortmunder Beiträge zur Raumplanung*, ed. Ursula von Petz and Klaus M. Schmals (Dortmund: Informationskreis für Raumplanung, 1992), 60.

18 "Turbo architecture is global, because it rejects modernism and embraces forms that either existed before modernism or else followed it. Turbo architecture tends, consciously or unconsciously, toward oriental forms and presents them as an authentic legacy." Srdjan Jovanovic Weiss, "Was war oder was ist Turbo-Kultur?," *Stadtbauwelt* 163, *Bauwelt* 95 (2004:36): 57.

19 This is not just the case in Prishtina. See: Choutiris/Heidenreich/Ipsen, (see note 17).

20 Weiss, (see note 18).

21 See: Elmar Altvater and Birgit Mahnkopf, "Die Informalisierung des städtischen Raums," http://www.polwiss.fuberlin.de/people/altvater/Aktuelles/informal.pdf (last accessed January 3, 2010).

22 See: Edward Luttwak, *Turbo-Capitalism: Winners and Losers in the Global Economy* (New York: HarperCollins Publishers, 1999).

23 Choutiris/Heidenreich/Ipsen, (see note 17), 49f. Kosovo is based on one of the oldest, most conservative social institutions: the traditional, patriarchal household consisting of several families. See: ESI (European Stability Initiative), "Das gekappte Rettungsseil. Auswanderung, Familien und die Zukunft des Kosovos," September 18, 2006, http://www.esiweb.org/index.php?lang=en&id=156&document_ID=80 (last accessed January 3, 2010).

ASTANA, ALMATY, AND AKTAU

Architectural Experiments
in the Steppes of Kazakhstan

Philipp Meuser

Astana

The tenth anniversary of Kazakhstan's new capital city, Astana took place on June 10, 2008. There were none of the festivities of the previous years, their absurdity recalling the worst excesses of the Soviet era: no central stage for propaganda performances, no press-ganged schoolgirls with bows in their hair, no boys in uniform waving small flags, no dancers and musicians performing a mix of Kazakh folklore and international pop. This year, the anniversary of the capital—which is located between the Kazakh steppe and the Siberian swamps—was a day like any other. In fact the celebrations took place exactly a month later, on the birthday of President Nursultan Nazarbayev, which has been declared a public holiday in the capital. The clocks run differently in this young nation, where the former Communist party chairman has been in power for almost two decades.

Astana, which was an insignificant place called Tselinograd (▶ 1) on the road from Moscow to Almaty until a few years ago, is now a two-speed city. While the local people try to live their modest lives in their rural homes, the omnipresent dredgers are testimony to its unstoppable urbanization, and to the government's preoccupation with rapid renewal (▶ 2). The inhabitants have already had a foretaste of the city's changing role over the coming years. The Ishim River has been artificially widened, and is now up to 200 meters in breadth, rivaling the Thames, Seine, or Danube, though on closer examination it looks more like a stagnant lake than a fast-flowing torrent. It is narrow at the best of times, snaking its way through the surrounding marshlands and grinding almost to a halt as it passes through the city; but at least Astana now has a promenade like those found in many riverside Russian cities.

1

1　Central Square, Tselinograd, today Astana, Kazakhstan, ca. 1985.

Aside from its somewhat controversial political importance as the new capital of Kazakhstan, Astana plays a major socioeconomic role in the region. In 1997, when the government decided to build it, 1.8 billion tenge, or about 10 billion euros, were budgeted for the project. The city's population doubled to more than 600,000 in the first ten years. In the past, most of its inhabitants were of Russian, Ukrainian, or German descent; today, 60 percent are Kazakhs, who formerly represented a minority of less than one in five.

To encourage investment and business growth, the 1,052-hectare capital has been declared a special economic zone with low taxes and duties. Early projects included the construction of factories for Nokian (tires), General Electric (locomotives), Nissan (vehicles), Lancaster Group Kazakhstan (silicon), and the Apple City logistics site. Many service and leisure facilities have also been built, sometimes on a massive scale; these include an ice skating rink, a 24,000-square-meter indoor cycling track, a cinema and a concert hall on the banks of the Ishim, two business centers, Sir Norman Foster's Abu Dhabi Plaza complex (▶ 3), and a cluster of skyscrapers containing offices, arts facilities, shops, restaurants, and expensive apartments.

A similar project, designed by Foster and built by a Turkish company, is the Khan Shatyry ("Royal Marquee") shopping and entertainment center (▶ 4). This also includes apartments, a five-star hotel, cinemas, cafés, an underground station, and sports and fitness facilities.

Some of the projects are fine examples of international contemporary architecture built as part of a comprehensive modernization and expansion plan, while others, personally promoted by President Nazarbayev, bear all the hallmarks of megalomania. These include the central government district with its huge pyramidal Palace of Peace and Concord, the 105-meter Bayterek Monument (▶ 5-9), and the proposed Batygai Indoor City, consisting of ten skyscrapers under a glass canopy and incorporating not only homes and shops, but a school, a hospital, and government offices. Another project, even vaster, is the planned sports and tourism complex in Borovoye, some 150 kilometers north of Astana. This includes new villages, hotels, and no fewer than twelve horse farms. President Nazarbayev intends to transform Borovoye into the Las Vegas of Kazakhstan, creating 50,000 jobs, attracting tourists from all over the world and providing a suitably elegant setting for state receptions. The government has also ordered the closure of all but two of the country's casinos: Borovoye and Kapchagai, near Almaty.

Social Politics

Despite all these pretensions to grandeur since Kazakhstan was created in 1991 and its status as the world's ninth largest country, it was a comedy film—a major box-office success—that truly put Kazakhstan on the map. *Borat* follows the fortunes of its eponymous Kazakh hero as he leaves his village on a blundering voyage of discovery across the United States, giving a jaundiced and politically incorrect glimpse both of Americans and of his own country's backwardness.

2

3

2   Presidential Palace and Ministerial Buildings in the Government District of Astana, architect Shochan Mataybekov, Astana, Kazakhstan, 2007.
3   Project Abu Dhabi Plaza, architects Foster and Partners, Astana, Kazakhstan, 2007.

4

4   Project Khan Shatyry Entertainment Center, architects Foster and Partners in cooperation with Linea
Tusavul Architecture and Gultekin Architecture, Astana, Kazakhstan, 2006–10.

5

5   Palace of Peace and Reconciliation, architects Foster and Partners in cooperation with Tabanlioglu Architecture & Consulting and Bureau Happold, Astana, Kazakhstan, 2007.

6

7

6   Ministerial Building, architect Shochan Mataybekov, Astana, Kazakhstan, 2007.
7   The Grand Alatau Waterfront Residential Towers, architect Shochan Mataybekov, Astana, Kazakhstan, 2007.

8   Bayterek Monument, architect Akmyrza I. Rustembekov, Astana, Kazakhstan, 2007.

9

The fact that Borat is a fictional character seemed to matter little in the ensuing controversy. The film's depiction of an impoverished central Asian country populated by illiterate yokels was too much for the government, which decided that moviegoers in places like Almaty and Aktau were incapable of making up their own minds, and promptly banned the movie. In an ironic twist, tourist numbers increased fivefold after the film was released worldwide.

With its wealth of natural resources, Kazakhstan is one of the world's leading exporters of raw materials. As well as oil and natural gas, it boasts a virtual periodic table of the elements, including uranium, selenium, and precious metals. Its population of 15.8 million is a quarter of that of the United Kingdom, living on an area of 2.7 million square kilometers, eleven times larger than the UK. At 42 percent of the total, the Kazakhs are the largest ethnic group, but the area is also home to Russians, Ukrainians, Germans, Uzbeks, Tatars, and some smaller, mainly Asiatic minorities.

There are large disparities in living standards. While the impoverished rural regions in the north and east are effectively cut off from the country's economic progress, cities such as the former capital Almaty and the former fishing village Atyrau are experiencing a rapid rise

9   View from the Palace of Peace and Reconciliation on the Presidential Palace, Astana, Kazakhstan, 2007.

in prosperity and causing a wave of rural depopulation. Life expectancy is way below the average for developed countries, at sixty-two years for men and seventy-three for women, compared to seventy-six and eighty-one in the UK. Because of these regional inequalities, the flight to the cities has been so great that, increasingly, the only people left behind in the country are those too poor, old or weak to make a new start.

Although Kazakhstan is nominally a democratic presidential republic, Nazarbayev has changed the constitution and engaged in other maneuvers to concentrate as much power as possible in his own hands. Although the constitution prevents him from serving more than two consecutive terms, in the spring of 2007 the parliament, in which his *Nur Otan* (Light of the Fatherland) party holds an absolute majority, voted to exempt him from this rule as the first president of the Republic of Kazakhstan.

There is no political opposition or free press; just before the parliamentary elections in the same year, small parties were banned from forming alliances with one another (as opposed to with larger parties), making it almost impossible to attain the 7 percent threshold required to win seats. Since 2007, the constitutional assembly has been peopled entirely by members of Nazarbayev's party, as have other key positions in the country. For many years the state television company has been controlled by the president's eldest daughter, Dariga Nazarbayeva; other leading companies are also managed by his cronies, and he has the final say on key investment projects.

Since 2000, Kazakhstan has experienced a dramatic growth of at least 9 percent per year, attracting more direct foreign investment than all of its Central Asian neighbors combined. The ubiquitous president and his nepotistic regime have exploited these successes to the full, building a propaganda machine against which the small and fragmented opposition is powerless, and riding roughshod over objections from such organizations as *Human Rights Watch*. The West has too much of a stake in Kazakhstan's oil and gas to rock the boat. The country has been awarded the presidency of the OECD in 2010, as well as permanent membership of the *World Trade Organization*, and has been chosen as the venue of the 2011 Asian Games.

Despite its protestations to the contrary, Kazakhstan is riddled with corruption, which is a particular problem for foreign companies. It is rated by *Transparency International* as the 122nd most corrupt country from a list of 145, placing it on a par with Sudan, Niger, and Guatemala. As the owner of the building that houses the German consulate general in Almaty points out, "You pay for everything in Kazakhstan, even a building permit for a diplomatic representation."

The payments are treated not as bribes but as fees for unspecified third-party services. Large sums are particularly common in the construction industry, where licensing authorities and materials suppliers exploit the fact that delays are expensive for contractors. In 2005, for example, a building permit for a four-story apartment block in Almaty cost US$30,000, and a permit to relocate a public road around US$5,000—which was also the price payable in Astana for sufficient land to build a house or for a zoning permit. The construction business is commonly transacted through nonexistent middlemen, with the real investors in the background "buying" the completed building at a fraction of the amount it cost to build.

The country still presents a contradictory picture to international eyes. Dark memories of the Soviet era are still fresh in people's minds, not least because of the disastrous consequences of decades of environmental neglect, including nuclear testing in the steppe near Semipalatinsk and the tragic disappearance of the Aral Sea. But observers also acknowledge that Kazakhstan has made a very orderly transition from planned economy to free market, and has been successful in encouraging foreign investment and gaining respect in the global community.

President Nazarbayev has announced plans to turn Kazakhstan into one of the world's biggest exporters over the next few years, with natural gas production increasing 50 percent to forty-five billion cubic meters by 2010. Kazakhstan and its neighbor Turkmenistan are participating in a Russian-led pipeline project to transport gas through Russia to Central and Western Europe. It is also involved in the construction of the Burgas-Alexandroupolis pipeline in Bulgaria and the expansion of the Caspian Pipeline Consortium system, transporting Kazakh oil from the Tengis basin at the Caspian Sea to the Russian Black Sea port of Novorossiysk.

10　Head Office of the Oil Company KazMunayGaz, architect Alexander Belovich et al., Astana, Kazakhstan, 2007.

Rapid Growth is Fueled by Oil

Since it gained independence, Kazakhstan has worked hard to become a major force on the economic map. Rising growth rates have marked the end of the painful transition that took place in all the former republics after the collapse of the Soviet Union, accompanied by decaying infrastructure, declining markets, and lack of regulation. The country's rich natural resources have lured long-term investors, enabling it to begin building a primary sector to transport raw materials reliably and efficiently and, with the help of foreign companies, processing facilities for oil and other products. The corporation Tengizchevroil, for example, is a joint venture between Chevron, ExxonMobil, Lukarco, and the local company KazMunayGaz (▶ 10), while Italy's Agip group has been chosen by the Kazakhs as a joint-venture partner to pump gas from the area around Uralsk.

The construction and mechanical engineering industries have also enjoyed rapid growth. The former accounted for 10 percent of gross domestic product in 2007, largely as a result of the huge investments made in the expansion of Astana and in well and pipeline construction. Many of the country's new oil and gas markets have been secured with the help of Russia, still its most important strategic partner. This could not have been achieved without massive foreign investment: in 2006, for example, direct investment totaled US$32.5 billion, compared to US$24.1 billion in Armenia, Azerbaijan, Georgia, Kyrgyzstan, Tajikistan, Turkmenistan, and Uzbekistan combined. In this respect, Kazakhstan has now overtaken countries such as South Africa, Poland, and Israel.

However, the country's strong dependence on the global economy also has its downside. In 2007, as the world recession began to bite, its previously unbroken growth dipped for the first time, thanks to a sharp fall in western investment and global economic insecurity. The construction industry was the worst hit by falling investment because it is highly dependent on bank loans: its growth rates more than halved, and the boom in residential construction slowed drastically. Lending income growth, which had previously been rising steadily, slumped from over 50 percent in 2007 to 14 percent in the following year. Investment was also hit by the rising cost of borrowing, and with inflation at just over 20 percent and food prices increasing sharply, real incomes declined. However, the effects of the recession were alleviated by a growing worldwide demand for oil and metals, Kazakhstan's most important exports, and this is likely to continue.

Oil drilling in the Tengis fields, which started in 1993, is expected to attract over US$20 billion in investment within four decades. Many of the key players are leading international oil and construction materials companies, committed to long-term expansion in Kazakhstan despite the current recession. They include the German ThyssenKrupp Corporation, which is building cement, silicon, and chemicals factories.

The government's intention to develop a flourishing raw materials sector is also reflected in improvements in the infrastructure, designed to make Kazakhstan attractive both to foreign investors and skilled workers. A very large proportion of the population is economically active, so the country needs to recruit more labor. There has already been an increase in immigration, with a healthy employment market drawing young men from Kazakhstan's southern neighbors—Kyrgyzstan, Uzbekistan and Tajikistan—into its industrial cities.

With almost every area of the economy seriously underdeveloped, the prospects for foreign investment are good. The government is using oil revenue to fund the construction and expansion of public services; in the Atyrau region alone, it is building 150 hospitals, 300 outpatient clinics, and 300 schools. It is also modernizing and extending the national road and transport system and updating the electricity grid. The service sector is gradually gaining in relative importance, mainly as a result of the medium-term fall in construction and manufacturing growth. Meanwhile, the property market in the big cities, particularly in the fast-expanding financial center of Almaty, is becoming much more diversified, with the demand for high-quality residential buildings and offices rising all the time.

11　View of the Financial District and the Al-Farabi Street from the JW Marriott Hotel, Almaty, Kazakhstan, 2008.

Before the banking crash in 2008, construction was one of the fastest-growing sectors, expanding sevenfold between 2000 and 2007 and worth US$7.8 billion by 2008. Property prices rose by 30 percent between 2001 and 2004, and then jumped 103 percent during 2005 and 2006. The figures reflect the huge shortage in this area, which is inevitably attracting speculators, but this is a disproportionately risky business. What impact the financial crisis will have on the construction business will be seen in the near future.

While the main focus at the turn of the millennium was on building factories and other industrial infrastructure, investors are now venturing into the gradually growing housing market and high-class offices, hotels, and leisure facilities. Most of the construction is concentrated in three regions, Almaty, Astana, and the Atyrau oilfields on the Caspian Sea, which together account for over 60 percent of volume.

Almaty

Almaty plays a particularly important role in this process. Although the government moved to Astana in 1997, it is still the country's economic and cultural hub, and is gradually being transformed into a major center for the finance sector (▶ 11).

There are several reasons for the city's continued attractiveness. It has a relatively high standard of living, a strong sense of history and a distinctly cosmopolitan feel. The government's relocation has freed up large areas of office space, which are being occupied mainly by start-ups. Many international business, cultural, and political organizations, such as Germany's *Goethe Institut*, have chosen to remain in Almaty rather than moving to Astana. These factors have created a continued long-term demand for high-quality property, and with many shopping centers and office buildings in the city occupied on long-term leases, many companies have set up their own offices.

The overheated property market has also resulted in the construction of poorly earthquake-proofed buildings in one of the world's most seismically active regions, with a high potential of experiencing tremors of 9 or even 10 on the Richter scale. Only Samal Towers, the CDC-1 Center and various buildings constructed by the Turkish/Kazakh developer Capital Partners qualify as 1A-class properties, meaning that they are centrally located, earthquake-proof, and with a high-quality finish, offering professional facility management, adequate parking, security, cleaning, restaurants, and central air-conditioning.

In the medium term, the demand for these upscale properties is likely to keep pace with the growth of the Kazakh economy, particularly since so many of the new arrivals are international companies demanding western standards. This in turn will result in increased inner-city building densities and cause Almaty to expand beyond its existing boundaries. Already, the planning authorities' inability to stand up to investors with deep pockets has resulted in encroachment on greenbelt land on the outskirts of the downtown area.

The continued growth in demand for office property is not the only problem facing the city. Office rents stood at up to US$60 per square meter in mid-2008, and housing was

also in short supply, sending rents spiraling upwards in the downtown area. These needs can only be met by a policy of large-scale urban development. Four new cities are planned to the north of Almaty; one of these, G4 City, is a self-contained conurbation of four satellite towns along the existing road between Almaty and Kapchagai.

The name of each of these projects reflects its function within the region. Gate City, in the Pervomaika district outside the entrance to Almaty, will serve as a business center for the new conurbation, while Golden City, near the Dmitriyevski Bridge, will be primarily residential in character. Growing City, close to the Nikolayevski Bridge, will be industrial, and Green City, on the banks of the Kapchagai reservoir, will be a tourist center. G4 City will provide new homes and jobs for 400,000 people, 100,000 at each site. This huge and ambitious project was planned by the Korean-Kazakh architect Alexander M. Chwan.

Rem Koolhaas' Science City

Naukograd is the Russian term for "science city," or Technopolis in Greek. The master plan for this futuristic and visionary project near Almaty is truly innovative. Rem Koolhaas' design for the Kazakh-British Technical University breaks down the boundaries between city and countryside, civilization and nature, in a location that encourages such a boldness of approach (▶ 12).

12   Project Kazakh-British Technical University (Naukograd) in Talgar near Almaty, Office for Metropolitan architecture OMA, Talgar, Kazakhstan 2007.

The area surrounding the former capital is one of Kazakhstan's most beautiful, and its development demanded a great deal of sensitivity on the part of the designer. Fortunately, university campuses tend to blend in with their surroundings, and their energy comes from within rather than from without. Koolhaas' design is inward-looking, making the natural landscape a key element of the physical structure. The campus buildings consist of modular bars, loops, and blocks with open spaces between them, and road traffic is replaced by a chairlift system. The architect has also created an additional level by planting the roofs and terraces with gardens, open spaces and water features.

The site combines all the standard features of a city, affording space for living, study, research, and leisure, with restaurants and public buildings complementing the university and providing shelter from the region's hot, dry summers and long, frigid winters. In warm weather, the buildings open up into the green hills surrounding them, while in the depths of winter they resemble nothing so much as warm, brightly lit UFOs offering no incentive to venture outside.

Aktau 2020: A City Reinvented

After Astana, the most ambitious urban project is the expansion of the city of Aktau on the Caspian Sea. The city was founded in 1963 after uranium was discovered on the Mangyshlak peninsula in the late nineteen-fifties, and designed to house miners and white-collar workers. As the mining expanded, it became necessary to build an entire city, complete with infrastructure. The result was Shevchenko, named after Ukraine's renowned nineteenth-century lyric poet, Taras Shevchenko.

Like other new cities of its time, it is a product of post-war Soviet architecture. The first apartment blocks were simple, temporary-looking low-rise structures, which were later replaced by multistory wooden buildings. Until the Soviet Union collapsed in 1991, Shevchenko was a closed city; the mining of uranium, which was used in nuclear power stations and for military purposes, required strict confidentiality. This created a sense of isolation, and to make the inhabitants' lives more pleasant, the planners deviated significantly from the schematic layout typical of such sites.

Eventually, the city acquired drinking water and energy supplies, and its administrative role in this thinly populated area increased. As a result, it grew constantly, and in 1975 was awarded the Sir Patrick Abercrombie prize for urban planning by the *Union Internationale des Architectes*. Like other new towns of the early nineteen-sixties, many of them influenced by Le Corbusier's Chandigarh, Shevchenko does not have street names, but instead is divided into sections known as mikrorayons, each with its own separate function.

When the state of Kazakhstan was created in 1991, the city was renamed Aktau. As the country severed its ties with Moscow and the planned economy began to crumble, it experienced a serious recession. Not until the late nineteen-nineties did Aktau gradually begin to profit from the growth of the oil industry, awakening from its slumbers to become an

13

important focus for international investors. As a result, it is now undergoing comprehensive restructuring and expansion which will change the appearance of this former Soviet planned city forever.

The biggest development is *Aktau City*, a huge project on the shores of the Caspian Sea next to Aktau. This 4,590-hectare site is being built on by a consortium from the Persian Gulf, a region with a long experience of building new cities on no man's land. This one will cost an extraordinary US$38 billion; each building will have an unobstructed view of the sea, and the business district will be studded with gleaming skyscraper office blocks.

Aktau City consists of six districts: one devoted to oil and technology, another housing the university, one located at the seafront, *Vista Park*, a ceremonial boulevard, a hotel, and entertainment district. The master plan is by the Boston architects Koetter Kim & Associates (▶ 13).

The oil and technology district will eventually be a bustling business center containing the city's trademark building, the *Energy Tower*, which will be 340 meters high and built in the shape of a drilling rig. Nearby is the *Crystal Bazaar*, grouping a large number of shops and restaurants under a huge glass roof. The science, research, and cultural facilities are concentrated in the university district: Aktau's new university will teach a full range of oil-and energy-related disciplines. A number of residential districts will be scattered throughout the

13 Urban extension of Aktau, architects Koetter Kim & Associates, project 2007–20, Kazakhstan.

city, while the seafront will comprise a chain of small artificial islands complete with exclusive villas and expensive apartment blocks designed to evoke the French Riviera.

Vista Park is a mixed-income housing area surrounded by parkland and sloping down to the sea, while the ceremonial boulevard is lined with museums and galleries chronicling the region's history and designed for the edification of residents and tourists. The foundation stone of Aktau City was laid by President Nazarbayev in September 2007, and the giant new development should be completed by 2020.

The Future for Kazakhstan's Neighbors

Such hugely ambitious projects are not the sole preserve of Kazakhstan: other central Asian nations have reaped the benefits of the oil and gas boom. Turkmenistan, for example, is planning its own tourist resort in the Caspian seaport of Turkmenbashi, formerly Krasnovodsk. This will be the first free trade zone in the country, which is still a dictatorship, and should provide a massive boost to the local economy. It will eventually include sixty new hotels, restaurants, a sports stadium, and a shopping center for pleasure-seeking Turkmen vacationers.

President Gurbanguly Berdimuhamedov, who came to power in February 2007, has announced plans to relax visa restrictions on visitors and proclaimed the establishment of a duty-free area. In a typical example of the spirit of a dictator's optimism, which prevails in central Asia, Turkmenistan plans to attract billions of dollars in foreign investment. These newly created states are seeking to emulate Dubai in their quest for national identity and rapid access to the global markets. Their success or failure will depend in no small measure on their ability to achieve political and social democracy.[1]

Endnotes

1   Further reading: Philipp Meuser, *Ästhetik der Leere. Moderne Architektur in Zentralasien* (Berlin: Braun, 2002); Philipp Meuser, "Building one's 'I.' In Search of National Identity," *Project Russia* 4 (2003); Simone Voigt, "Stararchitekten für die Steppe," *Ost-West Contact* 7 (2007): 10–12; *Vom roten Stern zur blauen Kuppel. Kunst und Architektur aus Zentralasien*, ifa Gallery exh. cat. Curators: Barbara Barsch, Philipp Meuser (Berlin: ifa, 2004).

POST-SOCIALIST OR POST-MODERNIST?

The Search for a New Urbanism in Armenia

Tigran Harutyunian

Introduction

After the collapse of the totalitarian regime in the Soviet Union and the creation of an independent Armenia in 1991, the government ceased to be the primary regulator of architecture. The once stable social structure fell apart; government control over urban planning and new construction waned.

The new capitalist reality heralded the reorientation of architecture to a focus on individuals rather than on society. Private commissions became the driving force of the new architecture that would likely have languished without them. The politicoeconomic climate in Armenia in the first years of its independence was not favorable to the development of architecture. Due to this, architectural activity over the course of seven years (roughly from 1991–98) was almost nonexistent. During this time, the majority of commissions were for buildings like private villas and other small projects (gas stations, restaurants, et cetera). Despite the considerable amount of such construction, these structures did not yet reflect the new paradigm of modern Armenian architecture.

The gradual improvement of the Armenian economy together with the involvement of foreign investors brought about increased demand for architecture. In a construction boom characteristic of developing economies, the construction sector became the primary industry of post-Soviet Armenia. This boom was centralized in the capital, as well as some popular resorts (the shores of Lake Sevan, Tsaghkadzor). Approximately 85 to 90 percent of new construction in the republic takes place in the capital city, Armenia's only metropolis. For this reason, the discussion of modern Armenian architecture in this work will focus primarily on examples found in Yerevan.

For roughly fifteen years, Yerevan was without any kind of urban development plan or regulations to guide the capital's growth. This had some unfortunate consequences for the city's infrastructure: such "organic" growth resulted in worsened ecological and transportation conditions in the capital, a reduction in the amount of gardens and green spaces, and so on. The construction boom and rising land prices in Yerevan's downtown led to generally poor architecture with many urban development and technical mistakes.[1] Before continuing our discussion of the particulars of Yerevan's post-communist development, let us briefly return to the history of the capital's urban development.

The Making of Yerevan

It is customary to trace the beginnings of the "new" Armenian architecture to 1828, the year in which Tsarist Russia conquered the fortress of Yerevan and annexed eastern Armenia. Russia's intention was to fortify its presence in the southern Caucasus, to which end it was important to establish a large population center. Yerevan turned out to be the best candidate. It was a middling town, consisting of the fortress to the southwest and four residential districts: Shahar to the north, Kond to the west, Dsoragukh to the southwest, and Damirbulag (populated primarily by Persians and Turks) to the south. The Armenians, having

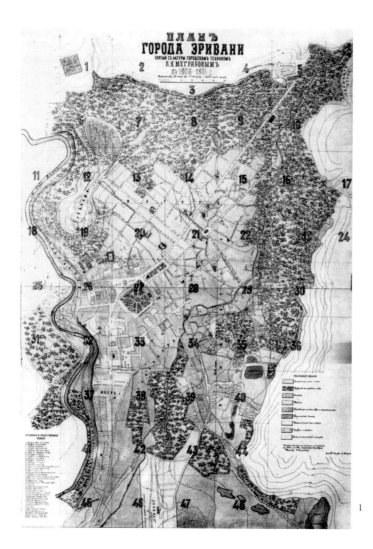

ПЛАНЪ
ГОРОДА ЭРИВАНИ
СНЯТЫЙ СЪ НАТУРЫ ГОРОДСКИМЪ ТЕХНИКОМЪ
К.Я.МЕГРАБОВЫМЪ
въ 1906-1911г.

until then been ruled by the Persians, assimilated elements of Persian culture. Yerevan consisted mostly of clay houses, churches, and mosques. The only significant structure from this era still remaining is the Blue Mosque. In 1856, the regional engineer A. Stotski drafted a general plan according to which the city of Yerevan was to develop. This general plan exemplified rationalist, geometric principles of city planning (▶ 1). According to this plan, the developed part of Yerevan would stretch from the northwest to the southeast (along Krepostnaya Street, now Abovian Street). During the end of the nineteenth century and the beginning of the twentieth century, construction began on many northwest-southeast and northeast-southwest streets.

1   Plan of Yerevan, architect A. Stotski, Yerevan, Armenia, 1865.

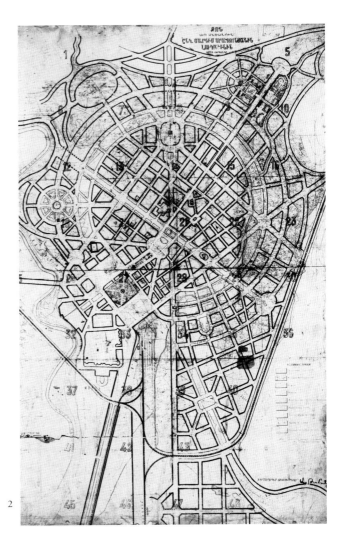

2

This period marks the paradigm shift in Armenian development. Armenian architecture changed its course, developing now in the context of European architectural processes (retaining, of course, its own regional character). With regard to style, architecture in Tsarist Armenia can generally be described as neoclassical and eclectic. Classical and Renaissance motifs, captured in the local black tuff, distinguish these structures—primarily apartment homes, mansions, gymnasiums, factories, hospitals, and the like.

2   General Plan for Yerevan's development, architect Aleksander Tamanian, Yerevan, Armenia, 1924.

Tamanian's Capital

In 1919, a year after the declaration of independence by the short-lived Democratic Republic of Armenia (1918–20), the young Armenian government invited the architect Aleksander Tamanian (1878–1936), a member of the *St. Petersburg Academy of Arts*, to draft a new general plan for Yerevan's development. When the plan was completed in 1924, it was approved by the government of the new Soviet Republic of Armenia (▶ 2). Tamanian had been tasked with designing the republic's capital. According to his plan, Yerevan was to open up towards Mount Ararat, a powerful national symbol. The mountain was to become the focal point of the city's perspective, the new, wide streets designed to admit the maximum possible amount of sunlight. Tamanian intended for the city to embody an Armenian Renaissance, following the 1915 genocide. Though a master of the classical school, Tamanian referred also to the regional architectural flavor in an attempt to revive and renew long-forgotten local traditions, masterfully synthesizing the classical with the uniquely Armenian.

The general plan accounted for a total population of 150,000 (with growth beginning from approximately 60,000). Even as Tamanian proposed radically new ideas for the city's development, he preserved the existing rectangular structure of the old plan. So, the new compositional axis lay from the north to the south. Several streets were to be widened. The general plan was grounded in the idea of a garden city. To this end, Tamanian proposed the construction of a ring-shaped boulevard that would circumscribe the residential district and act as the city's lungs. This new radial-ring system would allow for easier access to the city center from other neighborhoods. The majority of residential and administrative structures would be contained within the ring. A university district was planned for the northern part of the city. Another major component of the general plan was the construction of a major administrative center focused on Lenin Square—the focal point of the entire composition—and dominated by City Hall. Also proposed was a connection between the administrative center and Theater Square (the area surrounding the opera house), this connection to be realized via the Northern Avenue. In addition to calling for the construction of many landscaped boulevards, the general plan also included what was to become the city's Main Avenue, stretching from the northwest to the southeast. The industrial district was to be located in the south of the city on account of its flatter terrain and the direction of the dominant winds.

Aleksander Tamanian's general plan guided not only the architectural and urban planning development of Yerevan itself, but also of much of the rest of Armenia. Subsequent general plans for Yerevan were based on Tamanian's plan. Unfortunately, the majority of his ideas were not realized until after his death. His most significant projects were the City Hall (▶ 3) and the Opera House, completed in 1940 and 1953, respectively. Other projects, like the Northern Avenue, were realized only after the collapse of the USSR.

Due to the capital's rapid growth, Tamanian began work in 1935 on a new general plan, which, unfortunately, he was never able to finish (having died in 1936). The completion of

3

the new general plan, "Big Yerevan," intended to account for a total population of 450,000, was scheduled for 1939 ("Lengiprogor"—architects I. Malozemov, S. Klevitskii, and Norayr Zargarian). This further developed Yerevan was to include the Arabkir, Nork, and Saritag plateaus as well as the Nor Malatia and Nor Sebastia settlements on the west; the Dalmian garden district and Nor Butania on the south. Construction in the available northern and western areas of the city consisted equally of residential and industrial zones, leading eventually to considerable problems.

The Post-War Period

There was another attempt by a group of planners, led by Zargarian in 1951, to further develop Tamanian's general plan. The intensely ideological character of Soviet architecture imparted a certain conceptual unity to the city's development. This period was marked by the completion of several large-scale urban development projects including Lenin Square, the Cognac production facility, Matenadaran, the bridge "Pobeda," the central railway station, and so on. The current transportation infrastructure was put into place precisely during this period.

The city was expected to develop towards the northeast and southwest. The expansion of Yerevan was carried out in accordance with the general plan. The city's border stretched to include the right bank of the river Rasdan. Due to close relations with the capital, several nearby areas (Avan, Noragavit, Charbakh, Kharbert, Sebastia, Malatia, and others) became administrative districts of Yerevan. These districts began to develop in Tamanian's style,

3   City Hall, 1926–40, based on the design by Aleksander Tamanian, Yerevan, Armenia, 2009.

4

though changes in the Soviet architectural paradigm prevented them from developing fully and organically. These changes were also apparent in many large-scale urban development projects (avenues, streets, squares, et cetera) that already exhibited changes in style, though they were still built in accordance with a single concept of urban development (▶ 4).

Despite these changes, many of these new avenues, streets, and buildings served to underline Tamanian's urban planning and stylistic ideology. As a result, this sort of locally-flavored neoclassicism was often imitated.

Yerevan: Megalopolis

The industrialization of the nineteen-sixties and -seventies brought about rapid growth in the cities of Armenia. At this time, Yerevan was one of the fastest-growing cities in the Soviet Union. By the end of the nineteen-seventies, the total population of Yerevan had exceeded 1,000,000—over seven times Tamanian's expectations. A new general plan, intended to guide Yerevan's development until the year 2000, was approved in 1971 by the architects Mikael Mazmanian, Eduard Papian, Georgiy Murza, and Tsolak Chakhalian. This plan

4   District Malatia, with a typical building structure from the 1940s and 1950s, Yerevan, Armenia, 2009.

divided Yerevan into nine districts, as well as an additional three industrial districts in its suburbs. The territories added to Yerevan by the 1951 general plan began active development. This development employed new methodologies. New districts and microdistricts were formed; high-speed roads were planned; and so on. The most significant change of this period was the transformation of Yerevan into a megalopolis and the development that comes with such a transformation (the construction of a subway system, et cetera). It was during this period that the construction of the Main Avenue was completed—one of Tamanian's major projects, which, though designed to be functional, was primarily a stylistic choice by the time of its completion. These processes of urbanization, however, brought about a number of contradictions which are difficult to unequivocally regard as being positive. For example, a number of high-rises (mostly residential) were built in the city center, distorting the city's skyline and historic character.

Yerevan: Capital of an Independent State

The city, faced with a new sociopolitical climate, required a new general plan to guide its development; with such a plan to include modern solutions to the city's immediate problems. The new capitalist city had to be built upon the communist past. A major component of this transformation was the revision of land use statutes and zoning regulations.

The new general plan (developed by the "Yerevanproekt" Institute in 2005) anticipates a population growth of 100,000, up to a total population of 1.2 million, by the year 2020. Unlike previous general plans, this plan focuses on internal development rather than expansion. The principles of sustainable development lie at the core of the new general plan. The new plan's chief distinguishing characteristic is its focus on the development of Yerevan as the capital of an independent state. Its main provisions have to do with the reconstruction and reorganization of the city's infrastructure. There are provisions to develop downtown districts, update existing industrial zones, renovate and improve residential zones (largely by refurbishing and redeveloping territories that currently contain poorly constructed single-story and track homes), and so on. An attempt is being made to restore lost green spaces, almost doubling the total green area, generally at the expense of low-density, few-storied residential zones. Further details of Yerevan's development are to be decided taking into account individual districts' zoning projects. The existing transportation infrastructure has been expanded. During the last several years, a number of new arteries of transportation, some of which had been included in previous general plans but never implemented, have been completed—highways, streets, underground crosswalks, and so on. Of course, the most important accomplishment has been the completion of the high-speed highway circling the city center (▶ 5).

It is worth noting, however, that many of the major urban development and other large-scale projects had been planned (and some even completed) before the new zoning projects and the current general plan were finalized. The uniqueness of Yerevan's post-Soviet

development comes from its struggle to keep up with the chaotically growing city while accounting for private investments. For example, a rezoning plan was proposed for the city center to develop business centers in place of three existing territories: the first—Yerevan Berd—southwest of the city center, in place of the current residential district Kilikia; the second, west of the city center, in place of the current residential district Kond; the third, south of the city center, in place of an existing industrial district. Taking into account the significant scale of these projects, the plan's authors "Yerevanproekt" (2007) tried to maximize opportunities for future investors to develop the city center and other major projects while preserving "Tamanian's little center." In accordance with the general plan, the driving idea has been to reclaim old, low-density, poorly constructed residential districts and reutilize the territories more effectively. Setting aside the reasonable desire to depressurize the

5   Masterplan of Yerevan in the year 2020, developed in 2005, Yerevan, Armenia, 2005.

crowded center, however, it is worth noting that the development of so many administrative and business complexes around the city center is somewhat misguided, since a city of Yerevan's size is unlikely to need so many such complexes. It becomes clear that, due to the capital's political and economic needs, rapid expansion has become the city planners' dominant priority. It is only natural, in light of Armenia's difficult social and economic climate, that preserving the cultural heritage has become less of a priority.

The prestige factor has also played a not insignificant role in the change of the city's character. The central, prestigious districts of Yerevan are the most picturesque places to live, traits for which demand is high among the capital's affluent residents, foreigners among them.[2] The original residential structures were sufficient for a time but, as the economic situation improved, so did demand for new and improved residences. These new buildings were often called "elite," referring to the increased comfort and higher standard of living.

Unfortunately, the growth of the construction industry had its own set of side effects. The rapid development of the downtown districts precluded a more contextual approach during the planning stages. The limited amounts of available land in the city center have proven to be an insurmountable obstacle for many development projects which would have served to strengthen the economy, many of which also had government support. Because there is no room to build new structures, older buildings are often replaced by newer ones. Best suited to be replaced are pre-Soviet buildings, the majority of which have fallen into disrepair. Most of the buildings of this kind are (or were) poorly maintained historical monuments. Because maintaining and repairing such monuments is significantly more expensive than removing and replacing them, few restoration projects are undertaken. Even when such projects are undertaken, they generally have a largely formal character, often renovating only the building's façade while additions and new constructions displace the original spaces and styles (▶ 6).

According to the general plan, a historic architectural square called "Old Yerevan" is to be established along Main Avenue. The architect Levon Vardanian first proposed the idea (▶ 7). The territory (around Abovian Street, Arami Street, Byuzand Street, and Kogbatsi Street) is to contain restored, reconstructed, and recreated architectural monuments—some originally located there, others to be moved there—of Tsarist Yerevan. This area is distinguished by the multitude of structures of precisely that period, which of course played a fundamental role in its selection. This project aims to preserve architectural monuments that would otherwise doubtless be lost in Armenia's current political and economic climate. However, it should be noted that even these desperate measures do little to preserve the cultural heritage, a fact that leads the project's critics to declare it a "graveyard."

Unfortunately, it is impossible, given the current situation in Armenia, to adequately preserve the cultural heritage. This problem, of course, is not limited to Yerevan; similar changes are taking place in other countries and cities of the former Soviet Union, including Moscow.[3] In Yerevan's central districts—those most appealing to investors—historical

monuments have been demolished and replaced by new eclectic and pseudo-historical structures. Because the prestige of city centers attracts buyers and investors, many cities are faced with a similar situation.

Stylistic Idiosyncrasies of Modern Armenian Architecture

The first major project of the post-Soviet era was the construction of the Northern Avenue. Naturally, an undertaking of this magnitude required enormous resources and could not have been completed without foreign investments and government sponsorship. The avenue elicits mixed feelings: "being Modern, [it] embodies a reevaluation and rebirth of Tamanian's architecture, creating a new character with hints of the past."[4]

6   Multifunctional building at the crossroads of Anrapetunian and Byuzand streets, architect Karen Harutyunian, Yerevan, Armenia, 2009.

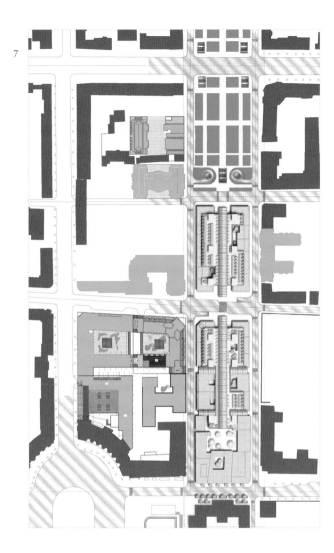

7

Tamanian imagined the Northern Avenue as a central axis connecting the cultural and administrative centers—the ballet and opera house—to City Hall. Today, constructing this axis would be a meaningless endeavor; during the nineteen-seventies, the construction of the State Art Gallery rendered the Northern Avenue idea impossible.[5] Tamanian's idea was instead reapplied in a social and business district near the capital's center. Critics, however, claim that this realization of his idea is artificial and meaningless, calling attention to the disharmony between the new avenue and the historic character of the city center.

Despite the fact that in terms of both urban development and stylistic approach, the Northern Avenue was intended to be a return to Tamanian's ideas, the execution (characterized by eclecticism and a distorted sense of scale) is inadequate to those ideas. The

7 Historical-architectural square "Old Yerevan," project by Levon Bardarian, Yerevan, Armenia, 2005.

8

avenue begins in a modernist style (the Nord complex, ▶ 8), undergoing a stylistic transformation on its way to the Republic Square, the buildings alongside it built in a more
traditional style merging the historic regional character with neoclassicism (the "Union
Armenia" complex).

Such backward-looking nostalgia also played a major role in another large-scale project:
the reconstruction of Myasnikian Square (now Moscow Square). This square serves as the
southwestern gate into the city center. Argishti Street, forming one of the square's boundaries, was built as part of this reconstruction. It is worth noting that in addition to traditional
(the Moscow House, ▶ 9) and reasonable modernist (the Renco business center) structures,
there have been attempts to complete construction projects begun by Armenian masters of
the Soviet era (the new Municipal Building, the restoration of the winery tower).

Yerevan's new Municipal Building (architect Jim Torosian) played a major role in establishing the square's character and has become one of the most significant architectural projects
of post-Soviet Yerevan. This building has become the dominant element not only of the
square, but also of the surrounding neighborhood. Planning for the project began in the
nineteen-seventies, during the Soviet era, and construction was started in the nineteen-
eighties. The collapse of the Soviet Union, however, put these plans on hiatus indefinitely.

8 Business center North, architects Gagik Oganissian and Oganes Mutafian, Yerevan, Armenia,
2009.

Construction of this indisputably interesting structure was finally completed in 2003; the building officially opened at the end of 2004. Of course, by the time the project had been realized, it had undergone considerable changes. However, according to the architect, these changes did not have a significant impact on the structure's ideological and aesthetic character. The building employs the theme of the twelve capitals of Armenia, including Yerevan. The façade alludes to the names of all of the existing capitals and the interior contains a museum of Yerevan's history, endeavoring to connect the past to the present.

The winery actively engaged the problem of preserving its own history; in 2007, the old Shustov Distillery was renovated and converted into a museum (architect Sarkis Sardarian). Work on a project to rebuild the winery tower based on Rafael Israelian's plans has already begun (▶ 10). This reconstruction project is unique in that the architect never settled on a final version of the tower. For a long time, during the nineteen-fifties, he developed many possible variants and produced countless sketches. By collaging these sketches, the new architect, Sarkis Sardarian, has recreated a "new" tower.

Post-Soviet Postmodernism

Opposite the decline of postmodernist tendencies in Western architecture during the nineteen-nineties, some characteristics of that movement began to manifest themselves in post-Soviet architecture. Communist Party rulings regarding architecture and urban planning

9   Moscow House, architect Levon Vardanian, Yerevan, Armenia, 2009.

precluded Soviet architecture from following a postmodernist path in parallel with the West. After the collapse of the USSR, postmodernist concepts, often somewhat distorted, began appearing in post-Soviet architecture. Despite this, post-Soviet architecture can generally be understood in a postmodernist context because during its development, it was strongly influenced by the concepts of postmodern architecture (a telling example of this might be the "Luzhkov style" in Moscow). "Postmodern architecture" here refers to architecture that regards the architectural object fundamentally as a "text"—architecture that establishes a dialogue between object and viewer, who must interpret that dialogue in terms of familiar codes and symbols. As a result, postmodern architecture can be characterized by collage, historicism, sensitivity to context, pluralism of styles, and ironic or grotesque reinterpretation of historical themes.

In light of this, the post-Soviet architecture of Armenia can be understood as the expansion of postmodernism into the East. This expansion of postmodern conceptions through the East was logical and predictable. Following the long period of faceless modernism during the Soviet era, the countries of Eastern Europe turned to their roots in an attempt to underline their uniqueness and traditions.

Despite differences in time, culture, and ideology, there is nevertheless a strong resemblance in terms of approaches to the methods and processes that establish architectural forms. The main similarity between postmodern and post-Soviet architecture is their emphasis on historicism. A further similarity is that both originated as a response to the previous dominant style—modernism. However, while one should regard postmodernism in Western architecture as a cultural and ideological revolution, post-Soviet postmodernism is better understood as a consequence of political regime change and a reevaluation of values.

10 Reconstruction of the Old Distillery, architects Rafael Israelian and Sarkis Sardarian, Yerevan, Armenia, 2008.

That said, post-Soviet postmodernism, unlike Western postmodernism, does not regard the architectural object as a "text." It includes historicism, pluralism of style, and sensitivity to context, but not irony, dialogue, or other characteristics of Western postmodern architecture. As a result, many post-Soviet buildings use historicism purely as a decorative element, thereby remaining within the modernist tradition.

In conclusion, it is worth noting that pluralism, the reappropriation of old codes and symbols, and eclecticism have been and continue to be dominant elements of the language of Armenian architecture. The use of regional neoclassicism as a stylistic device in Armenian architecture was already occurring even before the end of the Soviet era—as mentioned above, this style was being used during the nineteen-fifties and -sixties.

In its search for its own language, post-Soviet Armenian architecture similarly employed elements of regional neoclassicism, reinterpreting them through the lens of the contemporary social and political context. New building projects both in the city center and outside it, aiming to embellish the historical fabric of the capital while preserving its unique character, again returned to Yerevan's dominant architectural style. The absence of the ideology that defined Armenian architecture and urban planning during the Soviet era made room for an expanded architectural palette—one that, nevertheless, included many traditional tendencies. Despite the creative freedom afforded by political changes, traditionalism in Armenia (as compared to Russia and other former Soviet-Bloc nations) manifests in more rational and restrained ways. This movement, of course, should not be understood as a new tendency towards traditionalism or regional classicism in Armenian architecture. Simply put, the current socioeconomic situation has led investors to disregard architectural flourishes altogether, focusing instead on minimizing the time and capital necessary to erect new structures—structures that are themselves expected to bring in a maximized return per square meter.

Translated by Peter Kovalsky

Endnotes

1   Gurgen Mushegian, "12 Yerevanov ili edinyy gorod?" [12 Yerevans or a Single City?] (May 2006), http://www.armtown.com/news/ru/gol/20060525/2006052503/ (last accessed January 3, 2010).

2   The social conditions at the time gave rise to a sort of "castling" migration, the affluent moving in towards the city center while the less affluent residents of the center districts sold their homes and moved out.

3   Bart Goldhoorn and Philipp Meuser, Kaprealism. *Novaya arkhitektura v Rossii* [Capitalist Realism. New Architecture in Russia] (Berlin: DOM publishers, 2006).

4   Tigran Harutyunian, "Postmodernism i postsovetskaya arkhitektura Armenii," [Postmodernism and the Post-Soviet Armenian Architecture] in *Sbornik nauchnych trudov Yerevanskogo Gos. Universiteta arkhitektury i stroitel'stva* [Collection of Scientific Works of Yerevan State University of Architecture and Construction] 30 (2007:2): 64.

5   See: Karen Balian, *Sovremennaya nazional'naya arkhitektura Armenii* [Contemporary National Architecture of Armenia] (Yerevan: Hayastan, 1987).

LIST OF AUTHORS

Arnold Bartetzky Dr., studied History of Art, German Philology and Philosophy at Freiburg im Breisgau, Tübingen, and Cracow. Researcher at the Leipzig Center for the History and Culture of East Central Europe (GWZO) since 1995. Currently involved in research projects on visual state self-representation and the reconstruction of destroyed buildings in the nineteenth and twentieth centuries. Numerous publications on various aspects of architecture and urban planning from the Renaissance to the present day.

Eva Binder Dr., studied English and Russian Philology in Innsbruck and Moscow. Lecturer at the Department of Slavonic studies at the University of Innsbruck since 1999, where she teaches courses on Russian and Soviet film and literature. Her current field of research is twentieth-century Russian culture focusing on film, media, and cultural studies. Various publications on Soviet and Russian Cinema, and on Soviet visual culture.

Lydia Coudroy de Lille Dr., studied History and Geography at the École Normale Supérieure, Paris. Professor of Geography at the University of Lyon. Involved in the research center UMR 5600 "Environnement Ville Société" in Lyon. Research specializations and topics of publications: metropolization, housing, administrative reforms in Central and Eastern Europe, especially in Poland.

Mariusz Czepczyński Prof. Dr., Visiting Professor at the Eberhard-Karls-Universität Tübingen and the University of Gdansk. Researcher in several projects, consultant for municipalities and firms on development strategies and housing, transport, and tourism issues. His research activities include post-socialist landscape transformations, meanings of culture in urban conversion, social construction theory, local development and its strategies.

Marina Dmitrieva Dr., studied Art History and History at the Lomonossov-University of Moscow. Until 1992 worked at the Institute of Art History in Moscow. Teaching experience at the Universities of Moscow, Freiburg im Breisgau, Basel, Hamburg, and Bremen. Since 1996 researcher at the Leipzig Center for the History and Culture of East Central Europe (GWZO). Her fields of research are urban visual culture in Central and Eastern Europe, classical avant-garde, early modern art, and architecture in Central Europe.

Miléna Guest Assistant Prof. Dr., studied Geography at the Universities of Sofia and Paris I Panthéon-Sorbonne University. Research experience at the École Normale Supérieure Lettres et Sciences Humaines, Lyon, and at the University of Sofia. Currently teaching at the École Nationale Supérieure d'Architecture de Normandie. Several publications on urban planning, land tenure, and residential mobility of the inhabitants of urban areas in Central and Eastern Europe, especially in Bulgaria.

Cynthia Imogen Hammond Prof. Dr., studied Architectural History and Visual Art at Concordia University in Montreal. Since 2006 she has been Assistant Professor of Architectural History at Concordia University. In addition to her ongoing studio practice, she has published numerous articles and book chapters related to architecture, contemporary art, gender and urban space, and is currently completing a book on heritage, women's history, and public memory in the city of Bath, England.

Tigran Harutyunian Dr., architect and historian of architecture, studied at the Yerevan State University of Architecture and Construction. Postgraduate Student at the Institute of Arts at the National Academy of Sciences of Armenia from 2005 to 2008. Works as an architect and designer on numerous projects in Armenia. Publications on contemporary Armenian architecture, and the theory of architecture.

Augustin Ioan Prof. Dr., Professor at the University of Architecture and Urban Planning (UAUIM) in Bucharest, where he teaches architectural theory and the philosophy of space. Holds degrees in architecture, philosophy, and theology. Senior partner at the architect's offices Chora D.I. s.a. and Intergroupe Architecture srl in Bucharest. Numerous books and articles related to the communist built environment, contemporary sacred space, religious architecture, and the philosophy of public space.

Wilfried Jilge M.A., studied East European History, Slavic Philology and Economics at the Johannes-Gutenberg-University of Mainz. Researcher at the Leipzig Center for the History and Culture of East Central Europe (GWZO). Taught at the University of Potsdam and Humboldt University of Berlin. Various publications on nationalism and politics of history in East Central and Eastern Europe, particularly in Ukraine. Currently completing his doctoral dissertation on state symbolism, remembrance cultures, and nation-building in post-communist Ukraine.

Béla Kerékgyártó Prof. Dr., studied German Philology, Literature, and Philosophy at the Universities of Debrecen and Budapest. Associate Professor at the Department for Philosophy and History of Science of the Technical University in Budapest. His research fields are the theory and cultural history of modern architecture and urbanism. Publications include a comprehensive anthology of architectural theory in the twentieth century and articles on various aspects of architecture and urbanism in Berlin, Budapest, and Vienna.

Alfrun Kliems Dr., studied Russian and Czech Literature at Humboldt University of Berlin and Charles University in Prague. Literary theorist at the Leipzig Center for the History and Culture of East Central Europe (GWZO) since 1995. Her main interests are literature in exile and the poetics of migration, urban imagery, and underground literature in East Central Europe. Currently writing a book on underground art and its encroachment on urban space.

Philipp Meuser architect and publisher, studied Architecture in Berlin and Zurich. Co-founder of the architect's office Meuser Architekten GmbH in Berlin with Natascha Meuser. Founded the publishing house DOM publishers in 2005. Manages numerous design and construction projects in Russia and Kazakhstan. Writes books and articles on architecture, especially on the architecture of post-socialist urban space.

Małgorzata Omilanowska Prof. Dr., studied Art History at Warsaw University and the Technical University of Berlin. Professor at the History of Art Department of the University of Gdansk. Researcher at the Institute of Art, Polish Academy of Sciences. Specialized on such issues as engineering architecture, commercial architecture, spa architecture, educating architects in the nineteenth century, and the search for national and regional identity in the architecture of Central European countries.

Carmen Popescu Dr., studied Art History at the National University of Arts in Bucharest and Architectural History at the University Paris IV-Sorbonne. Assistant Lecturer at the Faculty of Art History and Theory in Bucharest from 1990 to 1996. Since 2008 Visiting Associate Professor at the University Paris I-Sorbonne. Works as an independent scholar and coordinates research projects, international conferences, and round tables in the field of architectural history. Various publications on the history of architecture in the nineteenth and twentieth centuries, related to politics, identity (nationalism, regionalism), and architecture in the Balkans.

Kai Vöckler urbanist and publicist, co-founder of Archis Interventions, a non-govern-mental organization that works together with local initiatives to solve urban development problems. Archis Interventions is supported by *ERSTE Stiftung* (FIRST Foundation) and currently active in Prishtina and Bucharest. Guest curator at European cultural institutions and program director for South Eastern Europe. Currently assembling a network of inde-pendent urban initiatives in this region. Writes on topics of urbanity.

IMAGE CREDITS

Representations and Images of "Recent History." The Transition of Post-Socialist Landscape Icons
Mariusz Czepczyński

▶ 1–13: Photographs by Mariusz Czepczyński, with all legal rights to them.

Towards Banalization? Trans-Forming the Legacies of the Post-Socialist City
Lydia Coudroy de Lille, Miléna Guest

▶ 1: Photograph by Miléna Guest, 1990.
▶ 2: Photograph by Miléna Guest, 2002.
▶ 3: Photograph by Lydia Coudroy de Lille, 2009.
▶ 4: Photograph by Lydia Coudroy de Lille, 1997.
▶ 5: Photograph by Lydia Coudroy de Lille, 2009.
▶ 6: Photograph by Chris Niedenthal, 1981.
▶ 7: Photograph by Lydia Coudroy de Lille, 2009.
▶ 8: Photograph by Lydia Coudroy de Lille, 2009.
▶ 9: Photograph by Edmund Kupiecki, 1973.
▶ 10: Photograph by Lydia Coudroy de Lille, 2009.
▶ 11: Photograph by Miléna Guest, 1990.
▶ 12: Photograph by Miléna Guest, 2000.

A Cumbersome Heritage. Political Monuments and Buildings of the GDR in Reunited Germany
Arnold Bartetzky

▶ 1: Photograph by Arnold Bartetzky, 2007.
▶ 2: Photograph by Arnold Bartetzky, 2007.
▶ 3: Photograph by Arnold Bartetzky, 2009.
▶ 4: Photograph by Arnold Bartetzky, 2009.
▶ 5: Photograph by Arnold Bartetzky, 2009.
▶ 6: Photograph by Arnold Bartetzky, 2009.
▶ 7: Kulturstiftung Leipzig.
▶ 8: Photographs a–c by Karin Wieckhorst, 1968, d: University of Leipzig.
▶ 9: Photograph by Heinz-Jürgen Böhme, 2001.
▶ 10: Photograph by Matthias Witt, 2007.
▶ 11: Photograph by Arnold Bartetzky, 2009.
▶ 12: Photograph by Arnold Bartetzky, 2008.
▶ 13: Photograph by Arnold Bartetzky, 2009.
▶ 14: Photograph by Neue Sächsische Galerie, 2008.
▶ 15: Photograph by Neue Sächsische Galerie, 2008.

Urban "Truths." Artistic Intervention in Post-Socialist Space
Cynthia Imogen Hammond

▶ 1: Image courtesy of TRUTH & amp; Dominik Art Projects.
▶ 2: Image courtesy of TRUTH & amp; Dominik Art Projects.
▶ 3: Image courtesy of TRUTH & amp; Dominik Art Projects.
▶ 4: Photograph by Kescior, 2008.
Source: http://commons.wikimedia.org/wiki/File:WarsawZloteTarasy.
License terms of this work:
http://creativecommons.org/licenses/by-sa/3.0/.
▶ 5: Photograph by Terence Faircloth, aka Atelier Teee, 2006.
Source: http://www.flickr.com/photos/atelier_tee/185793170/
License terms of this work:
http://creativecommons.org/licenses/by-nc-nd/2.0/.
▶ 6: Photograph by Shalom Alechem, 2005.
Source: http://upload.wikimedia.org/wikipedia/commons/5/57/Warsaw_-_Royal_Castle_Square.jpg.
License terms of this work:
Released into the public domain (by the author).
▶ 7: Image courtesy of TRUTH & amp; Dominik Art Projects.
▶ 8: Image courtesy of TRUTH & amp; Dominik Art Projects.

Screening the Post-Soviet Metropolis. Representations of Urbanity in Contemporary Russian Cinema
Eva Binder

▶ 1: With the kind permission of trigon-film, Brigitte Siegrist, http://www.trigon-film.org.
▶ 2: Kinokompania "STV," http://www.ctb.ru.
▶ 3: 20th Century Fox Home Entertainment, Copyright 2007.
▶ 4: 20th Century Fox Home Entertainment, Copyright 2007.
▶ 5: Robert Richter Distribution, Bern, http://home.tele2.ch/richterfilm.

The Golden City and the Golden Shot. Images from Prague after the Velvet Revolution

Alfrun Kliems

▸ 1–6: Scenes from *Angel Exit* (2000, director Vladimír Michálek).
With the kind permission of BUC-Film Prague.

Post-Totalitarian and Post-Colonial Experiences. The Palace of Culture and Science and Defilad Square in Warsaw

Małgorzata Omilanowska

▸ 1: *Skarpa Warszawska* 2 (1945): 5.
▸ 2: *Architektura* 2 (1948:6/7): 23.
▸ 3: Bolesław Bierut, *Sześcioletni plan odbudowy Warszawy* (Warsaw: Książka i Wiedza, 1950), plate 17.
▸ 4: *Architektura* 1 (1948:5): 119.
▸ 5: Edmund Goldzamt, *Architektura zespołów środmiejskich i problemy dziedzictwa* (Warsaw: Państwowe Wydawnictwo Naukowe, 1956), 497.
▸ 6: *Architektura* 7 (1954:7/8): 169.
▸ 7: Edmund Goldzamt, *Architektura zespołów środmiejskich i problemy dziedzictwa* (Warsaw: Państwowe Wydawnictwo Naukowe, 1956), 499.
▸ 8: Adolf Ciborowski, *Warszawa. O zniszczeniu i odbudowie miasta* (Warsaw: Polonia, 1964), 131.
▸ 9: Adolf Ciborowski, *Warszawa. O zniszczeniu i odbudowie miasta* (Warsaw: Polonia, 1964), 276.
▸ 10: Wojciech Włodarczyk, *Sztuka polska 1918–2000* (Warsaw: Arkady, 2000), 164.
▸ 11: *Gazeta Wyborcza* (Gazeta Stołeczna), January 23 (2008): 1.
▸ 12: *Gazeta Wyborcza* (Gazeta Stołeczna), February 8 (2008): 1.

Cultural Policy as the Politics of History. Independence Square in Kiev

Wilfried Jilge

▸ 1: Photograph by Christian Dietz, 2005.
▸ 2: Photograph by Christian Dietz, 2005.
▸ 3: Photograph by Marina Dmitrieva, 2002.
▸ 4: Photograph by Marina Dmitrieva, 2002.
▸ 5: Photograph by Christian Dietz, 2005.

The Presence of the Recent Past. Difficult Transformations of a "Paradigmatic Socialist City": Dunaújváros

Béla Kerékgyártó

▸ 1: Tibor Weiner, Károly Valentiny and Miklós Visontai, *Sztálinváros, Miskolc, Tatabánya. Városépítésünk fejlődése* (Budapest: Műszaki, 1959), 21.
▸ 2: Tibor Weiner, Károly Valentiny and Miklós Visontai, *Sztálinváros, Miskolc, Tatabánya. Városépítésünk fejlődése* (Budapest: Műszaki, 1959), 45.
▸ 3: *Magyar építészet 1945–1955*, ed. Jenő Szendrői et al. (Budapest: Képzőművészeti Alap Kiadóvállalat, 1955).
▸ 4: *Magyar építészet 1945–1955*, ed. Jenő Szendrői et al. (Budapest: Képzőművészeti Alap Kiadóvállalat, 1955).
▸ 5: Miklós Kapsza, *Dunaújváros. Az ötvenes évek épületei* (Dunaújváros, 1997), 17.
▸ 6: *Magyar építészet 1945–1955*, ed. Jenő Szendrői et al. (Budapest: Képzőművészeti Alap Kiadóvállalat, 1955).
▸ 7: Photograph by Béla Kerékgyártó, 2008.
▸ 8: Photograph by Béla Kerékgyártó, 2008.
▸ 9: Photograph by Béla Kerékgyártó, 2008.

Projected Happiness. Old Myths and New Ambitions in a Bucharest Neighborhood

Carmen Popescu

▸ 1: Map of Floreasca district and surroundings. Sketch by Romeo Negrescu.
▸ 2: Photograph by Carmen Popescu, 1994.
▸ 3: Research Library, The Getty Institute, Los Angeles, 2008. M.35.
▸ 4: Archive of the History Museum of the City of Bucharest.
▸ 5: *Bucureşti. Ghid* (Bucharest: Ed. Meridiane, 1962), 258.
▸ 6: *Arhitectura RPR 7* (1957): 4.
▸ 7: Collection of Mirela Ionescu, 1961.
▸ 8: *Arhitectura* 2–3 (1966): 53.
▸ 9: Collection of Mirela Ionescu, 1963.
▸ 10: *Arhitectura* 1 (1960): 34.
▸ 11: Photograph by Carmen Popescu, 2009.
▸ 12: Photograph by Carmen Popescu, 2009.
▸ 13: Photograph by Carmen Popescu, 2009.
▸ 14: Photograph by Aurelian Stroe, 2009.
▸ 15: Photograph by Carmen Popescu, 2009.
▸ 16: Photograph by Aurelian Stroe, 2009.
▸ 17: Photograph by Carmen Popescu, 2009.

Turbo Urbanism in Prishtina

Kai Vöckler

▶ 1, 8, 12: Graphics by Kai Vöckler and Heimann + Schwantes.

▶ 2–7, 9, 10, 11: Photographs by Vöckler/VG Bild Kunst.

Astana, Almaty, and Aktau. Architectural Experiments in the Steppes of Kazakhstan

Philipp Meuser

▶ 1: National Archives of Kazakhstan, Astana, ca. 1985.
▶ 2: Photograph by Alexei Naroditski, 2007.
▶ 3: Project by Foster and Partners, London, 2007.
▶ 4: Project by Foster and Partners, London, 2006–10.
▶ 5: Photograph by Alexei Naroditski, 2007.
▶ 6: Photograph by Alexei Naroditski, 2007.
▶ 7: Photograph by Alexei Naroditski, 2007.
▶ 8: Photograph by Alexei Naroditski, 2007.
▶ 9: Photograph by Alexei Naroditski, 2007.
▶ 10: Photograph by Alexei Naroditski, 2007.
▶ 11: Photograph by Philipp Meuser, 2008.
▶ 12: Project by Office for Metropolitan Architecture, Rotterdam, 2007.
▶ 13: Project by Koetter Kim & Associates, Boston, 2007–20.

Post-Socialist or Postmodernist? The Search for a New Urbanism in Armenia

Tigran Harutyunian

▶ 1: Plan of Yerevan, 1865, by A. Stotski.
▶ 2: Aleksander Tamanian Museum, Yerevan (General Plan for Yerevan's development, 1924).
▶ 3: Photograph by Merouzhan Minasian, 2009.
▶ 4: Photograph by Merouzhan Minasian, 2009.
▶ 5: Photograph by "Yerevanproekt," 2005.
▶ 6: Photograph by Merouzhan Minasian, 2009.
▶ 7: Project by "LV architects," 2005.
▶ 8: Photograph by Merouzhan Minasian, 2009.
▶ 9: Photograph by Merouzhan Minasian, 2009.
▶ 10: Project by Sarkis Sardarian, 2008.

This publication was generously supported by